Clem Beckett

to Trevor.
¡ No Pasaran !

Rob

Clem Beckett

Motorcycle Legend and War Hero

ROB HARGREAVES

Pen & Sword
MILITARY

AN IMPRINT OF PEN & SWORD BOOKS LTD.
YORKSHIRE – PHILADELPHIA

First published in Great Britain in 2022 by
PEN AND SWORD MILITARY
An imprint of
Pen & Sword Books Limited
Yorkshire – Philadelphia

ISBN 978 1 39909 842 7

Typeset in Times New Roman 11.5/14 by
SJmagic DESIGN SERVICES, India.
Printed and bound in the UK by CPI Group (UK) Ltd.

Pen & Sword Books Limited incorporates the imprints of Atlas, Archaeology,
Aviation, Discovery, Family History, Fiction, History, Maritime, Military, Military
Classics, Politics, Select, Transport, True Crime, Air World, Frontline Publishing,
Leo Cooper, Remember When, Seaforth Publishing, The Praetorian Press,
Wharncliffe Local History, Wharncliffe Transport, Wharncliffe True Crime and
White Owl.

For a complete list of Pen & Sword titles please contact
PEN & SWORD BOOKS LIMITED
47 Church Street, Barnsley, South Yorkshire S70 2AS, United Kingdom
E-mail: enquiries@pen-and-sword.co.uk
Website: www.pen-and-sword.co.uk

Or
PEN AND SWORD BOOKS
1950 Lawrence Rd, Havertown, PA 19083, USA
E-mail: Uspen-and-sword@casematepublishers.com
Website: www.penandswordbooks.com

Contents

Acknowledgements

I am grateful for the help of many individuals and organisations who checked facts and put me on the trail of diverse sources of information. Above all I have benefited from help freely given by my friend and neighbour Alan Hampson, researcher supreme.

Thanks especially to speedway aficionado Jim Henry who, in his dedication to preserving the memory of speedway pioneers, helped build the invaluable 'Speedway Researcher' website, and other notable records of the era. I was also helped in my understanding of early speedway by Trevor James, joint author with Barry Stephenson of *Speedway in Manchester*, while Phil Smith passed on inside information on Clem Beckett's time in Sheffield. Their painstaking research and detailed record-keeping, co-ordinated by webmaster Matt Jackson, enabled me to locate landmarks in Clem Beckett's Dirt Track career, otherwise eclipsed by the legends surrounding his political life and his death in Spain. Jim and Trevor patiently checked the text to head off howlers at the pass. Les Drury turned up illuminating press reports on the activities of International Speedways, Graham Gleave helped me identify old photographs, and John Somerville's vast collection of speedway images was also a fascinating reference point.

I am fortunate to have had access to the awe-inspiring collections of material accrued by the Working Class Movement Library, Salford, the Marx Memorial Library, Clerkenwell, and the National Fairground and Circus Archive at the University of Sheffield. Thanks to Lynette Cawthra at WCML, Meirian Jump at MML, and Matt O'Neill at NCFA, for guiding me through catalogues and retrieving documents. I am also grateful for Stuart Walsh's contribution to maintaining the Beckett files originally accrued by Edmund and Ruth Frow. The unique body of posters, letters, cuttings and diaries amassed by the late Alma Skinner, and housed at the NCFA, was revelatory of life as a Wall of Death rider, and the last period of Clem's life before going to Spain. Through Wall of Death historian Alan Mercer I was fortunate in obtaining information and images from the Skinner family. Resources at Oldham Local Studies Unit and Gallery and the Imperial War Museum Sound Archives were appreciatively mined. Peter Donnelly, curator of the King's Own Royal Regiment Museum, Lancaster, provided information about Alfred Beckett's First World War record.

Information collated by the International Brigade Memorial Trust provided detail as to the last dozen weeks or so of Clem Beckett's life as a volunteer in the Spanish Civil War. Likewise, I learned much from visits to the battlefields, organised by the IBMT and the North West Trade Union International Committee. Dolores Long provided me with fascinating insights into the life of her father, Sam Wild. Mark Garside and John Griffiths supplied learned information on motorcycle mechanics, and Ian Alderson helped me understand the subtle arts of cinder-shifting. John Whyatt lent me out-of-print books on speedway history, and Stephanie Turner carried out a necessary overview of the text.

The following websites were among those consulted: Academia, Ancestry UK, Alpha History, British Newspaper Archive, Defunct Speedway Tracks (John Skinner), Speedway Researcher (Jim Henry and Matt Jackson) Family Search (Latter Day Saints), Find My Past, Free BMD, The National Archives, Wikipedia, International Churchill Society, Gallery Oldham, Spartacus Educational, Steve Brown's In Memoriam, The Genealogist.

Sound Archives Imperial War Museum: interviews with Fred Copeman, Patrick Curry, Jack Jones, Joe Norman, Charles Sewell Bloom. Tameside Local Studies Library: various.

The International Brigades Remembered and Porta de las Historia Facebook sites, both coordinated by Alan Warren, have provided background information.

Where controversy still attaches to events I have endeavoured to admit opposing versions, while taking a view as to where truth lies. Photographs of contemporary landmarks are mine; otherwise every effort has been made to ascertain and acknowledge copyright holders or to verify those in the public domain.

Rob Hargreaves

Introduction

Clem Beckett, a working-class lad from Oldham, died in Spain manning a machine gun while covering the retreat of his comrades from the bloody slopes of Suicide Hill at the Battle of Jarama. Among survivors of the British Battalion of the XV (15th) International Brigade on that day was my father, Sam Wild, nursing four bullet wounds as he helped evacuate injured comrades.

Growing up in Manchester in the 1940s and 50s, my brothers and I learned a lot about the Spanish Civil War from our mother and father. In this we were unusual, because for most people, recollections of the war in Spain were eclipsed by personal sufferings brought upon them by the Great Depression and the Second World War. History paid little heed to the fate of these volunteer warriors, and were it not for Beckett's status as a speedway star, even I, in spite of all I was told by my parents, would probably only know of him as a name on the roll of honour of more than 500 British volunteers who died fighting for their beliefs.

Abridged and dramatised versions of Clem Beckett's life have come down the eighty-five years since his death through the misty lens of folklore, to which Beckett himself, a great spinner of yarns, contributed. But with *Motorcycle Legend and War Hero*, Rob Hargreaves has achieved a definitive account of Beckett's short life.

What a tale it is: motorbike-mad paper boy, dirt track superstar, jet-set aviator, speedboater, globe-trotting adventurer, Wall of Death stuntman and, throughout his adult life, dedicated member of the Communist Party.

Of Beckett's thirty action-packed years, only four months were in Spain. Most of it, one way or another, was about motorbikes, especially his part in the explosion of dirt track racing in the late 1920s. Hargreaves takes us through the mechanics of Beckett's speedway triumphs in some detail. Not really my thing, even though I was born in the shadow of

Manchester's Belle Vue stadium. But hold hard! His narrative is leavened by insights into the social and political context of the times, including reportage of remarkable women, who with Clem's support, broke down barriers to take part in motorcycle sport.

Above all, Hargreaves reveals Beckett's rip-roaring irreverence for authority; his warts-and-all decency as a human being. I commend his efforts.

Dolores Long
Manchester, 2020

Foreword

Forty years ago, before my twenty-five years as Clerk of the Course at Edinburgh's Powderhall and Armadale speedway stadiums (1989–2014) I realised that the sport's real history was lost in the mists of time – especially the unprecedented excitement and novelty of pioneering events in the 1920s and 1930s.

No internet in those days of course, so it was a case of foraging through old magazines and newspapers. However, trying to encourage mainstream speedway magazines to focus on early dirt track days proved fruitless, in spite of my certainty that the stories of pioneers like Clem Beckett were well worth telling. A solution was found when my friend Graham Fraser and I set up our own magazine, *The Speedway Researcher,* bringing together kindred spirits, keen to pool their knowledge and to find contemporary material.

Later, with the advent of the internet, the magazine became a website. Throughout, it has been gratifying to help fellow researchers and historians publish definitive accounts of various facets of speedway – including this, Rob Hargreaves's story of Clem Beckett, one of the most flamboyant and controversial characters in the history of the sport.

In turn I have been rewarded by information about Beckett which Rob and his associate, Alan Hampson, have dug out and of which I was largely ignorant – a fabulous *quid pro quo*. Moreover, given Beckett's strong socialist beliefs, I'd like to think that he now looks down with approval at the principles which have always guided *The Speedway Researcher* as a proud not-for-profit organisation based on co-operation and a common cause!

Over the years there have been other biographies of speedway riders. Most have described the early lives of their subjects, their on-track exploits and what they did when they retired. But by delving into Beckett's beliefs and motivations in the context of the economic and political turmoil of the inter-war years, Rob Hargreaves has produced a unique canvas of dramatic events both on and off the track.

This then is a biography of a speedway rider which breaks new ground, and I commend it to both speedway and social historians as a well-researched and well-written insight into the life of a man who was faithful to his creed.

Jim Henry
Edinburgh, 2020

Chapter One

King Cotton's Doorstep

'There is practically no local society – only multitudes of workers.'
Winston Churchill describing his first impressions
of Oldham to his mother.

For a Yorkshireman, Clem Beckett was born on the wrong side of the Pennines. His birthplace was Stone Rake, an isolated cottage on a windswept hillside, *west* of the Pennine watershed. It was part of Saddleworth, an anomalous amalgam of Yorkshire villages left on the doorstep of the Lancashire town of Oldham and miles away from the nearest town in the West Riding of the white-rose county.

Among the incomers to the booming textile town of Oldham were Clem's parents, Alfred Howard Beckett and Henrietta Price, married at the town's register office in September 1901. Alfred came from a family of metal-workers in Walsall, Staffordshire, his father having died a few months before his son's birth in 1876. At the time of the marriage he was a corporal in the army, giving his address – likely to have been lodgings – as 531 Huddersfield Road. Henrietta was living with her mother and father, four sisters and a brother at 46 Glodwick Road, close to the town centre. Like her mother and older sister she was employed as a velvet weaver; her father was a time-keeper in a textile machinery works and her brother was an apprentice 'fettler', probably in the same works as his father, almost certainly that of Oldham's biggest employer, Platt Brothers.

Also living with the family at the time of the Census in that year were Henrietta's two children: Herbert Price aged eight, and Elsie Price aged six. Both appear to have been born out of wedlock, but later on, Clem and her other children to Alfred may have been told that he was also the father of their much older siblings. That said, in later years Clem's sister

1

Hilda seems to have regarded Elsie and Herbert as step-siblings, and it is possible that Clem barely knew them, even if he knew *of* them.[1]

Alfred had lived in Oldham in the early 1890s before joining up, and at the time of his wedding to Henrietta was still serving with 1st Battalion, Royal Lancaster Regiment (RLR), recently returned from Singapore after five years' service in the Far East.[2] Henrietta was also born in the Black Country, at Wednesfield, six miles from Walsall, an area known for iron works and engineering. Like Oldham, its industry had attracted work-seekers from rural areas, especially Wales. But Oldham itself was enjoying a last great wave of mill building, and the fact that the entire Price family of working age was engaged in the textile industry manifestly determined the couple's decision to remain in Lancashire. No wonder the Becketts looked optimistically to the future. Between 1900 and 1908 fifty-five new mills were built in the town, thirty-seven of them between 1905 and 1907. Company profits soared, dividends to shareholders averaged fifteen per cent, and the prosperity of Oldham, with its reputation as the jewel in the crown of the Lancashire cotton industry, seemed assured.

Alfred and Henrietta were anxious to take any accommodation they could get. Their simple stone dwelling, perched on the edge of the moors and lodged between scattered outcrops of millstone grit, was set apart from the nearest hamlet of weavers' cottages by a steep hillside. Stone Rake was far from idyllic; it was likely to have been reliant on spring water, accessible only by field paths, and bereft of gas or electricity. Surrounded by rough pasture and moorland, it lay equidistant from the three Saddleworth villages of Springhead, Scouthead and Austerlands. Bleak, and separate from the settled community of Edwardian Oldham, Stone Rake might have been thought almost beyond the bounds of civilisation by better-off townsfolk who enjoyed the benefits of nearby council schools, tramcars, municipal parks, and a Co-operative store in every neighbourhood. For the most part, residents of terrace houses, blessed with running water and gas light, were served by well-paved and well-lit streets. Their relative prosperity was built, above all, on textiles, together with its off-shoot sister industries, especially the manufacture of spinning and weaving machinery. Given the family background (his father was a silver-plater) Alfred Beckett may have hoped for skilled work in Oldham's engineering industry after leaving the army, but in the event he never found a trade, always being described as 'labourer'.

For the Becketts, cries of nesting curlews and the sweet smell of drying hay in spring and summer were little consolation for the hardships dictated by the spartan conditions at Stone Rake. Denied the amenities of the town, exposed to the unforgiving upland weather, they lived life on the edge. Little consolation also, that on clear days, looking down the desolate clough (ravine) and southwards beyond the Pennine chain, Alfred and Henrietta could just make out the distant outline of the Staffordshire uplands, close to their native, and familiar, Black Country.

The Becketts' nearest neighbours at Stone Rake (sometimes rendered 'Stonerakes') lived at the bottom of the hill, in a grand terrace of three-storey cottages known as 'Laureate's Place'. Built for hand-loom weavers, they were part of the hamlet of Wood Brook, served by The Spinners Arms public house, a magnet for thirsty workers at Stone Breaks quarry on the other side of the clough, and close to the thriving Austerlands spinning mill with adjoining homes for its workers. Though hardly outcasts, the Becketts, as newcomers, were apart, socially as well as geographically, from this community. Their hope of betterment lay in Oldham itself. From the beginning, in spite of being surrounded by farms and fields, their lives were focused on the opportunities offered in the town below them.

The red-brick cotton mills and tall chimneys of the Oldham skyline symbolised England's phenomenal industrial growth. The town's population had expanded ten-fold in the preceding hundred years, and a mill-building boom at the end of the nineteenth century saw Oldham overtake other Lancashire towns – including Manchester – as the most productive cotton-spinning centre in the world. Just the place for Boer War hero and ambitious politician Winston Spencer Churchill to launch his Parliamentary career, being elected as Conservative MP for the town in 1900 – although in this dual-member constituency the other seat was held by the Liberals.

Before the Conservative government of Arthur Balfour had run its course, Churchill had crossed the floor of the House of Commons to join the Liberals and was disowned by Oldham Conservatives. Nor was he popular with militant Oldham suffragists, such as Annie Kenney, born at Springhead, who in 1905, after unfurling a banner reading 'Votes for Women', was arrested at a meeting in Manchester for interrupting Churchill and other Liberal politicians.

CLEM BECKETT: MOTORCYCLE LEGEND AND WAR HERO

Nothing expressed the hubris of the age, nor the self-confidence of Oldham, more than the splendours of its magnificent stone-built municipal library, its high walls adorned, like so many Victorian buildings, with the busts of those whom the worthy burghers of the town acknowledged as bringers of light, wisdom, and civilisation. On the north elevation, the lofty sculpted features of William Shakespeare, Michelangelo, Charles Darwin and Francis Bacon still look down on the town, alongside the likes of James Watt and George Stephenson, men whose contribution was as wealth creators, pioneers of the Industrial Revolution, engineers and inventors. On the same building, near the busy thoroughfare of Union Street, Samuel Crompton, inventor of the spinning mule, fixes his stony gaze on passers-by, as though to solicit their gratitude for a machine that revolutionised the spinning process and paved the way for Oldham's astonishing rise to predominance in the cotton industry. Moreover, the town's engineering tradition ensured that it remained at the forefront of technological developments in British industry (including an early venture into the manufacture of bicycles, and then motorcycles, by the firm of Bradbury and Co, which began life in the mid-nineteenth century making Europe's first sewing machines).

In the early years of the twentieth century, England still basked in its reputation as the workshop of the world. The British Empire covered a quarter of the globe, providing its industries with expanding markets and raw materials, while Oldham's mills housed more than a quarter of the spindles operating in the United Kingdom. It was inconceivable to the aspiring Becketts, as to all the good people of Oldham, that the bedrock of their hopes for the future, 'King Cotton', was soon to be dethroned.

On Christmas Eve 1904 Alfred and Henrietta, babe in arms, walked through the fields to St Paul's Church, Scouthead, where their child, John Griffiths Beckett, was baptised. He died in January 1905, barely a month old, and was buried at Greenacres (always pronounced *Grenner-kers*) Cemetery, Oldham. On 10 August 1906 Henrietta Beckett bore her third son, Clement Henry Beckett.

Chapter Two

Top o'th' Meadows

'Daddy, what did YOU do in the Great War?'
Words on a First World War recruitment poster.

The birth of Clement (a name he eschewed from an early age, preferring his friends to call him 'Joe') was followed within a few years by two daughters, Mary Alice and Hilda. The boys' Christian names, together with Henrietta's maiden name of Price, suggest Welsh ancestry. When, after a few years, the Becketts moved to a new home at 1, Top o'th' Meadows, it was a change for the better, a couple of miles to the west of Stone Rake and more sheltered from the fierce moorland winds. A mile above the village of Waterhead, the hamlet of Top o'th' Meadows consisted of a cluster of eighteenth-century cottages and farms. There had once been a mill there, but it had closed eighty years earlier. Pleasantly situated in a tongue of farmland, comfortably enfolded by the protective sides of the Strines valley, Top o'th' Meadows also lay just within the West Riding of Yorkshire, administered from faraway Wakefield.

Well above the height of Oldham's mill chimneys, the Beckett children had fresher air than contemporaries in the town. Cattle and horses grazed the meadows, and the yard between cottage and outbuildings was ideal for keeping hens. There was room to stable horses. In spite of Alfred's occupation as an iron-works labourer, the Becketts got to know local farmers, and Alfred may have taken the cottage on condition of providing occasional help at nearby Pastures Farm.

On 15 June 1910, not yet four, Clem was admitted to Waterhead Church School, possibly by mistake, or under protest. After two days he was removed, before being re-admitted, aged four years and six months, on 14 February 1911. For all the country air, life remained hard, and further tragedy attended the Becketts. Unhappily echoing the death of John Griffiths, another son, Henry Longville Beckett, born in September 1912, died at only one year old.

CLEM BECKETT: MOTORCYCLE LEGEND AND WAR HERO

As a young lad, Clem was close to the sights, sounds and smells of the countryside. On walks to and from school, through lanes and along the Strines brook, he saw the pattern of the seasons and observed life on adjacent farms. He got to know other children from Strinesdale making their way to school and back along the same lanes – Amy Brown from 7, Top o'th' Meadows, Joseph Smith of Strines Farm, and Harold Taylor, whose father was landlord of the Roebuck Inn higher up the hill. In this little piece of countryside close to the town, Clem would have had opportunities to lend a hand with hay-making or to look after animals. In any event, by the time he was in his teens he had set his heart on working with horses.

Yet the family's stay at Top o'th' Meadows did not last long. Within a short time of Clem's sister, Mary Alice, being enrolled in school at Waterhead (at the tender age of three-and-a-half) the Becketts were on the move again. On 27 October 1913 Clem, aged seven, was removed from Waterhead, where he had attended for nearly three years, and where he had already begun showing promise in sport. Two days later he was enrolled as a pupil at Roundthorn School, Glodwick, in the heart of industrial Oldham.

It is hard to see the family's move away from Top o'th' Meadows in terms of betterment. More likely the move was preceded by difficulty or discord. Perhaps father Alfred was put out of work or there was some other cause of a shortage of money. In any event, after a spell in accommodation in Roundthorn Road, the Becketts moved to a nearby terrace house at 17 Swinton Street.

Compared to the airy hillside at Top o'th' Meadows, the terrace houses of Roundthorn and adjacent Glodwick were suffocatingly confined. However, for the first time in his life, Clem was able to enjoy a home with the benefits of piped water, a lavatory in the backyard connected to a mains sewer, pavements beyond its little front garden, gas-lit streets, and shops within easy reach.

Close to a sprawling railway goods yard, overshadowed by mills and factories, Roundthorn was perpetually enveloped by the sounds and smells of industry. Dirty from soot and smoke emitted by steam locomotives and mill chimneys, the terraces gave onto busy cobbled streets echoing to the clip-clop of horse-drawn vehicles, and increasingly to the noise of internal combustion engines powering motorcars, lorries ... and motorcycles. Indeed, the town basked in the reflected glory of sporting victories accomplished by amateur riders on Bradbury's new, celebrated twin-cylinder 500cc machines replete with novel kick-start. In 1912 'H. Gibson and G. Wray' (for gentlemen amateurs, first names indicated only by initials was *de rigeur*) had completed the 886-mile John o'Groats to Land's End run in under thirty-nine hours, reducing the previous sidecar record by two hours.[1]

For a country lad, the move to the town must have been profound, but by no means traumatic. Oldham, it seemed, was set on a course forever upwards and onwards. The town hummed with optimism: its 320 textile mills offered employment to all and, so it seemed, infinite prosperity.

Clem was an easy-going, good-natured lad – adaptable, and usually up to something. He would have missed his chums from Waterhead, but the Oldham of 1913 offered infinite adventure, and in spite of its pervasive industry there were enticing open spaces all around. A few streets away lay the magnificent Alexandra Park, built by unemployed workers during the cotton famine of the 1860s, and financed by government loans and the largesse of local benefactors. Giving on to open space above the valley of the River Medlock, it was an awe-inspiring municipal creation, with a grand promenade, a boating lake, a playground, an observatory in the style of a Japanese pagoda and a domed hothouse growing tropical plants.

Oldham is unusual for an industrial town in that it was built on high ground, its steam-powered mills served by trickling streams rather than fast-flowing rivers. Weather and smoke permitting, therefore, it is always possible to find a vantage point from which to look out and down on the world below. One such is Oldham Edge, at the very top of the town; another is the renowned market at Tommyfield. Swinton Street, round the corner from a new Co-op store in Roundthorn Road, cheek by jowl with spinning mills and foundries, lay in the shadow of Glodwick Lows, an elevated hogsback of open land surrounded by outlying parts of the town. Pitted with abandoned mines and quarries reclaimed by nature, it was very different from the fields and farms at Top o'th' Meadows. Yet here also, from this island plateau Clem could look out on the world – south-west towards the great city of Manchester and the Welsh mountains beyond, and east towards the heather-clad Pennines. The muddy tracks and moonscape craters of the Lows offered the finest adventure playground a child might wish for. From here, Clem and his new friends could see a world stretching far beyond the claustrophobic mills and workshops of the town. For a young lad, as fearless and eager as Clem Beckett, it was a world of infinite opportunity.

But danger loomed large as the Becketts adapted to their new circumstances in the autumn of 1913. For half the world, for most of Europe, and for all of Britain, time was running out for the old order. Clem was almost eight when war was declared on Germany in August 1914. He would have witnessed the early enthusiasm shown by the town, sensed the optimism that 'Kaiser Bill' would soon be taught a lesson and that the war would be over by Christmas. Most vividly, he would have seen his own father join the rush to the recruiting office; and although he did not know it, he was witnessing the final days of his parents' married life together.

Very nearly forty years old, it seems Alfred Beckett rejoined the army within a month of war being declared, perhaps being called up as a reservist. At any rate, he was typical of men targeted by the campaign launched by Lord Kitchener, and famously remembered for its 'Your Country Needs YOU!' recruitment poster. Alfred enlisted in the King's Own Royal Lancaster (KORL) Regiment at Preston barracks, on 4 September, the same day that the iconic image first appeared in a London magazine. Lest marriage and fatherhood be seen as exempting circumstances, the War Office soon published other equally compelling posters. One showed a stern-faced mother, daughter by her side, urging her husband to join up, and in similar vein, another imagined a post-war father, child upon his lap, having to account for his war record. Unofficially, able-bodied men appearing in the streets in civilian clothes were shamed into joining up by women presenting them with a white feather as a symbolic accusation of cowardice. Voices raised against the war were drowned out in a din of jingoism. Members of the Independent Labour Party, who held protest meetings outside the gates of Alexandra Park, were chased and set upon.

From Preston barracks, following basic training in England, Private 4222 A. H. Beckett embarked for France and Flanders in September 1915, when Clem, the eldest child still at home, was nine years old.

As the war years went by the town fell into a state of endless mourning. In every street, curtains were drawn and blinds lowered as telegrams and newspapers told of the slaughter on the Western Front. Portrait galleries of the fallen appeared regularly in the *Oldham Chronicle* as politicians continually promised 'one last push' to bring about Germany's defeat.

In the meantime, as a pupil at Roundthorn Continuation School, Clem excelled at sport, especially rugby, assisted by his stocky physique, and inspired by the town's professional team, a founder member of the Northern Rugby Football Union. Academically, he performed well enough to be offered a scholarship at one of the town's prestigious grammar schools. He declined it, aware that, notwithstanding a bursary for fees, the incidental costs of formal education, such as uniform, were quite beyond his mother's means. Grammar school would also have prevented Clem from earning money, something he was determined to do at the first opportunity. It was, though, an act of self-denial, an altogether unremarkable occurrence in working-class families who simply took it for granted that higher education was beyond their reach. Yet it *was* to be both remembered and remarked on in the future. For this bright youngster it was class-defining, a crystal-clear demonstration of social injustice, and however uncomplainingly Clem got on with life, it was likely ever after to have been a source of resentment. Even so, a few years later it seems that Clem's sisters, Mary and Hilda, were able to accept scholarships. By that time, mother Henrietta was earning money as a nurse. It might have been hospital work, but with thousands of wounded men returning from the war, wrecked both physically and mentally, there would have been be a strong demand, from families who could afford to pay for them, for nurses and carers of all kinds.

In August 1917, still only eleven years old, Clem got a job as a paperboy with a newsagent on Roundthorn Road, round the corner from his home. Part of it was to meet the arrival of the newspaper train at Mumps station at 5.30am, and take a bundle of papers back to the shop. There, early one morning he met another lad, Eli Anderson, doing a similar job for a rival newsagent. They became friends, and the friendship was to last for the rest of Clem's life. They formed their own co-operative enterprise, sharing the profits of additional papers sold to workers on street corners and at mill-gates. To do this they needed to rise before dawn, perhaps even before the knocker-up had reached Swinton Street, and to traverse the cobbled streets to the station a mile away. Key to the business were two rickety bicycles kept in the Andersons' backyard shed, one left by Eli's father when he went off to the war, the other belonging to his sister.

For the papers, of course, the one big story was the war. At first, as the battle of Passchendaele raged in Flanders, they carried mostly upbeat accounts of a successful offensive. But then the army got bogged down in a sea of mud, losses mounted, casualty lists lengthened, and newspaper readers – Clem and Eli now among them – scanned the columns of the papers for names of loved ones with the same heightened anxiety that had accompanied the battle of the Somme the previous year.

The First World War robbed Oldham of more than 5,000 of its sons, and many hundreds more from the Saddleworth villages on its doorstep never returned. Clem's father survived, and his army service appears to have been exemplary, having been awarded the 1914-15 Star, and the British War and Allied Victory medals.[2]

However, the government delayed the demobilisation of troops, and as a result Alfred Beckett was unable – even had he wished it – to return home to take up his old job. Among soldiers stuck in France rumours circulated that the government was holding back demobilisation to allow laid-off munition workers to get the pick of the jobs. There were in fact more sinister reasons for the delay. Prime Minister David Lloyd George was concerned that a flood of demobbed soldiers would create an unsustainable demand for unemployment relief. While in the final months of the war, and amid a good deal of secrecy, his Secretary of State for War, Winston Churchill, sent troops to fight a new war against revolutionary forces in Russia.[3]

Accordingly, it was not until 23 May 1919, nine months after the Armistice, that Warrant Officer Class 2, Company Sergeant Major Beckett was discharged on medical grounds, possibly after contracting malaria while serving with the 9th Battalion of the King's Own (KO) in Salonika. As in every war, in addition to those who acted in a frenzy of patriotic zeal, there were those who joined up to escape the monotony of a dead-end job or an unhappy marriage. And there were also those whose experiences left them traumatised or utterly changed, unwilling or unable to return home. According to one of Clem's sisters, following his discharge from the army Alfred Beckett 'simply disappeared', and Clem never got the chance to ask his father what he had done in the war. But given that Alfred had served abroad as a soldier, on and off, over a period of more than twenty years, Henrietta herself may not have been all that surprised by his ultimate desertion.

Chapter Three

Mad Andy

'Oh no, the machine is necessary ... a man who rides up
on a great machine, this man is responsible,
this man exists.'
Dialogue from Act One, *A View from the*
Bridge by Arthur Miller.

Two days before his thirteenth birthday, and nine months after the
Armistice, Clem Beckett attended school as a 'full-timer' for the last
time. Now, above all, Clem was anxious to help his mother. It was three
months since his father had been discharged from the army, and perhaps
the family was still hoping he would return. If so, it would have a been
a painful time for mother and children as it slowly dawned on them that
they had been deserted. Their financial position would have been worse
than if Alfred had died in the war. Denied a widow's war pension, and
with her daughters still in full-time education, the family income was
limited to what Henrietta herself could bring in and Clem's part-time
earnings. We do not know if Henrietta applied for public assistance,
but if she did so the circumstances would have been humiliating. Men
who failed to maintain their wives and children featured regularly in
the columns of the *Oldham Chronicle* when they were hauled before
the town's magistrates. But you would first have to catch them, and if
Alfred had made a new life back in the Midlands, which appears likely,
the chances of enforcing maintenance payments on him were remote
indeed.

Clem grew up fast, starting work as a half-timer with Platt Brothers,
Oldham's leading textile engineers. The scale of Platt's operations was
immense. Its offices in Werneth resembled a French chateau, and it was
said that the town's heart beat in time with the great clock that looked
down on its vast works occupying 85 acres and served by a network

of private railway sidings. With some 15,000 workers, it was far and away the largest employer in the town. At the start of the war it had been the biggest maker of cotton-processing machinery in the world. In 1919, following a spell producing munitions, it resumed peace-time production, still expanding and soon to announce record profits.

No doubt then, that when Clem began work as an apprentice card-fitter at the firm's Lower House works, Henrietta Beckett breathed a sigh of relief that her son had secured a position in a skilled trade with the prospect of a job for life.[1] It would have helped Clem no end to have had – as appears to have been the case – both an uncle and a grandfather on the payroll at Platts. But Henrietta was in for a shock. Before long Clem quit his job with Platts to become an apprentice blacksmith.

The reason given for Clem's sudden move was that he seized an opportunity to work with horses. Perhaps his father had once made him aware of metal-worker ancestors back in Staffordshire who made horse brasses. As farriers, Frank Bowman's firm in Glodwick was contracted by the Lancashire and Yorkshire Railway to shoe horses used to haul its fleet of delivery vans. It seemed an unwise move, because following the war motorised lorries were already taking over from horse-drawn transport. It was all the more surprising because, love of horses aside, no one was more fascinated by the possibilities of the internal combustion engine than Clem Beckett. It remains possible, of course, that the departure from Platt's was prompted by other factors; the absence of fatherly advice being one of them. He was fast becoming a bit of a tearaway, no respecter of rules and regulations, mischievous and adventurous. Clem's sister Mary was later to say that at this time her brother had to be prevented from accepting the offer of a job as an ostler in Arabia!

Post-war England yearned to return to business as usual. Supplying markets that had been starved during hostilities, there was a cotton boom in 1919 and 1920. Accordingly, Clem's introduction to full-time employment coincided with increased militancy within trade unions. In 1919 almost 35 million days were lost due to strikes, and overall union membership doubled from its pre-war level. Lloyd George, unable to deliver on his promises of post-war prosperity, warned Cabinet colleagues of the increasing threat posed by a labour force composed of 'millions of men who had been trained to arms'.

It was, too, a nation characterised by social division, in which wealth accumulated by land and capital existed in stark contrast with the struggle for survival faced by mill workers and their families. Many returning soldiers were unable to take up their old jobs. When, in May 1919, Oldham's new Labour Exchange opened, it reported 11,000 unemployed, including 3,000 women.

Even a teenage boy consumed by his own interests – sport, horses, and a growing preoccupation with motorcycles – would have understood that times were changing. There was a chronic housing shortage, and people worried about the future of Oldham's textile industry amid all the uncertainties of the post-war world. The obvious truth was that war had bled the country dry, and the coalition government of David Lloyd George was in a state of panic over how to win the peace. There was a new mood of militancy in the workforce, and even Oldham teachers gave notice of an intention to strike if their salary demands were not met.

At the same time, rumours of the British government's best efforts to crush the Russian Revolution were seeping through to believers in International Socialism. British military intervention in northern Russia, intended to prop up the Czarist state, was a disastrous failure, and in October 1919 it required the despatch of former commander-in-chief on the Western Front, Sir Henry Rawlinson, to extricate troops from Murmansk. The experience of senior army officers in Russia, such as Generals Ironside and Maynard, was to inform British foreign policy for years to come.[2] So far as they were concerned, the Bolsheviks were 'the blood-lusting wolves of Moscow [...] wanton, brutal, barbaric, inhuman, repellent and abhorrent'. Right or wrong, officers of the British Expeditionary Force brought home stories of the Bolshevik revolution which terrified even the majority of working-class voters.

Clem began riding motorcycles at the age of fourteen. He graduated from pushbikes to motorbikes with obsessive enthusiasm, and shortage of money was overcome by hard work and ingenuity. He and friend Irving Anderson (no relation to Eli) scraped together £5 between them to buy an ancient machine. This was a tidy sum – more than an entire month's pay for an army sergeant. The bike had automatic inlet-valves, and was fuelled by ether. The lads stripped it down to its tiniest parts and put it back together. Not content to stay on the handy off-road paths and tracks of Glodwick Lows, they roared through busy Oldham streets, unrestrained by rules or regulations, one riding, the other hanging on as pillion passenger. Elders gasped their disapproval, but younger eyes followed their antics with envy. A motorcycle 'craze' was sweeping the country. Machines retrieved from army-surplus dumps following the Armistice were being pressed back into service. In their Oldham works, a short distance from the town centre, Bradbury and Co were producing a range of motorbikes, with optional sidecars, for those with the money to pay for them. Featuring in a series of cigarette cards produced by Lambert and Butler, the combination version of the latest Bradbury machine, with stylish sidecar attached, had every appearance of being top of the range, and way beyond the means of Clem and his pals in Roundthorn. The firm also cashed in on its pre-war reputation as market-leader in machines for competitive hill-climbing events.[3]

Noisy, flamboyant and fearless, Clem and Irving attracted a good deal of attention. Naturally, when it came to servicing and repairs, it was a case of self-help, and the boys became proficient in motorcycle mechanics. Though barely out of school, they began repairing motorbikes for friends and acquaintances. A builder erected a shed for them. They were soon earning enough to pay a weekly rent of four shillings, and to buy themselves better bikes – an *Indian* for Irving and a *Harley Davidson* for Clem. To the annoyance of the general public, the sight and sound of motorbikes ridden by young working-class lads became commonplace. Of course, the temptation to race was irresistible, and there were confrontations with the police. Occasionally, they were caught, but were let off with cautions. A favourite wheeze when stopped for having unlicensed machines was to say they had borrowed them. Clem's exploits had by now earned him the nickname of 'Daredevil' Beckett, while Irving gloried in the soubriquet 'Mad Andy'. Eli Anderson, too, was just as motorbike-mad as the other two, but, alas, as time would tell, not quite so lucky in his encounters with the authorities.

The lads were growing up in a world that prided itself on settled values and secure employment, but was, at the same time, increasingly nervous about its future. Victory over Germany had been bought at a high price. During the course of the 1920s unemployment declined, but the nation's basic industries continued to suffer the effects of international competition. Textiles, especially cotton, were having a hard time in the face of 'a decline in the Eastern market'. For the mills of Oldham this was passed on to workers by way of short-time working. Hardly surprising that given the dearth of obvious reasons for these developments, and the absence of practical solutions, young Clem eventually came to see the world as a conspiracy of greedy and incompetent old fogeys.

This contrasted, however, with the prevailing mood amongst his elders, which was at first stoical, mixed with relief the war was over, and the hope that pre-war prosperity would soon return.

Accordingly, mill-owners resolved to go on taking profits. Typically, shares in Oldham's spinning mills were still paying a five per cent dividend, and gullible investors were likewise offered five per cent on loan stock by way of debentures. Prescient owners realised, however, that only investment on a massive scale, beyond their means, could save their industry. 'Smart money' was already moving out of textiles. A mill-buying boom, financed by rash bank lending, reached its peak in 1920. Mill workers, taking advantage of the post-war demand, secured as much as thirty per cent wage increases. The stage was set for what was later described as 'the most sordid and tragic episode' in the history of Oldham's industry.[4]

Unscrupulous speculators, intent on profit-taking, bid up the share prices of the mills. In a scenario redolent of the worldwide financial crash in 2008, they were assisted in this by irresponsible bank lending. Two-thirds of the mills succumbed to the frenzy, and once acquired at an inflated value, companies were re-floated at even higher values. Tradesmen, clerks, mill-managers and overlookers took up shares, as the *Oldham Evening Chronicle* warned that profits were being taken by men who were 'not of the highest probity'. Syndicates of anonymous City speculators moved in, and were assisted in their acquisitions by self-made William ('Billy') Hopwood, of Shaw, who because of his local roots and humble beginnings as a 'piecer' enjoyed the trust of local people. Hopwood, said to have been 'a typical Lancashire man of broad speech and brusque manner' was duped. At the height of the boom he had nominal control of more than thirty mills in the Oldham district. But it all ended in tears. In 1921 trade collapsed, as did share prices. Over the next few years firms resorted to calling in millions of pounds of unpaid share capital, and those who been misled into buying shares at below face value were asked to foot the bill.

Post-war shortages had been met. The market for cotton had changed. The world had changed. High-cost production in Lancashire now faced competition from countries such as India and China, many of whose mills relied on Platt's machinery. Japan had doubled its pre-war capacity. Between 1914 and 1921 the volume of raw cotton consumed by Oldham's mills almost halved.

In human terms all this meant hard times: rising unemployment, short-time working, falling wages, and a wave of mill closures. True, unemployed workers could now draw a modest dole, provided they were insured, but in fatherless families like the Becketts there was real poverty. In late 1922, as winter drew on, the mayor launched a public appeal for the relief of distress, and harking back to the days of the cotton famine, work on a new road, Broadway, through the meadows of Chadderton was begun to provide jobs for some 600 men. The long-term decline of cotton would mean the decline of Oldham. Pre-war prosperity would not return. Of the 320 mills in the district in 1914, only 200 remained by 1939, many of them having ceased production.

Chapter Four

Bill o' Jack's

'Yet when we achieved, and the new world dawned, the
old men came out again and took our victory to remake it
in the likeness of the former world they knew. Youth was
pitiably weak against age.'
T.E. Lawrence in *Seven Pillars of Wisdom*
reflecting on the aftermath of the First World War.

In spite of his absorbing motorbike hobby Clem remained restless. Perhaps wishing to follow in his absent father's footsteps, and willing to falsify his age, he tried to join the army, hoping to serve in a horse regiment. Had it not been for the fact that he was still a bound apprentice he might have succeeded. He was thwarted by his employer, Frank Bowman, who intervened with the army authorities on the grounds that their new recruit was indentured to him. Clem was ignominiously, though not dishonourably, discharged, and soon found himself back at work in Glodwick.

Resolving to stick at the apprenticeship with Bowmans, Clem settled down to life in Oldham, his meagre wages supplemented by what he and Irving were able to charge for motorbike repairs. At the same time, he acquired a reputation as a tough guy. On the rugby pitch, an opponent recalled that tackling Clem was 'like trying to stop a tank'. When he was called in to deal with cousin Elsie's vicious Alsatian dog, he fought it to a standstill, hand-to-paw, inside a locked barn. In the process he was bitten on the arm, and a few days later astonished onlookers at work by lancing the festering wound with his jack-knife. Workmates also remembered Clem's reaction to being kicked by a horse, a farrier's occupational hazard. Refusing advice to go home and rest, and fortified by a glass of brandy, he resumed work, declaring 'I will shoe that horse even if I have to lift it up.'[1]

Above all, however, Clem's reputation rested on his amazing resilience to motorbike crashes, and his irresistible urge to accept a challenge. Riding home one night, he was catapulted through the air when his machine lost its front wheel. Bruised, cut and shaken from the hard landing, he was back on his bike three days later. On the lofty heights of Oldham Edge, a mile or so from Glodwick, he took up a dare from two Royton lads, Bob Kennedy and Eddie Hulton, to ride to the top up a ferociously steep quarry face. None of them made it, but not for want of trying. They rode until their bikes fell backwards on top of them.

Undeterred by his abortive attempt to become a full-time soldier, Clem joined the Territorial Army. His military training was probably brief and rudimentary but it was to be a significant – and fatal – enhancement of his CV.

And, of course, for this good-looking, daredevil lad with grey-blue eyes, there were girls eager to share the thrill of a motorbike ride as Clem's pillion passenger. Sometimes, he had two up at a time. Irving Anderson's future wife, Elsie, described how Clem became 'a great womaniser, with no thought of marriage', adding, 'but for his kindness and courage he was loved by all.' Clem was a charmer all right.

For a bright lad who could travel about under his own steam, Clem was well placed to see evidence of a divided society. Moreover, a socialist shoesmith (farrier) at Bowmans took the young apprentice under his wing, bending his ear with a commentary on contemporary events, and the glories of the new workers' paradise in Soviet Russia.

And so began the politicisation of Clem Beckett. Absorbing socialist vocabulary from his old sweat of a Marxist tutor in the heat of the Bowmans forge, he would have identified Victorian mansions on the outskirts of the town as homes of 'capitalists' or 'bosses', and newer, larger detached houses in Grotton and Grasscroft as those of the 'bourgeoisie'. What neither the shoesmith nor politicians of any party were able to explain, however, was the reason for the decline in Oldham's traditional industries. Nor did they understand the intermittent spikes of recovery and bubbles of false confidence that were to plague the economy for another dozen years. Along with shipbuilding towns on Merseyside, at Barrow-in-Furness and in the North East, as well as mining communities all over the country, textile towns in Lancashire and Yorkshire were to be hardest hit of all by economic forces over which they had no control.

Apprentice Clem was encouraged to join a trade union as matter of course. By the early 1920s the blacksmiths' union had been absorbed into the United Society of Boilermakers and Iron and Steel Shipbuilders. The Society emerged from the war as a pillar of the respectable working class, representing skilled workers across the engineering trades. Members were required to serve a seven-year apprenticeship, their contributions funded members' sick pay and superannuation, and records were kept with scrupulous thoroughness – even to the point of detailing the cause of death of members' widows. The union's officials served on government committees, set up to boost the war effort by ensuring industrial peace. Its monthly reports labelled 'For the Use of Members Only' suggested a superior exclusiveness, but the information they carried consisted of statistics collected by the Board of Trade, firmly in the public domain. Alas, the enhanced status conferred on unions by the war-time government could not protect members from the endemic decline of their industry, caused by lack of investment and foreign competition. Lloyd George's promises took on a hollow ring, and Clem began to see even trade unions and the Labour Party as part of a respectable cabal looking after its own interests, incapable of decisive action.

The conventional wisdom of industrialists and politicians was that British industry could only regain its pre-war prosperity by reducing costs and becoming more competitive in world markets: the fashionable word for it, very much favoured by Oldham mill-owners, was 'rationalisation'. In reality it meant an attack on living standards of workers by way of job cuts, wage cuts, and short-time working.

In the face of foreign competition, British exports slumped by almost half between 1919 and 1922, and men in traditional heavy industries such as textiles and engineering were laid off in their thousands. Apprentices like Clem Beckett faced the prospect of being out of work once they were 'out of their time' – a depressing prospect for lads who had spent seven years or so indentured to masters, on low wages, learning their trade, and perhaps hoping to marry once they were better paid as 'time-served' men. The idea of waiting patiently for improvements brought about by long-term rationalisation was as unattractive to Clem and his contemporaries as it was to the economist John Maynard Keynes, already exercised by government ineptitude. 'In the long run', Keynes famously said, 'we are all dead'.

Moreover, even the Labour Party, some of whose leaders had opposed the war, had no clear answer to the problem of unemployment, which in national terms had been as low as three per cent of the work force in 1914. By 1922 it had risen to eighteen per cent. Between 1920 and 1924 average income per head fell by fifteen per cent, but for families like the Becketts, living from hand-to-mouth, the situation was much worse.

Nor could politicians agree on how prosperity might be restored. With the break-up of the war-time coalition, the general election of 1922 failed to produce a party with an overall majority. This virtually guaranteed weak government, and those who had believed – or who had been told – that winning the war would create a better world became disillusioned. The confidence of Edwardian England had been irretrievably shattered, as traditional conservative values of once-prosperous towns such as Oldham came under pressure. The behaviour of voters in Oldham's dual-member constituency expressed a qualified vote of no confidence in the post-war government. It elected William Tout as its first Labour Member of Parliament, but the second candidate elected was Liberal Sir Edward Grigg – a result symbolic of the national mood of dissatisfaction with the old order combined with fear of the future. The mood at Labour's 'victory social' in the Greenacres Co-op Hall was distinctly restrained.

Britain's first Labour Cabinet entered office. As leader of a minority government, however, Ramsay MacDonald soon found that his party was a hostage to fortune, easy to blame when it emerged that it did not possess a magic wand. That MacDonald was hamstrung and hemmed in from the beginning by the combined majority of Conservatives and Liberals was a mitigation too feeble and mundane to appeal to impatient youngsters like Clem Beckett, to whom, in the ardour of youth, all things seemed possible. The experiences of the first Labour government would have provided an apposite Marxist text for the socialist farrier at Bowmans, reinforcing Clem's contempt for weak-kneed social democrats.

The unveiling of Oldham's war memorial in 1923 gave focus to the town's mourning, and the ceremony brought it to a standstill. Thousands of people crowded round the Parish Church of St Mary with St Peter to see the names of loved ones cast in bronze on huge plaques fixed to marble columns. Yet, for Clem and his sisters, it must have been a strange feeling to be mourning the loss of a father who was still alive, and whose name was absent from the memorial, although almost certainly on the police wanted list of husbands who had deserted their wives and children. Smaller memorials were erected in surrounding towns and hamlets, including the one at Austerlands, a short distance from Clem's birthplace. Hardly a family had escaped loss. Limbless ex-service men had become a familiar sight on the streets, as were their cumbersome black government-issue invalid carriages. And many who survived in one piece had invisible scars.

Euphemistically referred to as 'neurasthenia', there was an epidemic of men suffering with their 'nerves'. In some cases this was delayed reaction to the horrors of the trenches; what would, today, be referred to as post-traumatic stress disorder. The only help available was a strong cup of tea or one of numerous quack remedies advertised in the press. But at least the effects of war upon those who returned from the trenches were beginning to be understood. When ex-soldier William Gibbons appeared before Oldham magistrates for being drunk and disorderly, Police Superintendent Musgrave asked the court to take into account that he was still suffering the effects of 'shell shock'. Disabled or not, men like Gibbons who survived the trenches came to see Lloyd George's prophesy of 'a land fit for heroes' as a cynical insult.

There was, however, rough justice of small satisfaction to the victims of the reflotation boom. Some of the men who had fuelled it so recklessly were caught in the trap of their own making. In 1923 William Hopwood, who had picked up a knighthood at the zenith of his mercurial career, was declared bankrupt, with debts of £140,000. Sir William and others, who between them owed millions, were mercifully granted 'allowances' from the banks, and pensioned off to boarding houses in Prestatyn, a safe distance from the many thousands of Oldhamers who were enduring penury as a result of their misjudgments.

By 1924 Clem Beckett stood on the verge of manhood, fatherless and fighting-fit, good-natured, and for all his mischief-making on a motorbike, a good man imbued with well-meaning idealism. He was a prime recruit to any good cause, and all the more so if the likelihood was that he would be sacked when his apprenticeship came to an end. Clem himself, in spite of his love of horses, and perhaps because of his love of machines, would have foreseen the demise of the railway company horse fleet, on which his own blacksmith's firm depended.[2] Looking round for alternative employment across a landscape of unemployment and short-time working, Clem viewed the future with apprehension.

The war had brought some Labour politicians and trade unionists into government. Lloyd George had engaged them in the war effort by setting up joint committees to help absorb women and unskilled workers in industries depleted of manpower by army recruitment, and a Labour front-bencher, John Robert Clynes, an Oldhamer, had joined the War Cabinet. At local level, Labour politicians had become part of the war-time bureaucracy which carried on into peace-time. So it was that early in 1924 the weekly edition of the *Oldham Chronicle* took as its subject, in a series entitled *Some Local Men,* 'Mr James Bell, JP'.

Bell, a career politician, union organiser, and magistrate, had stood unsuccessfully as Labour candidate in several constituencies. Under a cartoon showing a dapper, moustachioed, besuited figure wearing a trilby hat and carrying what was doubtless meant to suggest an important portfolio of documents, the *Chronicle* recited a long list of Bell's official positions. These included 'executive member of the Weavers' Amalgamation, member of the Legislative Council of the Textile Factory Workers' Association, and member of the Joint Committee of Employers and Operatives' Representatives,' the latter body 'still sitting to consider ways and means of bringing about an improvement in the trade'. In times of austerity, when short-time working was becoming the norm, Bell personified the radical socialist notion of the Labour Party as a prop of the capitalist system. He was precisely the kind of ineffectual 'old fogey' authority figure that Clem and his pals would have no time for.

Improving trade for the benefit of employees, and not the war effort, was a function beyond the purpose for which the Joint Committee had been set up, but it suited employers resisting wage rises or attempting to impose cuts to have the imprimatur of a hand-wringing workers' representative endorsing their decisions. Bell was also chairman of the 'Oldham Insurance Committee' in which capacity he had 'done much valuable work in carrying out the Act'.

In fairness, one reason that Labour was making steady inroads into local government was that men like Bell had demonstrated its inherent moderation and respectability. But in the eyes of bright young men like Clem Beckett, Labour councillors appointed as magistrates or as members of government committees had simply become part of the status quo, representatives of a moribund establishment.

Meanwhile, there was laughter in Oldham Police Court on 2 October 1924, when Eli Anderson appeared before magistrates charged with dangerous use of an unlicensed motorcycle. Riding erratically through the streets of Greenacres, he had been spotted by Constables Lally and Bourne being shoved off from a standing start by a group of youths. There was a loud bang from the exhaust and PC Lally had to jump clear of Eli's machine as it careered past him. When it finally came to a halt at the bottom of Roundthorn Road, Eli fell off, and was apprehended. The court heard that the bike was 'home-made', had been built from scrap and spare parts, had no working brakes, no silencer, and could reach a maximum speed of only 10mph. Without naming names, Eli claimed that it was a team effort and that he was simply the test pilot. Given the manifest deficiencies of the machine, this might have been all to the good so far as Clem's reputation as a mechanic was concerned.

No doubt the matter provided light relief for Their Worships as they ploughed through a long list of cases brought against husbands in desertion of wives, as well as prosecutions following a spate of hooliganism on the town's trams. There was, too, an increasing burden on the courts as a result of motorcar accidents, so that in nearby Royton summonses for driving offences made up the majority of cases. Almost every edition of Oldham's two daily papers carried news of pedestrians, often children, killed or seriously injured as a result of the reckless, dangerous or drunken driving of motorcars. With middle-class car ownership rising steadily, the carnage would only get worse. Casualties in motorcycle accidents, however, were usually limited to riders and pillion passengers. Accordingly, the chairman of the Bench, which included the town's mayor, expressed his admiration for the ingenuity, inventiveness and industry of the boys, and declined to impose any penalty on Eli beyond court costs.

Even so, the authorities remained vigilant as to the menace of motorcycling and its dangers. In the same week as Eli's case before the magistrates, the town's Watch Committee passed a resolution calling on the government to make pillion riding illegal.[3] Councillor Freeman lamented that it was impossible for riders to balance their machines with a pillion passenger on the back, and the chairman, Alderman Dr Low, commented: 'How the heels of some of the girls who ride in this way do not get into the spokes of the wheels, I do not know.' Oh dear, perhaps he had seen Clem cavorting round the streets with *two* girls riding behind him!

CLEM BECKETT: MOTORCYCLE LEGEND AND WAR HERO

For many, the sight of working-class youths on noisy, ramshackle motorbikes was an affront to social order. It challenged the assumption that beyond commercial and military use, motorcars and motorcycles were the preserve of the well-heeled. Better-off mill managers and office employees living along quiet roads leading up to the moors were disturbed and irritated by the sight, and sound, of these harum-scarum lads racing past their substantial homes. Imagine their reaction, then, to 'Road Louse', a homemade car put together by Clem from all manner of spare parts, and reputedly capable of speeds up to 90mph. But it was not only youngsters who caused problems on the roads. In the early hours of the morning, a local doctor returning from a social call on a colleague crashed his car into the new war memorial at Springhead, demolishing it.

More often than not, Clem and friends, including the Anderson boys, headed for a wayside inn, The Moorcock, known to regulars as Bill o' Jack's, perched on moorland above the village of Greenfield, overlooking the Dovestones valley. From there, a narrow road snaked over the hills towards Holmfirth, passing another landmark hostelry, The Isle of Skye. These bikers were not interested in drinking. Their chief amusement of a summer's evening was racing their machines at speed. Moreover, the Roundthorn boys took on all-comers, and usually won.

In their daring and youthful exuberance, Clem and his pals gave expression to post-war optimism, to a feeling that the 'war to ends all wars' had bequeathed them a new era. They were disinclined to share in the pessimism which others felt in the context of shrinking international markets for cotton. They were young and confident. The growth in car and motorcycle ownership promised excitement and mobility beyond the wildest dreams of their parents. They did not hanker after the 'good old days' before the war. Rather they anticipated an era of technological change, and wanted to be part of it. In contrast, the motorcycle correspondent of the *Oldham Evening Chronicle* perfectly summed up the complacent attitude of the 'old fogeys' who seemed to be holding back progress. 'It is really difficult to see how the modern machine, so reliable, and so efficient, can be much improved.' Unfortunately, his attitude mirrored that of Oldham's mill-owning aristocracy, who in the face of increasing foreign competition, were unable or unwilling to recognise the need for modernisation and innovation.

And although Britain, unlike much of Europe, had emerged from the war with its old order intact, it too was having to come to terms with changes of a revolutionary nature, forced upon it by the exigencies of war. Oldham women Annie Kenney and Marjorie Lees had been at the forefront of pre-war agitation for the enfranchisement of women. While the passing of the Representation of the People Act in 1918 had given the vote to women over the age of thirty, they continued to agitate for the same rights as men. Soldiers' wounds had been dressed by women nurses, home fires had been kept burning by mothers, sisters and wives, and the wheels of industry only kept turning because women had filled the jobs of men away at the front.

Chapter Five

Temperance Hall

*'The class struggle is being waged in every country; with
the experience of Russia to guide us I entirely agree there
will be a period when the dictatorship of the proletariat
must be resorted to.'*
Tom Mann, writing in 1923, after his return
from a visit to Russia.

Against a backdrop of uncertainty and electoral stasis, the nascent
Communist Party of Great Britain (CPGB) sought to kindle support for
a revolutionary solution to society's problems. Communists believed
they had fertile ground to plough in the industrial heartlands of Britain,
and that freedom from want, and full employment would follow if only
they could bring about the downfall of the capitalist system. Formed in
1920 as an amalgam of socialist societies, the Party had strong roots
in Lancashire. There, it made great strides as post-war disillusionment
set in, creating an image of decisiveness bound to appeal to the likes
of Clem and other young men whose future was at stake. Among its
founding members was Harry Pollitt, a charismatic Lancastrian, born
in Droylsden, a few miles from Oldham. The Party's early leadership
consisted of old guard socialists such as folk-hero Tom Mann, combined
with a new breed of younger middle-class intellectuals. What both groups
had in common was an unswerving belief in Karl Marx's paradigm
theory of dialectical materialism: an assertion that the tide of human
history was determined by unstoppable evolutionary forces destined to
bring down the tyranny of capitalism and replace it with a just society
controlled by the working classes. The cause to which Party members
pledged allegiance was backed up by Marx's scholarly research, much
of it carried out in England, some in Manchester. But above all the Party
was inspired by the success of the Russian Revolution in 1917.

So it was, in the autumn of 1924, as the minority Labour government struggled to cope with economic crisis amid soaring unemployment, that Clem Beckett and friends waited in eager anticipation for the Communist Party of Great Britain to bring its travelling road show to town.[1] Oldham was certainly promising ground for recruitment. The general malaise of the post-war economy had been exacerbated locally by the collapse of the flotation boom. The shockwaves were such that even Bradbury and Co had been forced to close their factory, and anyone preaching conspiracy theory politics was assured of a hearing. The venue was the Temperance Hall and the star of the show was Tom Mann, a firebrand speaker who had been a pre-war trade union leader and who, even before the First World War, had served a term of imprisonment for incitement to mutiny in the armed forces. Mann, a socialist mountebank, was a brilliant itinerant orator, who had spent time in Australia and South Africa. Invariably he attracted the attention of the authorities, and appeared to relish prosecutions as a means of amplifying his reputation. A founding member of the CPGB, Mann had been invited, along with other foreign sympathisers, to visit Russia as a guest of the Soviet government. They were given a sanitised view of life under the Bolsheviks, and, of course, it was easy to castigate critics of the new regime as apologists for capitalism. Mann's speaking tour took him the length and breadth of Britain, and wherever he spoke, Party loyalists ensured a good attendance.

The meeting at Oldham Temperance Hall heard from various speakers that Communists were committed to expose every crisis in society, and that sooner or later one such crisis would bring about the promised land. When he came to hear Tom Mann, Clem was mesmerised by his well-practised eloquence. What he was not told, however, was that from the beginning, the Communist Party of Great Britain had been under orders from the Comintern, the international directorate of the Russian government. This would certainly not have assisted recruitment, nor indeed in advancing the Party's aim of attracting membership from other socialist parties such as the Labour Party, and its constituent body, the Independent Labour Party.

Disingenuously, Tom Mann made it clear that he saw a role for Communists as a pressure group *within* the Labour Party. Accordingly, he was at pains to express his support for traditional Labour institutions such as the Co-op. It was all part of the Communist plan to infiltrate established bodies in the Labour movement, and in these early days there was nothing in the Labour Party rule book to exclude members who were also members of the CPGB. Indeed, Mann was going round saying that there would soon be a complete reconciliation between the Communists and the Labour Party. The Soviet charm offensive on Britain also included the formation of an organisation known as the Society for Cultural Relations, open to anyone with a benign view towards Russia even if they were not Communists. In July the Society's inaugural meeting in London had been presided over by Margaret Llewelyn Davies, a stalwart of Britain's Co-operative movement.

By praising the Co-operative movement, whose working-class pedigree predated Marxism by half a century, and whose street-corner stores were as familiar to Oldhamers as mill chimneys, Mann was trying to poach typical Labour voters. The Oldham Co-operative Society was indeed enjoying its golden age. The ornately decorated tile facades of its neighbourhood stores, like the one round the corner from Clem's home in Swinton Street, were as much a part of the landscape as porticoed Nonconformist chapels. Mann was pitching to identify working-class values of self-help with the idea of revolution. His style of speaking was in the great tradition of radical and socialist orators, passionate as a Christian evangelist, working his audience up to a fever-pitch of righteous indignation with homilies of deprivation spiced with references to the languorous lives of the idle rich. Those who were moved by his version of a better world were invited to come forward and publicly demonstrate their conversion, with Communist Party organisers sitting at a little table below the platform, ready with application forms. That night five young Oldhamers stepped up to join the Young Communist League: Leslie Smith, Bob Mayall, Jimmy Barnes, Eli Anderson, and eighteen-year-old apprentice blacksmith Clem Beckett. The meeting at the Temperance Hall was Clem's epiphany. Communism became his creed.

It is easy to understand the appeal of Communism to Clem. The chance to belong to an elite group of activists had a powerful attraction for youngsters with a sense of adventure as well as a social conscience. Tom Mann was at the height of his powers, and while allegations that he was in cahoots with Russian leaders would alienate many, it would only add to his charisma among others. Clem Beckett was quite a catch. He and his friends believed what they were told about the good life in post-revolutionary Russia, lauded as a template to cure all society's ills, much in the way that a century earlier idealists had looked across the Channel to the French Revolution.

MacDonald's government fell within weeks of Mann's visit to Oldham, caught in a vice between hysterical anti-Communist scaremongering and the disillusionment of first-time Labour voters who could only see things getting worse. As a marginal dual-member constituency, Oldham was honoured by campaign visits from MacDonald himself, and Conservative leader Stanley Baldwin, both of whom addressed large meetings at the gates of Alexandra Park. Tout's short stint in Parliament was brought to an end when he lost his seat to Conservative opponent Alfred Duff Cooper. Clem was among the ranks of YCL members who demonstrated their scorn and impatience with all main-party candidates.

Tom Mann himself was linked to the infamous 'Zinoviev Letter' episode, a plot to scare off Labour voters, hatched by members of the British Secret Service. Yet however many reports were to come out of Soviet Russia alleging totalitarian excesses, the CPGB had a ready answer to the right-wing press and others: they would say that, wouldn't they? As the election approached, the Oldham Board of Guardians reported an increase in those receiving 'indoor relief' (in the workhouse) to a figure of 1,175, and a worrying number of smallpox cases in 'casual wards'. In the same week, the Short Time Organisation Committee of the Federation of Master Cotton Spinners resolved to hold its meeting in camera and subsequently announced there would be no change in the existing arrangements.

As a member of the Young Communist League, Clem Beckett was expected to toe the line and to put in time selling or distributing pamphlets or copies of the *Workers' Weekly,* the Party's propaganda mouthpiece. According to Party tributes following his death it was a responsibility Clem took seriously, but speaking some thirty years later, Clem's sister Mary gave a different account. She maintained that Clem was never politically active, and only attended Party meetings 'occasionally'. However, with the final years of his apprenticeship characterised by economic crisis and unrest, all of which was grist to the Communist mill, it would have been easy for Clem to accept the Party's central doctrine that a breakdown of society, leading to revolution, was imminent.

In 1925 leaders of the CPGB, in pursuit of their revolutionary aims, were prosecuted for sedition. The case provided them with much publicity and the resulting guilty verdicts, followed by short prison sentences, enhanced their reputation as men of action. Among them was Tom Wintringham, an egotistical middle-class apostle of Communism, whose life as a Party propagandist was destined to impact profoundly on that of Clem Beckett and thousands of his contemporaries. Guilty verdicts resulted in only short terms of imprisonment. These men regarded themselves as victims of a corrupt capitalist system, and their loyalty was indeed, as the prosecution alleged, to the Communist Party of the Soviet Union. What Clem Beckett did not know was that the machinery of the CPGB, and the expenses of its leaders, were heavily subsidised by payments secretly made by the Comintern. Even the purchase of Party headquarters in King Street, London, was facilitated by 'red gold'. Some of the money was smuggled across from the Continent in used dollar bills. Party membership fees raised at home accounted for only a small fraction of total expenses.

Accordingly, when a Parliamentary by-election took place in Oldham the same year, William Tout, trying to recover his seat, had once again to contend not only with scaremongering tactics from his Conservative opponent, but also open criticism from Clem and the YCL. It was no surprise, then, that when Conservatives and Liberals joined forces with the express intention of keeping Labour out, they succeeded. The Liberal candidate beat Tout with a big majority. Tout was out for good, and it would be a long time before voters in Oldham could be persuaded to return a Labour candidate to Parliament.

The CPGB continued its campaign of resistance to wage cuts. In April 1925 Oldham's former Liberal Member of Parliament, Winston Churchill, Chancellor of the Exchequer in Stanley Baldwin's Conservative government, restored the pound to the 'Gold Standard'. Then, as now, there was little popular understanding of economics, and Churchill's grasp of monetary policy was no better than that of ordinary citizens such as Clem Beckett. Churchill acted on the advice of Montagu Norman, Governor of the Bank of England, who believed that strong currency would cure economic ills 'in the long run'. Its more immediate effect, however, was to make British exports less competitive, and to provoke a new round of wage cuts. When, the following year, British trade unionists organised a General Strike to oppose industrial wage cuts, CPGB members prepared for action. But its hopes that a revolution would emerge from the chaos were dashed. Even its most ardent members must have begun to realise that although Britain still retained a fully-functioning class system, with huge sections of its people living on the breadline, there was little prospect of a general uprising. In Oldham the strike collapsed within a few days. To avoid future victimisation, apprentices like Clem were exempted from their union's call to take part. But the continuing miners' strike imposed hardship on working-class homes in Oldham, and as winter closed in families like the Becketts were obliged to scavenge for coal themselves wherever spoil heaps could be found. Oldham Edge witnessed a procession of raggedy children, sent to scoop up coal into buckets, prams and tin baths.

Clem Beckett and other raw recruits to the CPGB did not believe stories they read or heard about suppression of freedoms in Russia, or allegations that Party funds were subsidised by secret payments from the Comintern, swelled by vast amounts of jewellery expropriated from the deposed Russian aristocracy and sold on the international black market. Nor would Clem have known that the miners' strike was being prolonged by funds received from Russia. Again, the capitalist press would say that, wouldn't they? Moreover, the Party remained devout in its belief that Soviet Russia was the perfect template for a better society. In every pamphlet and newspaper produced by the Party, in every meeting and at every demonstration, Clem Beckett and comrades of the Young Communist League loyally toed the party line: that society's ills emanated from the 'capitalist system' and could only be cured by its total destruction. Nor would they know that by now there were hundreds of Russians in Britain, ostensibly part of a trade delegation, but many in fact reporting to the Comintern as spies or tasked to liaise with British comrades to foment revolution.

For dedicated Communists who would otherwise have been trapped in dead-end jobs in declining industries, politics offered a way out. A few contemporaries were able, with the help of Russian gold, to follow professional careers as Party organisers. One such was Ernie Woolley, born in Gorton, Manchester, who, relishing subterfuge and all manner of clandestine activity, became a paid organiser for the YCL in the north-west of England. His penchant for coded communications, his organising of a cyclist division ready to carry messages between comrades in the hour of need, reflected the prevailing optimism that one day *soon,* the workers would rise up and the Party would be there to lead them. For new recruits like Clem, Woolley, who had served in the Royal Flying Corps during the war, was an inspirational figure in stark contrast to the likes of Bell and his Labour colleagues who sat on committees, collaborating with employers in reducing wages and imposing short-time working. Woolley saw himself as a fearless man of action, cultivating an heroic image designed to appeal to his followers in the Young Communist League. In turn he would have viewed Clem as an ideal recruit to an elite group of activists who might one day be in the vanguard of revolution. Clem's reputation as a tough rugby player, and his prowess as a motorcyclist were strong recommendations, as was his service in the Territorial Army.

The possibility of a revolutionary overthrow of the traditional institutions in Britain existed in the minds of some politicians and civil servants as much as it was part of the Communist mantra. Hardly surprising, given that at this time a Party recruitment leaflet began with the words: 'The Communist Party honestly and frankly stands for the abolition of the capitalist State, and all its machinery, such as Parliament and the British Constitution.' Given that the authorities were increasingly alarmed at the activities of the CPGB, it seems unlikely that, as a known Communist, Clem would have been able to remain in the Territorial Army for as long as six years – as claimed by some contemporaries. It is possible, of course, that Clem just kept his head down during the years of his apprenticeship, and this is consistent with sister Mary's recollections that Clem was never really an active Party member. But it is contradicted by the statement of Oldham Party organiser Herbert Liversage, who claimed that Clem was a dedicated door-to-door canvasser for Party newspapers.

Concerned about Party propaganda, the government leaned on the British Board of Film Censorship to prevent the showing of a Soviet film, *Battleship Potemkin*. The Admiralty, having got wind of the film, was desperate to ban the depiction of mutiny on board a Russian battleship, 'so as to constitute very objectionable propaganda against the discipline of the Fighting Forces.' Indeed, throughout the 1920s British Intelligence, through MI5 and Special Branch, never let up in its surveillance of Communist Party members and the activities of Russians in Britain. Although the Party of the mid-1920s had fewer than 5,000 members, the authorities even became alarmed at the activities of the Society for Cultural Relations. The SCR was enjoying considerable success recruiting sympathisers from among Britain's liberal elite, focusing on extolling the achievements of Soviet art, literature and science.

Loyal Party member though he was, there is no evidence that Clem Beckett ever showed the slightest interest in these esoteric posturings. To him, the appeal of Party membership lay in the call to action. Beyond that, he was like any other young man, devoting his energies – in no particular order – to work, girls, family and motorbikes.

Communist Party membership doubled in the summer that followed the General Strike, but many workers remained deeply suspicious of the CPGB's links with Russia. While its leadership held firmly to the belief that revolution was only a matter of time, the fact was that the CPGB was a revolutionary party in a non-revolutionary situation. Love stories and Charlie Chaplin slapstick, not *Battleship Potemkin*, were the staple diet of patrons at Oldham's new art deco cinemas. In September 1927, as Clem's apprenticeship was coming to an end, Warner Brothers released *The Jazz Singer*, the first 'talkie' to be shown in cinemas. Its star was Al Jolson, who, like Karl Marx, was a Jewish émigré from Russia. The film was soon showing in cinemas all over the world, and Clem Beckett, girl on his arm, would have been just as keen as other Oldhamers to see it. But the fact remains that the majority of cinema-goers were far more likely to have heard of Hollywood than Petrograd.

Chapter Six

Besting Mr Toad

*'Who in his right mind would sit astride a potent,
streamlined 500 c.c. motor cycle with no brakes, and fling
it though a series of tight turns on a loose surface? What
orthodox motorcyclist would point his front wheel to the
right in order to turn left? But then speedway has never
followed the orthodox or the obvious.'*
Martin Rogers, speedway journalist.

Some recruits to the ranks of the CPGB – men like Harry Pollitt and Ernie Woolley – became absolutists, their conversion to Communism resulting in the unshakable, all-consuming belief that in the revolution that was just around the corner they would find their destiny. Clem Beckett was not among their number. For all his honest belief in Communism, he was not ready to dedicate himself to the cause to the exclusion of all else. Pending the revolution, he had other priorities, especially girls, but more importantly to him, motorcycles.

As with motorcars, ownership of motorbikes in the 1920s was largely confined to better-off younger men and women who did not care to be chauffeur-driven, and who enjoyed the novelty of machines that brought thrills, speed and freedom on quiet country roads. Black and white photographs of the time depict them, Wooster-like, donned in tweeds and goggles, posing astride their machines. Typically for northerners, the objective of a weekend *run-out* was a country pub or the promenade of a Lancashire coastal resort, such as Morecambe or Southport. Like so many 'Mr Toads', middle-class people with money to buy motorcars and motorbikes thought they owned the road to the exclusion of lesser mortals. Indeed, until Parliament intervened, motorcyclists had recklessly indulged in organised races on public roads, with inevitable consequences.

Early motor sport, including motorcycle racing, was also dominated by middle-class competitors and organisations such as the Royal Automobile Club, whose powerful offshoot, the Auto-Cycle Union (ACU), was responsible for regulating it. Contemporary journals like the *Motor Cycle,* produced to cater for these amateur enthusiasts, reflected nothing of the post-war economic crisis affecting staple industries such as textiles and mining. Rather they took an upbeat approach, reflecting the energy and optimism of growing enterprises centred on the internal combustion engine.

Not surprisingly, when the new craze of dirt track motorcycle racing reached Britain from Australia and America, it was an irresistible draw for a tearaway youngster like Clem. Later in life Clem enjoyed recounting the legend that dirt track racing – or speedway, as it soon became known – was invented by accident. According to him, a sudden torrential downpour at a grass track event in Australia left the surface so sodden that officials pronounced it too dangerous to race upon. Then somebody suggested it would be all right to race on cinders round the perimeter. When the cinders got ploughed up the machines began to skid, and in a Eureka moment riders realised they could still keep control while accelerating. The resultant noise amid showers of cinders produced the perfect spectacle – and the birth of 'broadsiding'. It was a good story, which Clem enjoyed telling, even though the truth was more prosaic. It came to be generally acknowledged that the sport was, in effect, devised as a variant of grass track racing by Australian Johnnie Hoskins and friends, who, in turn introduced it to Britain. That said, patriots still insist that even before the invasion from Down Under, 'dirt track demonstrations' were being given by motorcyclists who were members of the Ilford (Essex) and Camberley (Surrey) Motor Clubs. As early as 1915 a single motorcyclist, Charlie McEvoy, was demonstrating cinder-shifting at Paddington Recreation Ground.

Clem did not have far to go to see the new sport for himself. Only five miles from Oldham a new track was opened at the Audenshaw Race Course, on 3 March 1928, days after the first dirt track event at High Beech in rural Essex, where an incredible 30,000 spectators had turned up, astounding everybody, including the organisers who had anticipated only 2,000.[1] The event at High Beech was front page news in the *Daily Mirror*; it was filmed for *Pathé News*, and shown in cinemas the length and breadth of the country. While motorcycles and other types of motorcycle sport were familiar to everyone, the phenomenon of 'broadsiding' was completely novel.

There was an explosion of interest in the new sport, although more traditional, and far more gentle aspects of motorcycle competition continued. Five days after the momentous event at High Beech, the *Motor Cycle* described the Sunbeam Club's London to Bognor 'Trial' with 232 entrants enjoying hill-climbs over the South Downs on a perfect spring day with a leisurely lunch taken on Bognor Pier. Tame stuff for a working-class lad like Clem Beckett who had neither the time nor the means to affect tweedy gentility, but was equally attracted to the promise of excitement offered by motorbikes and motorcycling. Besides, Clem cut quite a dash racing through the streets of Oldham, with a girl – sometimes two – riding pillion and holding on for dear life.

Clawed out of fertile ground on the edge of Ashton Moss, an area known for its market gardens and small-holdings, Audenshaw Racecourse had formerly been used for trotting horses. The trotting course was sometimes referred to as 'The Snipe', located close to a public house of that name, suggesting that the Moss had once provided a habitat for England's most secretive game bird. Only a quarter of a mile across the Moss was the site of another course, at Dodds Farm, Droylsden, where northern aficionados still claim that the first British dirt track meeting took place on 27 June the previous year. The Droylsden track was surfaced with cinders recycled from nearby coal-fired East Manchester power station, further symbolising the new sport as a product of the fossil-fuelled industrial age.[2] However, the promoters at Audenshaw, the South Manchester Motor Club, were bound to be encouraged to put on further meetings by the support for their first venture – with estimated attendance figures varying between 10,000 and 20,000.

Clem, now aged twenty-one, together with Irving Anderson, was among spectators at the Audenshaw event, which – in spite of the rival claimant over the Moss – was announced by organisers to be the first dirt track meeting in Britain 'run as is done in Australia'. In no time they were hooked by the furious spectacle of machines, some specially adapted, racing over the half-mile oval circuit. Aping the razzmatazz of American speedway, the promoters did all they could to spice the races with excitement, and in this they were helped by a pervasive atmosphere of cavalier amateurism.

One of the riders in the first race, the eccentric, one-legged G.E. 'Pa' Cowley, was more than seventy years old. Cowley had begun motorcycling in 1889, and his equally unconventional daughter, 'Dot', was soon to appear among the dirt track pioneers. In the third race, for machines up to 500cc, the joint winner, Alec Jackson, set off smoking a cigarette, which doubtless appealed to Clem, an habitual smoker, who was frequently photographed with a cigarette in his mouth. Many riders obliged promoters and spectators alike by recklessness, verging on suicidal risk-taking. They fell off, were catapulted over handlebars, and got pinned under their machines. On rare occasions they suffered 'frost' burns to their most tender parts from leaking fuel tanks filled with methanol. Most commonly they sustained cuts and bruises (especially to the face) and at the very first meeting Clem saw at least four riders injured.

The inherent risks of dirt track racing were myriad. On poorly constructed or maintained tracks, often pot-holed, with cinders packed too tightly or too loosely, riders were at greater risk of being thrown to the ground at speed. Any falling rider might be hit by his own machine, gashed by handlebars, lacerated by the revolving chain, or stabbed by a foot-rest. Worse impact injuries were inflicted in frequent collisions, particularly on bends. Riders might part company with their machines by a side-swipe or by being projected over the handlebars. Carelessly positioned fencing and fence posts were especially dangerous. The risk of injury was not confined to the track. About 400 spectators intent on achieving a better view at Audenshaw climbed onto the roof of the stand, and were only persuaded to come down by officials and police when people underneath noticed sagging beams.[3]

Nevertheless, some commentators on the new sport, supported by vested interests, minimised the dangers. A columnist in the *Motor Cycle* even opined that the risk of serious injury was 'infinitesimal': 'I have already seen two riders loop the loop [...] neither man was hurt.' Tellingly, however, the writer admitted that he had still only attended two meetings. At the second Audenshaw meeting one rider who fell sustained a broken collar-bone, but nevertheless remounted to finish. The phenomenon of gallant, sometimes injured, riders getting back onto their machines pleased the crowd no end – but it was not so pleasing for other riders, who frequently collided with them.

In the meantime, back in his shed in Oldham, and with help from the Anderson boys, Clem was busy constructing a machine suitable for dirt track racing. In order to be eligible for competitions, Clem and Irving were obliged to apply for licences from the Auto-Cycle Union, and this required application for membership of its affiliate body, Stalybridge Motor Club. Clem was later to allege that one of the conditions of the licence was an undertaking *not* to take part in dirt track events! Indeed, this is more than likely in view of the diehard resistance to the new sport being put up by traditionally minded members of the ACU. Early in May, at a meeting behind the grand terracotta facade of the Metropole Hotel in Leeds, northern members of the ACU demanded a special meeting of its national rule-making council to prevent recognition 'of any syndicate or organisation formed for the promotion of events for gain'. The dramatic intrusion of dirt track racing into the genteel world of amateur competition had sparked a fresh round in the age-old conflict between amateur and professional values, and traditionalists were already bemoaning the 'speedway problem' – a product, in their view, of undesirable foreign and colonial influence.

But for the likes of Clem Beckett and other working-class lads there was no problem. Observing the huge crowds turning up wherever dirt track events were staged, they reasoned that the best way to enjoy the thrill of motorcycling was to make it pay. From Clem's perspective, here was an opportunity infinitely more attractive than the alternative of shoeing horses, and certainly more possible than a revolution that might never come.

Within weeks, probably at the second Audenshaw meeting on Saturday, 12 May, Clem Beckett made his debut appearance on the track. He had to pay the promoters 3s 6d for the privilege, and thought it was worth every penny. With most machines bereft of a clutch, riders required a 'pusher-off', and doubtless Clem would have turned to one or other of the Anderson lads. A strong pusher-off to ensure the engine started quickly was essential with standing starts, where a good shove could give the rider a crucial advantage. As well as an estimated 10,000 spectators, several uninvited bookmakers got into the rickety Audenshaw stand, and when officials asked them to leave, police refused to intervene. There would have been long odds against the unknown rider from Oldham on a homemade machine with a side-valve engine. But even in these very early days of the new sport, Clem was ahead of the game. He had cottoned on to the benefits of fuel 'additives', and contemporaries remember him mixing ether with petrol in order to achieve a maximum surge of acceleration – crucial in the charge towards the first bend at the start of a race.

However, in another early example of lax safety standards at Audenshaw, the earth and cinder track had been insufficiently watered. Typically, though, Clem's sanguine acceptance of the risks was complemented by determination to win. Sure enough, in a brave challenge to an established rider called Tattersall, a wheel-to-wheel battle developed over the dusty track. Having taken the lead, Clem fell off in front of his rival's machine. Tattersall mercifully swerved to avoid Clem, who was lucky to escape with bruises. It was not his first fall from a motorbike, nor would it be his last. Daredevil Clem Beckett had found his forte, and his days as a blacksmith were numbered.

Clem's career as a dirt rack rider was meteoric. In the week following his debut, he obtained the use of a better, purpose-built machine, a Velocete. On 19 May, in pouring rain and with treacherous track conditions, he again made his mark. In spite of another bruising accident in a qualifying heat, he finished third in the final 350cc class. Spectators observed his natural mastery of the broadside – a quintessential feature of the sport, and its most dangerous manoeuvre – involving the rider cutting out his motor to induce the machine to skid or slide round the bends, with the rider trailing or dabbing his inside foot on the ground to maintain stability.[4] This itself presented extra danger, not only for riders but also spectators. At a later Audenshaw meeting the iron sheath worn over a rider's broadsiding foot came off and was launched into the air, narrowly missing officials standing on the inside of the circuit near to the judge's box. There was no doubt that the new sport was as dangerous as it was exciting.

Clem was riding for fun, as were most of the other riders. At the same time he would have noted that victories could bring riches. On a winning streak at one of the May meetings, leading rider Harold Riley 'Ginger' Lees, of Bury, was able to scoop £60 (worth about £500 today) in prize money. There were in addition awards in kind, namely, according to programme notes, '3 Solid Gold Watches' valued at £7-10 shillings, '6 Canteens of Cutlery' valued at £3-10s, and '6 Solid Silver Cigarette Cases' valued at £1-10s each.

Naturally riders took risks, and there were injuries at every meeting. Danger was the sport's main selling point, and from the beginning Audenshaw acquired a notorious safety record. Whenever a rider fell, the crowd lapsed into an eerie silence. Usually – but by no means always – the rider managed to get to his feet, upon which the crowd broke into enthusiastic cheering. In addition to the usual hazards, the cinders at Audenshaw had been packed down too hard, which hindered broadsiding by making it more difficult for riders to stay in control of their machines.

Dirt track racing quickly became second only to association football as a spectator sport. Although some organisers, guided by the Auto-Cycle Union, clung to the term 'dirt track' racing, the American alternative of 'speedway' was increasingly used by the public, warming to the cinematic glamour of all things American.

Transplanted to Europe, however, where political and economic crises had become the norm, the nascent world of speedway was a natural milieu for promoters keen to cash in. And there was no shortage of chancers ready to exploit young men desperate to make a name for themselves. Attracted by glamour and the opportunity to escape humdrum and uncertain employment in mill or factory, they were easy meat. Like prize-fighters, they were willing to provide entertainment and spectacle by taking risks with their lives, and in no time the new sport was creating a mythology of mystique and heroism. Riders adopted snappy – sometimes ludicrous – nicknames: 'Stiffy' Aston, 'Acorn' Dobson, 'Crazy' Hutchins, 'Crasher' Myhill, 'Riskit' Riley, and 'Slider' Shuttleworth were among them, while spectators had special affection for plucky men such as the Newcastle rider 'Onandoff' Johnson, who remounted their machines, sometimes serially in the same race, after spills. The reputation Clem had enjoyed since his youthful exploits at Bill o'Jack's led to the sobriquet 'Daredevil' Beckett (sometimes spelled 'Dare-devil' or 'Dare-Devil' in the press and on race programmes), though this gradually faded away as Clem's career progressed. He did not, however, become less of a daredevil.

The arrival of the dirt track in Britain triggered howls of outrage from traditionalists – the sort of motorcyclists who enjoyed leisurely weekend trial runs to the coast. Writing to the *Motor Cycle,* 'B.H.C.' of Birmingham purported to represent 'all lovers of the sport of motor cycling' when he declared that 'dirt track racing is an evil […] for which there appears to be no remedy.' It was a *tour de force* of class bias: half of the spectators were neither motorcyclists nor even motorists, attracted only by the prospect of witnessing spectacular accidents, while riders of 'dirt irons' were of a 'distinct type' (that is to say the *wrong* type) requiring 'freak' machines. The dirt track 'circus show' would influence any self-respecting father against allowing his 'modern son – or daughter' to take up 'the most desirable and healthy hobby for youth today.' Sitting at his writing desk long ago in May 1928, perhaps not having taken enough water with his usual evening snifter, there was no stopping B.H.C, who claimed that with greedy promoters and professional riders leaving amateurs with no chance of winning, genuine members of the 'motor cycle movement' would soon be regarded as 'social lepers'.

As new dirt tracks sprang up across the country, there were at first insufficient riders to satisfy demand. So long as star men were in short supply, riders could make good money. The problem was that, unlike association football, speedway had no settled organisation or regulation. This meant that individual riders like Clem had to go from one race meeting to another, negotiating appearance fees with promoters and track owners as best they could. Of course, a rough-hewn man like Clem had, at first, no idea what his services were worth. Gossip in the riders' paddock was an unreliable source of information.

When it came to the 'dirt track problem' it was soon obvious that ACU diehards were fighting a losing battle, and that the best line of retreat was to argue its indispensable role as a rule-maker, bringing order to chaos. Speedway was a volatile business, which matched the frenetic mood of the 'Roaring Twenties', and whatever its upper-class associations and cherished links to the Royal Automobile Club, there was a general acceptance that the ACU was the only body that could bring law and order to the speedway gold-rush. It was a very English solution, stated succinctly by an editorial in the *Motor Cycle:* the new sport could only thrive if it accepted ACU control; promoters must work in co-operation with the governing body.

When the series of five speedway meetings at Audenshaw came to an end in May 1928, Clem was inevitably drawn to try his luck on a bigger stage, and a better arena for his talents was the stadium at White City, Manchester. Indeed, given that in June the British Dirt Track Racing Association forsook its original venue at Audenshaw in favour of White City, it was a natural progression. The track was part of a leisure complex two miles south of the city centre, close to Manchester United Football Club and the Lancashire County Cricket Club's ground at Old Trafford. Amid a fanfare of publicity at the opening meeting in June, American 'star' Lloyd 'Sprouts' Elder demonstrated the art of broadsiding to a crowd of 13,000 before the start of the race programme. Home-grown Arthur Franklyn, even younger than Clem, soon established himself as a favourite with the crowds, and riders who had raced alongside Clem at Audenshaw, including Ginger Lees and Tommy Hatch, were also anxious to make their mark.[5]

However, new corporate interests quickly realised that speedway on the grand scale required promotion and publicity akin to that which had already created professional football stars and top clubs. Stardom was one thing – and it was not long before Clem was being stopped in the street to sign autographs – but 'club loyalty', a much-vaunted concept in the ACU, was another, and it did not sit easily with the drive for financial gain being pursued by some promoters and some riders. Noting the shenanigans at 'flapping' tracks like Audenshaw, Clem soon learned that it was a case of every man for himself, and gradually formed the opinion that the ACU did not adequately protect the interests of riders.[6] Even so, there followed a period in his life which by his own account was happy, exciting, and punctuated by adventure.

Chapter Seven

Flying High

*'Heavens, the noise! It is like a million mechanical drills
performing in unison. It swells and falls as the riders take
the corners; it echoes about the cavernous concrete halls,
drowning the feeble acclamations of the crowd;
it dies slowly as the riders stop, and at the end of
the race it seems like the end of a battle.'*

A.P. Herbert, writing after attending a
speedway stadium in 1928.

It was not until 21 July 1928 that Clem made his first appearance at
White City, still very much junior to the better known riders. He made
an immediate impression by beating Abel (A.B.) Drew, one of three
Irish brothers, in a 'challenge' match. It was, however, in a race two
weeks later during the August Bank Holiday that he established his 'star'
reputation by beating Arthur Franklyn, and setting a new track record. A
few weeks later he won another match race, against Ron Johnson, part of
the Australian 'invasion' (although born in Scotland), breaking the track
record again in front of 38,000 cheering spectators. Crowds at White
City were soon above 45,000, far exceeding those watching Manchester
United or the Lancashire cricket team.

This was speedway's golden hour. Even the lofty *Manchester Guardian*
was obliged to enlighten its middle-class readers as to the impact of the
'new sport'. A 'new type of athlete' was attracting a 'new type of audience,
extraordinarily versed in motorcycling matters'. In an uncannily prescient
aside the paper's 'Special Correspondent' encapsulated the national
obsession with the internal combustion engine, describing the scene at the
end of a meeting at White City: 'When the racing was over, they streamed
away from the track in cars, on motorbicycles, in sidecars, on pillions –
exploding, ejecting blue fumes, honking, rattling like machine guns: the
mechanised army of the modern city.'

43

CLEM BECKETT: MOTORCYCLE LEGEND AND WAR HERO

A sure-fire formula for exciting the crowds was to pitch a relatively unknown and inexperienced local rider against a star man in a challenge match, such as that between Clem and Abel Drew. Clem Beckett duly obliged once more, taking on Sprouts Elder, riding a machine lent to him by another established rider, Karl Snape. He scored a notable victory over Elder, with whom he soon became friends, but received not a penny in remuneration. Thereafter Clem's reputation soared, and although there were still experienced riders who had the edge on him, his star status was confirmed. The speedway reporter of the *Manchester Evening News* waxed lyrical: 'Beckett's riding of late has been a revelation [...] the Oldham lad is the finest broadsider the White City has seen, and will likely go on from triumph to triumph.'

Unlike meetings at Audenshaw, which were always held on either a Saturday or Sunday, White City put on a number of midweek meetings starting in the afternoons. Clem, like many riders, was obliged to use subterfuge such as sudden illness in order to appear. It was no use inventing a family bereavement, he later admitted, because most of the Beckett family were known to his boss at Bowmans. Cuts and bruises, which often marked Clem's face on his return to work the day following a race meeting, were an obvious giveaway. Weighing up the lure of fame and fortune on the dirt track against the prospects of employment at Bowmans, Clem did not hesitate when push came to shove. He later wrote: 'I forget now who spoke first, the boss saying, "You're sacked", or me saying, "I'm finished."' Otherwise Clem seems not to have said a word against Bowman, and the tale suggests that his boss had turned a blind eye to Clem taking liberties. It was a small family business, giving employment to local people, and Bowman was nothing like the bloated capitalist beloved of Communist Party propaganda. Nevertheless, Clem's decision was taken against the background of anti-trade union legislation in the aftermath of the failed General Strike. Conservative Prime Minister Stanley Baldwin, while trying not to provoke further unrest, enacted the Trade Disputes and Trade Unions Bill intending to hobble the unions and deter strikes.

At the same time, the promoters of White City speedway, the British Dirt Track Racing Association, faced a challenge from the appearance of a rival track in Manchester, based at Belle Vue Greyhound Stadium, and which put on its opening meeting on 28 July 1928 – a month after speedway commenced at White City. At first, the feeling was that there would be room in the city for two speedway venues, with the added bonus of local derby matches after the manner of Manchester's two famous football clubs. Such a benign outlook, however, was to prove naive. Belle Vue's Australian owners, International Speedways Ltd, had other ideas. Within a short time Belle Vue was putting on evening meetings under floodlights and readers of the *Manchester Evening News* were being entertained by colourful accounts of 'Roaring Engines of the Night'.

Such was the adoration generated by Clem's performances at White City that, according to the *Manchester Evening News*, 'a group of admirers' got together to present him with a new Douglas machine. The real benefactor, however, was almost certainly Manchester businessman Edgar Hart, who already had his own plans to promote dirt track ventures, and had his eye on Clem as likely protégé. Alas, Clem may have been a little too eager to show his gratitude. At the August Bank Holiday Monday meeting on 6 August, he came a spectacular cropper in the second heat of the White City Challenge Cup event. In a crash on the straight he was hurled over the handlebars, completing two full somersaults before hitting the ground. He was picked up unconscious, face and hands covered in cuts and scratches, and with a badly bruised back. Still game to reward his fans, only the intervention of the Clerk of the Course prevented him from entering a later race. But Clem was soon back in the saddle. On 15 August, during a contrived 'international' meeting fought out between English and Scottish riders, he established a new White City track record.

Throughout the summer and autumn of 1928 dozens of new dirt tracks opened all over Britain, often constructed inside greyhound circuits, which had the advantage of fans being able to use existing stands and other facilities. By the end of the year there were at least fifty, twenty or so of which were within a thirty-mile radius of Manchester. They had varying degrees of success, and for good riders the rapid expansion created a sellers' market. For Clem and others who had established reputations it was a happy hunting ground; they were in demand, and could command large appearance fees.

Clem revelled in it. Within months of his first appearance at Audenshaw he was racing on speedway tracks all over the North and Midlands. The world beat a path to his door. Later he recalled the reverence shown towards talented riders by track owners anxious to recruit star men. Clem cashed in by appearing at two, sometimes three meetings a day, with eager promoters and owners ready to arrange travel between tracks.

Sometimes, at the end of an afternoon meeting, a director would be waiting to chauffeur him to another venue in time for the evening event.

Speedway riders, including Clem, were among the first sportsmen to use air travel. Arthur Franklyn got into trouble for flying his plane without a licence, and it was probably he who taught Clem to fly. Not that Clem ever made much of it; the likelihood is that he, too, never bothered to become a qualified pilot. In addition, he was usually air-sick, as on the occasion he flew from Manchester's aerodrome at Barton to Coventry for a meeting beginning at 2pm. He was, however, able to recover sufficiently to win a match race against star rider Syd Jackson, and to set a new track record. Then he was back on the plane to Manchester for a White City race due to start at 4pm, which was delayed because of his late arrival. Alas, a broken chain resulted in Clem being spectacularly catapulted over the handlebars.[1] Despite this, he was still able to compete in an evening meeting at Rochdale. At all three venues Clem broke records. No wonder the Rochdale track owners presented him with a motorcar to enable him to reach their stadium without worrying about train connections.

It was at this time that Clem struck up a friendship with Hector 'Skid' Skinner, another homegrown rising star who made his mark before the Manchester crowds. Like Clem, Skinner, born in Epworth, north Lincolnshire, delighted fans by getting the better of big-name riders from America and Australia. As the season progressed the pair of them continued to register shock victories over more experienced men; Clem achieved another win over A.B. Drew at Liverpool, and Skinner defeated Arthur Franklyn to win the *Evening News* Challenge Trophy.

This was indeed the fast life. Clem was making big money – as much as £100 a night, and £10,000 over a few months. Years later he admitted: 'I spent it almost as fast as I got it. Easy come, easy go.' Rewards on this scale enabled Clem to indulge his passion for speed and adventure in a way that would have been unthinkable only a year before. He and Skid Skinner rubbed shoulders with the 'Cheshire set', taking flying lessons and enjoying speedboat racing on the Cheshire lakes (or meres). They raced their boats as recklessly as they rode their bikes, swimming ashore when they crashed, and laughing it off. With their natural daring and love of adventure, Clem and Skid cemented an enduring friendship. Each of them, in his own way, possessed a stubborn streak and a natural irreverence towards authority. Clem's own unique style of broadsiding was matched by pint-size Skinner's crab-like posture in the saddle, leaning forward over the petrol tank, broadsiding foot trailing behind him. He also shared Clem's gut feeling that the sport of speedway was not just about winning; it was also about doing things in style for the spectators. Win or lose, Skid always finished off his public performance by riding at speed towards the paddock after a race. He would then effect a nifty little semi-circular skid-cum-broadside with the aim of bringing his machine to rest as close to the paddock gate as possible. It was a final flourish which combined skill and artistic genius. Sometimes he miscalculated, ending up by scraping along the perimeter fence – a minor mishap which no doubt prompted an even bigger cheer from an adoring crowd.

As Clem's fame spread, a good many slapdash and inaccurate compliments were paid to him by journalists. The assertion that Clem had been a professional speedboat racer was one of them. When the *Rover* comic for boys brought out a series of collectors' cards, the one featuring Clem alleged that he had left the North to ride at Cardiff, but Clem only rode on the Welsh track occasionally. Likewise, although Clem was a good rugby league player, who may have played for Oldham at junior level, he did not go on to play for the town's senior side. Clem might not, however, have objected to being described as having 'a magnificent physique'; stocky and muscular, and 5ft 7in tall, rugby opponents testified he was very hard to stop. As to being labelled 'Australian', Clem, a simple 'roughyed' from Oldham, would have merely smiled.[2] On the other hand, who would have argued with the claim made by tobacco manufacturer J.A. Pattreiouex Ltd., in their series of dirt track rider cigarette cards, that Clem Beckett was 'the most daring and spectacular rider ever seen'?

And, of course, Daredevil Clem Beckett was a big pull for girls, happy to be seen as his pillion passenger, arms round their heart-throb, hanging on for dear life. Clem enjoyed the attention and the company of girls. But he does not seem to have taken these relationships very seriously. Once, when a tyre came off his car while returning from the Rochdale track, he and a girlfriend were obliged to walk the six miles back to Oldham. Wearing red leathers and dragging the heavy steel protector worn on his broadsiding foot, it was not to be the romantic evening he had in mind – but he relished telling the tale. On another occasion, when chided for having two girl pillion passengers, Clem replied: 'I need one of 'em to hold the bike'. No thought of political correctness in 1928. And, it seems, no thought of tomorrow either.

Chapter Eight

Taming the Beast

*'We looked round, like Alexander, for fresh
worlds to conquer.'*
A.J. Hunting, Managing Director of
International Speedways, announcing
his company's plans for expansion in Britain.

Although Clem could not have known it at the time, the role played
by International Speedways (ISL) and its parent company, Speedways
Trust Ltd, was already beginning to match the Communist Party's notion
of exploitative 'monopoly' capitalism. Launched on the London Stock
Exchange only weeks before the Belle Vue takeover, with a share capital
of £80,000, Speedays Trust was busy establishing its base at three
London stadiums: White City, Harringay and Wimbledon. The value of
shares in International Speedways had already more than quadrupled,
on a prospectus that promised a phenomenal sixty per cent return on
capital, and which was boosted by American investors. As the 1920s
roared to a conclusion the era of frenzied speculation which was to end
a year later with the Wall Street crash was well underway. Moreover, as
well as seeking to dominate the London speedway scene, ISL had its
sights set on other provincial stadiums. Unsurprisingly, it began 'co-
operating' with the ACU to establish a central speedway authority with
power to 'standardise' regulations, a development that would inevitably
make life harder for competing stadiums and riders.

In truth, White City promoters were slow to realise the danger from
ISL, whose managing director, A.J. Hunting, an 'ideas man' and a master
manipulator of the media, had already secured generous publicity in
the sports columns of Manchester's newspapers. As well as making
the dubious claim to be the originator of dirt track racing in his native
Australia, Hunting made the even more dubious averment that once

riders had mastered the new sport 'no serious accidents could occur'. In fairness, however, Hunting stressed the paramount importance of safety in Australia by way of carefully constructed tracks, with cinders topped by brick dust, and bounded by wire-mesh fences supported by spiral springs. As Clem knew only too well, it was impossible to deny that such features were manifestly absent from British tracks. However, buried in the detail of a long article printed in the *Manchester Evening News* was a candid admission by Hunting that it was the intention of ISL to 'conquer' Britain, and, more ominously, to ensure that speedway would 'come under the control of a central body, with complete authority to take any steps it thinks proper for the good of the game'. As the *Evening News'* own motorcycling correspondent noted, the growing commercialisation of speedway by ISL would soon mean that it controlled riders' remuneration and other matters such as transfers between stadiums, just as autocratically as the Football Association was able to control the pay and conditions of professional footballers.

The upstart Belle Vue club lost two early challenge meetings against White City, and when a third was proposed they presumptuously suggested a challenge match between their star Australian riders, Vic Huxley and Frank Arthur, and White City men Arthur Franklyn and Clem. White City, however, wanted the meeting format to include qualifying heats, and in the end new-boy Clem was denied a crack at taking on the two big-name Australian stars.

But eventually the Old Trafford outfit made extra efforts to sparkle. On Saturday, 18 August, White City spectators, there to see the *Manchester Evening News* Fifty Guineas Challenge Trophy, probably witnessed the first occasion on which riders wore coloured leathers. According to the press, 'the vermillion and delphinium-blue leathers worn respectively by Clem Beckett and Arthur Franklyn added gaiety to the scene.'

A week later, at another Saturday afternoon meeting which coincided with Manchester United's first match of the season, the White City crowd was in excess of the 20,129 spectators who witnessed United's disappointing 1-1 draw with Leicester City. Arthur Franklyn won the Golden Helmet, and a reporter picked out Skid Skinner as a future champion. Taking note of Clem's distinctive style, he added: 'C. H. Beckett is a slider of the broadsiding school, but he can do his skids as close to the inside of the track as the "straight" riders can.' All seemed well in the camp, but the reporter added a prophetic warning to White City that it needed to up its game to avoid the disheartening sight of the same riders carrying off all the prizes. The remedy, he opined, was for White City to introduce handicapping – as had already happened at Belle Vue.

Moreover, in contrast to what was on offer at International Speedway venues, not one Australian rider had taken part in the meeting. It was, the reporter said, ungrateful and inadvisable to neglect the golden goose on the assumption that it would continue to lay golden eggs. Yet, even now White City promoters could be forgiven for being a tad complacent about their rivals on the other side of the city. In early September, at short notice, ISL instructed Belle Vue to cancel a Thursday evening meeting, and although no reason was given, the conclusion drawn by the press was that these evening meetings were proving unprofitable. But a Friday evening charity event at White City on 7 September was attended by more than 50,000 people, including the Lord Mayor of Manchester, and more than a thousand spectators were claimed to have rushed the gates to get in.

Clem was also at home on the new Rochdale track, where, on 12 September, before a record crowd, he again broke the track record, prompting the *Motor Cycle* to describe him as 'the wonderful rider from Oldham'. At another autumn meeting in Rochdale Sprouts Elder thrilled the crowd in a three-way match race with Clem and Skid Skinner. Skid fell off, and Clem 'had the misfortune to break a chain'. Elder, a free spirit, tried to stay clear of contractual encumbrances – or blithely broke those he entered into – and played out his speedway days as a freelance maverick, and a thorn in the side of ISL. Unlike Australian riders who were kept close to heel by ISL, Elder ploughed his own furrow and accepted frequent invitations to ride on northern tracks. For that, of course, he, like Clem, was to become a marked man.

But still the fact was that the proliferation of speedway tracks was creating a situation of over-supply, which was good for riders in the short-term, but potentially disastrous for investors. Typical of these fly-by-night ventures was the speedway track laid inside the newly built South Shore greyhound stadium on St Anne's Road, Blackpool. There was already a dirt track stadium in Blackpool, barely a mile away at Highfield Road, to say nothing of the myriad competing holiday attractions, including the town's famous Pleasure Beach close by. The promoter of the South Shore venue was the grandly named British Dirt Track Racing Association Ltd., which also owned Manchester White City, and was supported by the

Blackpool and Fylde Motor and Aero Club. The nearby airfield offered a convenient commute for Manchester-based dirt track aviators such as Franklyn and Clem. Sure enough, both took part in the opening meeting on 11 September, along with other White City regulars, Arthur Jervis and 'Smoky' Stratton. Clem was on top form. He beat New Zealander Stewie St George in a series of match races, setting a track record, and going on to win the open senior race ahead of Lees and Skinner. These were all men whom Clem would get to know well. They were fiercely competitive on the track, but the realities of their close-knit world, and their shared dangers, created a bond of camaraderie.

Clem was at the height of his popularity in Manchester. Riding at White City, the day after appearing at Blackpool, he crashed and fell in the final of the Senior race. The crowd, fearing he had sustained serious injury, refused to leave and waited for more than an hour after racing ended, only leaving after Clem, back on his feet, had been brought to the main gate to speak to them. The scene is one to savour, because for all the posthumous praise heaped on Clem for his allegiance to the Communist Party, there is no record of him ever making a speech. With the crowd clamouring for a glimpse of their hero, Clem stood in the shadows of the magnificent porticoed columns of White City receiving the plaudits of the multitude like a god at the altar of a Greek temple, while, as one commentator put it, cheering 'filled the welkin'. Shy and taciturn, Clem reassured his adoring fans that his injured ankle was nothing to worry about. It was an oration brief and to the point, perhaps because Clem was already beginning to sense that what part of the crowd really wanted was another sacrifice to the gods.

Clem's friendship with Skid Skinner developed into a sort of dirt track double-act, as in a lively meeting at Rochdale in late September, when they put on a great show to compensate the crowd for the disappointment arising from the inability of local idol Paddy Dean to ride owing to injury. Clem broke the track record for four laps, and Skid narrowly failed to better it. On the last lap of the final senior event, Clem and Skinner appeared to ride alongside each other, before Clem inched ahead. By the end of 1928 Clem Beckett held twenty-eight track records, including the record for the 'Flying Mile' at Halifax.

International Speedways Ltd were just as aware as their rivals at White City that they faced competition from the two city's football clubs once the soccer season started in August. Accordingly, to avoid the clash with

51

Saturday football fixtures, they brought in midweek evening matches, but after initial success attendances declined. White City looked secure in its status as the city's premiere speedway venue.

They had, however, reckoned without ISL's resourcefulness, and cash available from shareholders. Unbeknown to White City, or the speedway fans of Manchester, Belle Vue began conducting secret negotiations to obtain a new stadium. Big business went to work in smoke-filled rooms. On 17 October Belle Vue (M/c) Ltd reached agreement with the North Manchester Motor Club for the promotion of dirt track racing on a new circuit within Belle Vue Gardens on Hyde Road, slightly nearer the city centre. As part of Manchester's biggest leisure complex, the new venue was located on a huge site which accommodated a zoo, exhibition hall, fairground, miniature railway, boating lake, dance hall and travelling circuses. It brought speedway firmly into mainstream popular entertainment. The deal, masterminded by Belle Vue manager Eric Oswald Spence, who had close ties with the ACU, involved a series of collateral agreements, including one with the Northern Dirt Track Owners' Association. The NMMC was to be guaranteed a commission on any gate revenue in excess of £500. Crucially, Arthur Franklyn was audaciously poached from White City, with a promise of guaranteed rides and a permanent appointment as the club's riding instructor for the following season. But while Franklyn was a key part in Spence's ambitions for Belle Vue, Clem was not. So far as the business of speedway was concerned, the Belle Vue deal taught Clem an early lesson. Money, as well as sporting ability, did the talking.

It was at Rochdale, on Saturday, 30 October that horrified spectators witnessed the first fatal casualty on a northern track. It happened shortly after Clem had won a closely fought 'triple' challenge match, ahead of Skid Skinner and Australian rider Charlie Datson. In an incident involving three machines, Bradford rider Cliff Mawson was hurled against the rails on the outside of the circuit. Several spectators required treatment for shock; Mawson died of his injuries the following day. Giving evidence at the inquest, Norman Dawson of Salford, who had been thrown from his machine after it developed a 'wheel wobble', maintained that Rochdale was the 'best and safest in the country', but Dawson's claim that he had ridden on 'every track in the country' was later to be doubted.[1]

The ACU realised that if it could not force the dirt track beast back into its cage, it would be best to tame it. By now, through its Competitions and

Track Licensing Committees, it had licensed over forty tracks and drafted a set of regulations that it hoped would preserve the role of affiliated motor clubs such as Stalybridge and North Manchester. Moreover, British motorcycle manufacturers had at last realised the market potential of machines specially adapted for speedway, hammering the final nail in the coffin for anti-speedway diehards who had always claimed that the sport did nothing to improve 'the breed'. In November, at the annual Motor Cycle Show at London's Olympia, John Douglas, maker of Clem's favourite mount, boasted that his family firm had learned more practical design lessons from one year's dirt track racing than it had from ten years' involvement in other motorcycle competitions.[2]

Track owners were now organising to protect their interest at the expense of riders. The enigmatic and wily Spence gave his support. As Clerk of the Belle Vue course, he pioneered arrangements to improve facilities for spectators and track safety, but when it came to riders he was a no-nonsense authoritarian. In spite of his abrasive relationship with the NDTOA, Spence was happy with the association's decision to introduce a grading system for riders' appearance money. The grades were cunningly related to track records, so that whenever the record was broken, the grades and the fees paid to lesser riders were lowered. Atop the pyramid, 'star' men were put on £3 appearance money; Grade A riders coming within four seconds of the record got £2; while grade B riders on £1 had to be within eight seconds. Even *Motor Cycling* magazine thought this was 'cutting things a little fine', and suggested more generous timings. The owners exploited the scheme by contriving with fast riders to break the track record. It was a sublime example of divide and conquer, with inevitable ill-will between the star men and their not-so-fast competitors.

To cap it all, a prize-money maximum of £80 per meeting was set, inclusive of other payments. In their determination to impose a master-servant relationship on riders, speedway rulers were little different from administrators in other sports, typically Association Football, where amateur values were giving way to professionalism. As early as September the ACU had issued a specimen contract dealing with the terms of 'transfers' and 'temporary transfers' between promoters and riders, providing notice periods, and in some cases limiting a rider to tracks owned by his 'employer'. By imposing one-sided contract terms, such as the maximum wage, the Football League left no doubt in the minds of players who was boss, and it was a precedent that speedway was quick to follow. Drawing a parallel with professional soccer, The *Motor Cycle* commented: 'Everywhere contracts and agreements are being fluttered in riders' faces.'

These developments were hardly welcomed by the riders, and they led to resentment – especially against star men who clipped track records and thereby reduced other riders' grades and remuneration. Clem, along with most riders, had put his faith in the Auto-Cycle Union to protect their interests as competitive motorcyclists. The NDTOA was manifestly in it for the owners, but the ACU was ostensibly bound to protect the interests of motorcyclists – both amateur *and* professional. Dirt track riders felt, however, that they were being neglected in favour of track owners. The charging of fees by the ACU for inspecting riders' helmets was a bone of contention, and inevitably fees levied for track inspections were used by the owners as a reason to limit prize money.

While the public gasped with envy at the level of prize money, they did not understand the heavy costs incurred by riders. Typically, a top rider like Clem, racing several times a week, would need to replace damaged parts or even complete machines, and overheads of £40-50 a week were not uncommon.[3] New Douglas DT5s – the dirt track bike to beat – were selling at £85, with riders paying an extra £10 for a works-tuned engine. In an interview with the *Motor Cycle*, Australian rider Frank Arthur spoke up for the majority of riders: 'I've no firm behind me to pay me a salary; manufacturers do not give me the machines I ride, there is no job being kept open for me at the end of my riding career – and one cannot keep on at this game indefinitely.' So far as Clem Beckett's career was to work out, Arthur's words amounted to a prophetic dose of realism.

Chapter Nine

Icicles in Marseille

'Clem Beckett was now a star attraction; to hold a
meeting without him was unthinkable.'
From *Speedway in Manchester 1927-1945*
by Trevor James and Barry Stephenson.

In spite of signs that owners were organising to limit riders' pay, it would have seemed to most dirt track hopefuls that the new sport offered them a fair chance of fame and fortune – provided they could avoid serious injury. Realising the scope for advertising, tobacco companies such as Players added speedway riders to the gallery of footballers and cricketers whose images, together with brief pen portraits, featured on 'cigarette cards'. Typically, smokers – Clem himself was rarely seen without a cigarette in his mouth – were met at the door of the tobacconist by youthful collectors soliciting cards tucked into cigarette packets, and hoping to complete a 'set'. Duplicates, of course, could be swapped.

The advertising industry had cottoned on to the essential appeal of dirt track racing to members of the public. In spite of – or maybe *because* of – its dogged resistance to on-track gambling, crowds were still flocking to speedway events. The spectacle of men and machines in combat amid flying cinders was attracting middle-aged devotees, male and female: handsome Clem Beckett attracted hero worship and adulation from autograph-hunting female fans on a par with that heaped on film star Rudolph Valentino.

The unprecedented surge of interest in the new sport even drew the attention of academics and psychologists. One of them opined that a typical dirt track spectator, identifying himself with the winning rider, 'enjoys, at second hand, a sense of relief and triumph'. Uniquely, a high-powered motorcycle was 'almost part of the rider, a physical extension of his own body', and those who could tame and direct its ferocious power might rise to the heights of a 'Grecian demi-god'.[1] Clem Beckett was just such a 'mechanical superman', who lived to hold his own amongst the best philosophers and poets of his generation, was well aware that in sixty seconds of 50mph virility an ordinary mortal could live like a god. Before long, speedway was to receive more censorious attention from persons claiming to be psychologists, but as the start of the new season approached, the editor of International Speedways' house magazine, Norman Pritchard, was happy to have them on his side, and he was confident that with the help of the new Promoters Association a successful season was assured.

A step down from such ethereal contemplation, the nuts and bolts of speedway superstars were being supplied by one particular manufacturer of motorcycles: Douglas, a company which had supplied 70,000 motorbikes to the army during the First World War, had, after a good deal of hesitation, hit on the ideal formula for dirt track machines. Their engines, known as 'flat-twin', consisted of horizontally opposed cylinders, arranged 'fore and aft' rather than across the frame. This gave them a very low centre of gravity, while not projecting outwards so as not to impede banking, and likewise avoiding 'grounding' when cornering. And so, as claimed by the manufacturers, a 1928 500cc 'Dirt Track' Douglas, with three-speed gearbox, no clutch, no brakes, and hand pump lubrication, was pretty well unbeatable in the early days of speedway.

However, unlike football, dirt track meetings were less frequent in the winter, obliging Clem to travel as far afield as Bristol and Southampton for engagements. Indeed, even in these pioneering days of speedway, meetings after the end of October and before the end of March were very rare, a fact which required riders to supplement their incomes wherever opportunities arose.

Unsurprisingly, therefore, and following the example set by the speedway missionaries who had come to England from Australia, New Zealand and America, Clem was tempted to try his luck abroad. Towards the end of 1928 he was among the first British riders to blaze the dirt track trail in Denmark and Sweden, and he was to be a regular visitor to Scandinavia for the rest of his life.

Clem ended the year with a Boxing Day appearance in Cardiff, one of a small number of stadiums owned by Manchester entrepreneur Edgar W. Hart. This was at the personal invitation of Hart who had been following Clem's career at White City. Hart was to play an important role in Clem's life, and was already planning business deals that would involve him.

Even so, perhaps miffed by the move of Franklyn to Belle Vue, or by his being denied a chance to participate in the sport at a higher level, Clem again considered his options. Only twenty-two, it was less than a year since he had walked out of Bowmans blacksmiths shop, yet even he was beginning to sense that the novelty of the English dirt track was wearing off. Still, despite the occupational hazard of track falls, he was fit, footloose and fancy-free, with enough money in the bank to take care of his immediate needs and to help look after his mother. What better time to go in search of adventure?

On 15 January 1929 Clem Beckett and a small group of English dirt track riders set sail for Europe, taking their machines and a considerable quantity of spares. The aim was to put on a road show, consisting of exhibition matches, wherever they could find paying spectators. It must have been something of a whistle-stop tour relying on machines being transported by train. Performing in Turkey, Romania, and Bulgaria, these speedway adventurers ill-fitted the period image of Englishmen venturing eastwards.[2] Accordingly, the travels of these motorbike-mad working-class lads never made it into the realms of romantic fiction readily devoured by middle-class readers. Clem and his playboy pals were a couple of years ahead of Agatha Christie's 1931 journey on the Orient Express, but their exploits became legendary, and Clem was said to have left a trail of broken hearts all over the Continent. As travelling troubadours of the dirt track, the boys had no inclination to become involved in the political tumult of eastern European countries in the wake of the Treaty of Versailles. Hardly surprising, therefore, that when, a few years later, Clem was writing articles for Communist publications, he had virtually nothing to say about them. It is always possible, of course, that the tour was highly profitable for riders and promoters alike, and that there was little to be gained from recounting their travels, other than stirring up unwanted interest from His Majesty's tax inspectors.

At any rate, when Clem arrived in France with other British riders they had money to invest. The group was managed by Norman Coates, boss of the Leicester speedway, and included Leicester rider Cyril 'Squib' Burton (also known as 'Broadside' and occasionally 'Squibs' Burton), another amateur aviator who had broken into the top flight of speedway and had built up his reputation as a rider at the new stadium in Rochdale.

Other Leicester men were Stan Baines, Arthur Sherlock, and Neville Wheeler. Also in the party was Clem's boon-companion from White City days, Skid Skinner, and – in spite of his preferment by EOS – Arthur Franklyn. Given these riders' common pastime of aviation, they might have become known as the 'Flying Squad'. Riders Alec Bowerman and Mark Sheldon were also members of the team. Their goal was Marseille, France's second city, and given the exponential rise of speedway in England, it no doubt seemed a good idea at the time – as many inherently risky ventures do to the young and fearless. The plan was to set up a dirt track for speedway at the Jean Bouin cycle velodrome, and to compete against French rivals.

The scenario in which these intrepid English adventurers pursued their plans was an unlikely one. In 1929 Marseille, whose citizens had once marched to the French Revolution singing the stirring song which became France's national anthem, was notorious for organised crime and gangsters. Its *gendarmerie* was riddled with corruption, and there was widespread poverty and homelessness. It was always going to be a hard track to ride. Not only that, whereas the original idea had been for the Englishmen to take on teams of French riders, a dearth of local opposition meant that it was virtually impossible to put on international team events. The best that could be done to flavour events with excitement was to have the seven or eight riders competing for the Handicap de Provence, with the top challenge matches being fought out between Clem and Skid Skinner.

Alas, the stadium on which all hopes were pinned had recently been vandalised by disappointed boxing fans who, having paid to see a match between champions, recognised the respective protagonists as a local navvy and a ship's cook. Moreover, the riders had put their trust in a backer, who, it transpired, was an habitué of the English bankruptcy court, and, not surprisingly, legal issues concerning title to the land began to arise. Clem and colleagues nevertheless set about preparing the track and carrying out urgent repairs to the stadium.

If the riders had relied on the benign climate of the Côte d'Azur to favour their enterprise they were disappointed. They had not taken into account the Mistral wind, a seasonal discomfort well-known to the *Marseillois*. Just as the track was about to open amid hopes of warm spring days bringing in the crowds, the Mistral struck, triggering the coldest spell of weather inflicted on the city for years. Water pipes burst;

the harbour froze over; dangerous 60ft-long icicles hung from the sides of buildings and had to be shot down by the police. All the daredevil broadsiding and cinder-shifting in the world could not induce the locals to turn out for a speedway meeting in a blizzard. The team's hapless manager fled back to England, allowing a short time for Clem to have a look around. In a snow-bound festival at nearby Aix he was angered by the sight of rich socialites throwing flowers at each other, while on the streets of the city homeless old men were sleeping rough. Clem's anger was such that he imagined lobbing a Mills bomb into the midst of the revellers. There was an eerie prescience in this. Before his time was up, Clem Beckett was destined to have at least two real-life encounters with hand-grenades. In the meantime, to relieve the boredom of the enforced lay-off, Skid Skinner organised shooting matches for the riders, with tin cans and pigeons as targets.

As they were about to cut their losses and also head for home, the riders were offered a lifeline by the appearance of a mysterious benefactor, whom Clem described as a supporter of the Rochdale speedway track. But the man was a rogue, who relieved the riders of their remaining cash with what turned out to be another broken promise of repayment in order to launch an advertising campaign. This, too, failed, and in a last-gasp attempt to rescue the scheme, the riders responded to a plea from the exiled manager to provide photographs or film which might encourage backers in England. The riders duly laid on free buses to bring spectators from the city centre, only to discover that when they alighted most of them joined the queue for admission to the meeting at the adjacent horse racing course. What few spectators there were at the dirt track were cajoled into moving round to be filmed in different parts of the stadium so as to create an entirely exaggerated impression of support. It was all to no avail; there were not even sufficient funds left to pay for processing the film. The riders threw in the towel and returned to England.

Evoking a scene from the *Keystone Cops*, Clem's last recollection of Marseille was of police intervention in a brawl between unpaid landladies, track assistants and riders. Clem commented laconically, 'As usual the police got most satisfaction'. They did indeed. Outraged by the behaviour of *'les motocyclists Anglais'* the *gendarmerie* struck back. Aware of the pigeon shooting competitions between Skid Skinner and Mark Sheldon inside the stadium, and in spite of the fact that revolvers could be bought without restriction in France, they set up an ambush.

As soon as the two of them stepped outside the stadium, still 'armed', the police pounced. Skinner and Sheldon were remanded to prison for ten days. Fortunately for them, and thanks to the British Consul, proceedings were expedited, and after three days confined to a diet of black bread and water, they were released in time to join the team's hasty retreat back to England.

Back home, Clem made light of the mishaps in France, and enjoyed joshing with reporters. Referring to the substantial board fence at the Bouin stadium, he reckoned he had ridden up it to overtake opponents, and that when, in a fog of dust, he had misjudged the manoeuvre and run smack into the fence, the impact had fortuitously straightened a pair of bent forks. Clem was a sociable creature. He dined out on his mad-cap adventure in Marseille for the rest of his life. It widened his horizons and whetted his appetite for foreign travel. It taught him lessons in human nature, and his losses were put down to experience. And, this time, nobody died.

However, while the boys were capering about in Marseille, a dirt track turf war was being fought out at home. Concerned at the expansion of International Speedways, and deals being done through EOS, their 'man in the north', track owners who had previously been rivals got together determined to fight their corner. Their main concern was that International Speedways would corner the market in star riders. Negotiations progressed slowly, perhaps because no one could quite believe that the boom was over. Eventually, the *Daily Express* informed readers that the British Dirt Track Racing Association Ltd (BDTRA), owners of tracks at Manchester White City, Bolton, Blackpool and Bristol had completed negotiations with Dirt Track Speedways Ltd., owners of other far-flung stadiums, on the formation of a 'combine'. Also included in the arrangement were Midland Speedways Ltd., with tracks at Coventry and Leicester, and the independent owners of the Middlesbrough track. The BDTRA spokesman talked big: not only had they acquired a site in Sheffield destined to have 'the finest stadium in the country', but they also had plans for tracks in Belgium, Germany and Scandinavia, while sites had already been earmarked for Paris, Milan and Italy.

The much-vaunted development at Sheffield was to be spearheaded by business-savvy Edgar Hart, a dab hand at promotion and publicity, who had arranged Clem's press interview on his return from France. Hart lost no time in announcing to the *Yorkshire Telegraph* that dirt track would only be one of the attractions laid on for Sheffield sports enthusiasts. The new stadium at Owlerton, on the banks of the River Don, would have accommodation for football, cricket, cycling and athletics; there were plans to introduce new sports such as 'Motor-polo on both cars and motor cycles' and even 'chariot racing'! Hart was anxious to impress the *Telegraph*'s reporter with his credentials as a speedway aficionado: he had never missed a meeting in Manchester since the beginning of the sport. More significantly, he heaped praise on two 'brilliant' riders in particular, and made it clear that he wanted them at Owlerton. They were Skid Skinner and Clem Beckett.

Alas, the best laid schemes of mice and men … the BDTRA's plans depended on generous support from the banks. A few months later, as the British economy reeled under the effects of the Wall Street Crash, belts were tightened, interest rates rose sharply, and loans were called in. The Twenties were already losing their roar. The war on International Speedways was to end in an ignominious defeat, and the eventual surrender to EOS was to have a profound effect on the course of Clem's life.

Chapter Ten

Tin Cans and Dead Cats

*'Unlike many other popular spectator and participant
sports, it allows the emphasis upon entertainment to equal
that laid upon the final result.'*
Martin Rogers on the appeal of speedway.

When Clem returned to England in the spring of 1929 he was most
likely broke, but glad to get back to the familiar streets of Oldham, to
the comfort of his mother's home in Swinton Street, and to regale the
Anderson boys with tales of his travels.

Resting and recuperating, Clem surveyed the rapidly changing
speedway scene at home, where E.O. Spence was busy consolidating
his grip on Manchester. In this endeavour he was part of the master-
plan being pushed forward by International Speedways Limited. Their
general manager, Vivian Van Damm, confident of backing from the
ACU and the Southern Promoters Association, announced that where
'sympathy between riders' on the track was detected, the race would be
stopped, with no award of prize money.[1] His concern was directed at
'one or two leading riders' who had 'got their heads together' in match
races, with the idea of splitting the prize money. He also threatened that
riders who failed to keep engagements, or made unreasonable demands
on promoters, would be asked to provide a doctor's certificate, and those
who could not would be shamed over the stadium's loudspeaker. Van
Damm added that a comprehensive set of ACU 'Rules and Regulations'
was at hand for the new season, but he failed to mention that the ACU
had more or less accepted the rules as drafted by A.J. Hunting, his
managing director.

In the meantime, rebel riders in the North, who objected to the new
grading system, had found a champion in the form of Edgar Hart, who,
assisted by a Bury businessman and amateur rider named Lees, began

negotiating with track owners and promoters on their behalf. Clem and like-minded colleagues formed the Dirt Track Riders Association, and Hart made a donation of £20 towards running costs. Moreover, from now on Hart began acting as Clem's promoter and manager, having reputedly exclaimed on first seeing Clem race: 'I want that boy!'

The Riders Association put up stout resistance to high-handed promoters, combining the roles of agent and quasi trade union. There were successful riders' strikes, when promoters had to give way to riders' demands, and at some tracks owners were obliged to accept safety measures put forward by riders' representatives. Clem's part in the Riders Association obviously alienated him from track owners. Not for the first time, he stuck his neck out for a principle, and so far as the authorities were concerned he was, from now on, a marked man.

The success of the Riders Association was threatened by the number of new riders willing to undercut members, and the inevitable effects of unemployment and short-time working on the incomes of paying customers, which reduced spectator attendances. In the battle that was to follow for control of English speedway, neither Hart nor Clem was a match for the wily Spence, master of the deal, and bankrolled by International Speedways, the sport's biggest player.

As Clem himself admitted, much of the early support for speedway arose from its sheer novelty value, and as the novelty wore off so attendances declined. One factor was the number of mechanical failures – broken frames, 'burst' engines, collapsed wheels, and derailed chains – which led to fans being disappointed, especially in the case of match races between big name riders. Accordingly, a knowledgeable commentator was moved to lament that manufacturers were not putting enough effort into improving frame and engine design. Unlike football, where the League formula had created an enduring model to sustain spectator interest, speedway was still struggling to find a format that would maintain fan loyalty. Track 'speed charts' converting average speeds to lap times as published in *Speedway News* were not exactly riveting reading, and neither were headlines such as 'The following are Points scored by the various Riders in the Competitions for the various Trophies.' Complicated rules awarding points cumulatively, and varying from track to track, determined the award of individual trophies. Most prestigious of all was the 'Golden Helmet' with which winning riders on ISL tracks were ceremoniously crowned by company directors, glamorous actresses or minor aristocrats.[2] Bejewelled and decorated with ornate wings suggesting the Greek god Mercury, golden helmets made their wearers look faintly ridiculous in their moment of triumph, and they were glad to take them off once the photographers' flash-bulbs had stopped popping. Observing the gangling figure of Sprouts Elder thus adorned as he walked round the White City track to the applause of the crowd, the *Manchester Guardian*'s 'Special Correspondent' was moved to compare him with 'a fireman looking for a fire'. True, work was not drying up, but for all except the superstar 'cracks' it was still a hand-to-mouth existence, with the threat of a career-ending injury hanging over every rider's every appearance on the track.

Through his company, Provincial Dirt Tracks Ltd., Edgar Hart pressed on with his plans for a purpose-built dirt track stadium in Sheffield on a site known as Owlerton Meadows. For some reason Hart had not gone in with the BDTRA's 'combine', although he may have indicated support privately earlier in the year when it had boasted of its plans for a 'super track' at Sheffield.

So determined was Hart to have Clem as the star man at Sheffield that he offered him a directorship in his company, which at that time also controlled stadiums in Cardiff and Wolverhampton. Clem accepted, although his role as 'director' was later to cause him embarrassment among Communist Party purists. To them, company directors were synonymous with exploitative employers, whom Party publications routinely caricatured as top-hatted, pot-bellied, cigar-smoking capitalists. True, Clem later developed a taste for cigars, but *sans* crash-helmet his preferred headgear was the flat cap, typical of a working man. Other riders persuaded to invest hard-won savings in Provincial included Jimmy Hindle, a Mancunian, and the New Zealander Spencer 'Smoky' Stratton, who, like Clem, was back in England after speedway adventures in Europe. None of them bore the slightest resemblance to a bloated capitalist. Moreover, these directors were very much hands-on when it came to developing the new stadium. Clem had a major input into the design of the track – at 395yds, one of the longest in the country, and ever afterwards thought to be among the best, with its long bends and well-built surface providing ample scope for broadsiding.

For Clem Beckett Sheffield was to provide the best – and the worst – of times. He made his mark immediately, when 15,000 spectators turned up for the first meeting of the season on the evening of Easter Saturday,

30 March 1929. Clem won the Golden Helmet in a final contested with local hero George Wigfield, beating his own time in the heats by five seconds. In an afternoon meeting at the Olympic Speedway stadium, Nottingham, Clem shared top billing with Wigfield, fancifully described as 'Northern Champion', and established Australian star Stewie St George. In a short space of time, Clem was challenging Barnsley-born Wigfield as the idol of the crowd, spearheading the newly formed Sheffield team in its encounters with other clubs.

Although it would eventually end in tears, Edgar Hart deserves credit for his unique initiative in ensuring riders had a commercial stake in the speedway business. Hart was ahead of his time, thinking outside the box, and Clem never doubted his good faith. Hart was also a master self-publicist, never short of ideas, and given Clem's flair for record breaking put forward a canny proposal to the ACU to sponsor a 'perpetual' British Mile Record Trophy. But somebody up there did not like him: the idea was imperiously dismissed because it contravened Clause (a) Appendix J of the Union's General Competition Rules. Perhaps the grandees of the ACU felt that Hart's idea was a tad self-serving, given that in early April Clem smashed the 'unofficial' flying mile record at Owlerton, with a time of 80.6 seconds. But three weeks later Clem's friend Sprouts Elder lowered it to dead-on 80 seconds. It was not long, however, before Clem reclaimed it with a time of 78.8 seconds. It was worth winning back. Hart had cleverly spiced the trophy with a stipend of £2 per week for the holder, and over the next twelve months other 'cracks' – including Elder, Frank Arthur, Vic Huxley, Squib Burton, Stewie St George, and Frank Varey – tried in vain to dispossess him.

Naturally, Clem's high-flying lifestyle continued. Thwarted by a storm from piloting his plane back from Cardiff to Sheffield for a meeting at Rochdale, he accepted the challenge in his Chrysler car, completing the journey of 230 miles on pre-motorway 'A' roads in a record time (which probably survives to this day) of 4 hours 50 minutes. Such risk-taking on public roads typified Clem Beckett's cavalier, if youthful, attitude to authority – even though it was to be another six years before Parliament imposed speed limits in built-up areas.

Clem was now at the peak of his fame nationally. When the *Motor Cycle* magazine invited correspondents to nominate the best dirt track star, 'C.H. Beckett' attracted widespread support from its readers. According to one fan, not even Arthur Franklyn or Sprouts Elder could 'do the mile' with such ease as Clem. Other nominees for the title included London-based riders Dickie Smythe, Billy 'Cyclone' Lamont and Jack Parker. But E. Hayes sounded a sour note, claiming that Clem had recently turned in disappointing performances at Manchester White City. Mr Hayes's contribution perfectly and prophetically expressed the fickleness of fans in the early days of speedway, and a reason for riders' insecurity: in the eyes of many fans you were only as good as your last race.

However, it was not just Clem's winning ways that endeared him to the crowds. He was uniquely stylish. According to one commentator, Clem was 'the first Englishman to adopt the Australian style of broadsiding'. And whereas the majority of riders used a 'knee-hook' to assist in broadsiding, Clem still preferred to rely on his own strength. According to Eli Anderson, Clem was also the only speedway rider not to use a steering damper, a device intended to eliminate uncontrolled oscillation of the front wheel. That said, towards the end of his career, when he was suffering the effects of serial injuries, there were good reasons for Clem to use whatever protections were available.

Spence had not yet reached the peak of his power, and as the dirt track boom entered its most frenetic phase, 'Daredevil' Beckett was in great demand. It was a hectic life of speedway appearances up and down the country, but it was on the cinder tracks of Owlerton, in his native county of Yorkshire, that Clem achieved the pinnacle of his speedway career.

Clem kept up ties with his home town, anxious about his mother's welfare, and maintaining friendships with the Anderson boys. While he may have overnighted in Sheffield from time to time, especially after race meetings, likely as not staying with other riders, his official address remained 17 Swinton Street, Roundthorn. One night, traversing the Pennines over the Woodhead Pass, he was stopped by police who pointed out the absence of rear lights on his car. 'Bugger the lights!' he responded, 'Where's my trailer?' Somewhere behind him, on the lonely moorland road, the trailer he had been towing had become detached. It was a typical Clem Beckett yarn.

By now it was obvious that speedway would benefit from the creation of a competitive league, along the lines of the most popular spectator sport, association football. Accordingly, the 1929 season saw the launch of the English Dirt Track League, under the auspices of the Northern Dirt Track Owners Association. At the outset there were eighteen League members, including White City and Belle Vue in Manchester, and teams from other cities in the North and Midlands such as Liverpool, Leeds, Newcastle, Leicester and Sheffield. To Clem and other riders, the League at first offered the prospect of well-paid employment as a member of a team with regular fixtures. Furthermore, the League was not yet part of the amalgam of various bodies over which E.O. Spence increasingly exercised de facto control.

In May Clem was back at Trent Bridge and top of the bill. Leading his Sheffield teammates, and with Northern League fixtures underway, he confirmed his status as Sheffield's star man, along with fellow director Spencer Stratton. Typically, in a Yorkshire derby match with Halifax, both men came off, sustaining leg injuries which prevented them from taking part in later races. This was small beer for Stratton, who, a few years earlier, had lain unconscious for twenty-three days following a crash in Australia. In the same month, Clem turned in a virtuoso performance at Manchester Belle Vue, equalling Frank Varey's lap record, and going on to beat Varey in two straight runs of a challenge match. The *Motor Cycle's* man in the press-box observed: 'Beckett's win-or-crash tactics are becoming a thing of the past. These days he uses his head quite a lot, but his riding is no less spectacular,' while the reporter from *Motor Cycling* magazine noted that Clem's 'beautifully controlled slides were a tonic to watch.' More than 30,000 spectators cheered Clem to the echo – in spite of having to contend with an ACU steward who did not like his brightly coloured helmet and only reluctantly approved it.

Controlled by Spence and financed by ISL, Belle Vue was now well established as a model track, renowned for its efficiency. Typically, Spence directed proceedings from an elevated control tower close to the starting line, with telephone links to the paddock, the track-manager's office, the judges' box below, and the 'music purveyor'. Switches controlling flood lighting and track lights – green for 'go' and red for 'stop'- were personally operated by Spence. Naturally, the microphone for the public address system was also located in the tower, and whenever possible Spence composed speeches to be delivered by the announcer. In between races twenty-two men dressed in white, eleven at each end, waited for their cue to leap onto the track to rake the cinders.

For all their daring, it is doubtful that Clem or Stratton, or any of the other riders retained by Hart, ever made much money through their commitment to Sheffield Speedway. In spite of regular attendances of more than 20,000, gate receipts were insufficient to pay dividends, and income was being diverted to pay for improved stadium facilities. Indeed, although he was a fighter, Hart was struggling to keep the show on the road. The economy was ailing and unemployment was rising. There was another political crisis, and once again a minority Labour government led by MacDonald took office, this time enjoying the support of two Labour MPs elected for Oldham.

With the launch of a charm offensive against 'Gadfly', the erudite sports columnist of the *Sheffield Star,* Hart pulled out all the stops to promote Owlerton speedway. Clem himself had a lean spell, failing to finish, typically by coming off at speed going into the home bend. Even so, Gadfly described him as 'the best and cleverest rider we have seen on the Sheffield track.' The opinion was not shared, however, by 'Talmage' of the *Motor Cycle,* who reckoned that in Frank Arthur's narrow match race victory over Clem, the Australian had turned in 'the most spectacular ride that has ever been seen on the Sheffield track.'[3] At any rate, given the polar opposite riding styles of the two men – Clem broadsiding out to towards the fence, Arthur sticking close to the white line – the contest must have been an occasion for dirt track connoisseurs.

Spectators observed Clem's unfailing sense of fair play, typified by an episode at the end of a Saturday 'derby' League tie between Sheffield and Barnsley, at the Lundwood stadium on 15 June 1929. Before a record crowd, the visitors were beaten 37 points to 24, performances from Barnsley's homegrown 'crack' Bert Round being decisive. The subsequent challenge match between Clem and Round was therefore an opportunity for Sheffield to achieve some consolation. In the first of three races, Clem came off; a similar mishap befell Round in the second. The stage was set for a dramatic decider, but at the very start of the race, and to the dismay of home fans, an over-enthusiastic Round lost control of his machine and fell to the ground. Clem immediately offered to race again, with the result being decided in Round's favour. It was the kind of impulsive behaviour that defined Clem Beckett – an unforgettable gesture that fathers might relate to sons as an example of good sportsmanship, and still be telling it to their grandchildren years later.

Alas, the League was beset with problems from its inception, with smaller clubs struggling to meet minimum standards. Embarrassed by its safety record, the League, backed by the ACU, refused membership to Audenshaw, and attempted to blacklist riders who appeared there. This resulted in riders adopting *nomes de guerre* to avoid suspension from NDTOA tracks, and fully masked riders using names of prisons such as 'Pentonville', 'Dartmoor', and 'Strangeways' lent the track an outlaw reputation, not to mention an aura of farce. This was not quite the scenario that had been envisaged by Major T.W. Loughborough, ACU secretary, when, anticipating future transgressions of 'get-rich-quick' promoters, he threatened them with the 'iron hand of the Union'.

At the same time, stadium owners and promoters were coming to terms with the fact that they did not, after all, have a licence to print money. Even at Belle Vue there were warning signs that the bubble had burst. A reporter noted that, compared with the euphoria of the previous season, crowds seemed 'wooden and unemotional'. When Clem was upended at a meeting at Halifax and left the stadium with his arm in a sling, a cynical motorcycle journalist suggested he was swinging the lead by pointing out that Clem was on the grid the following evening at Middlesbrough.

League match attendances were disappointing and in order to revive them, individual entrepreneurs such as Percy Platt, managing director at Rochdale stadium, and John Thomas Wolfenden, at Audenshaw, were dreaming up events 'with a difference'. Platt and Wolfenden told the press that they planned a series of matches between Rochdale 'crack' Squib Burton and top Coventry rider Syd Jackson, with a 'Three-Venue' theme. Adding extra spice, the £200 prize money was to be raised by way of a wager between Platt and Wolfenden, with the loser stumping up. But there is no evidence that the matches ever took place.

Platt, who, like Clem, had grown up in Glodwick, was the owner of Oldham's biggest motorcycle shop, situated in Union Street, and had shrewdly bought out the cherished 'Bradbury' name associated with the town's defunct motorcycle manufacturers. As well as acquiring additional premises in Bell Buildings, Platt had obtained several of Oldham's first dealerships in motorcars, all the while keeping an eye on Clem's meteoric career, and looking out for new business opportunities.

Tracks were still being built with scant regard to safety. True, riders wore crash-helmets and usually leathers (an expensive item) for protection, but deaths and serious injuries were frequent. Riders' safety reps helped, but desperate to attract spectators, owners and promoters had other priorities. Where tracks had been built inside greyhound circuits, there were complaints that dogs were injuring their paws on cinders sprayed over the fence by broadsiders. This necessitated the extra expense of laying canvasses across dog-tracks, although some venues refused to entertain speedway on this ground alone. Many tracks, including Audenshaw, defaulted into perpetual crisis and rogue management. On 18 June twenty-eight-year-old rider George Rowlands died from head injuries. At the inquest the coroner urged the ACU representative, Captain Gilchrist, to make greater efforts to ensure the track was kept in good repair, and to see that riders wore adequate protective clothing. Showing an obvious lack of understanding of the sport, he thought that tyres of 'an anti-skid type' would make things safer, while a local journalist made the more realistic recommendation that all competitors should be tested by the ACU on how to fall from a machine safely, and how to do 'double skidding at speed'.[4] Other tragedies were to follow at Audenshaw, and Clem no doubt breathed a sigh of relief that he had survived his baptism of fire there.

Spence, whose unchallenged authority led rapidly to him becoming known by the diminutive 'EOS' to friend and foe alike, was a Machiavellian schemer. He knew that in the long run there was no room for speedway at flapping tracks like Audenshaw. His solution to the problem of supply in excess of demand was as simple as that of the Oldham mill-owners: rationalisation. It was, therefore, in the interests of ambitious, well-financed tracks such as Belle Vue to be rid of smaller concerns that siphoned off spectators from their own tracks. The model was being driven by Spence's ultimate paymasters, Speedway Trust Ltd., parent company of ISL, who now announced its intention to increase its share capital from £80,000 to £150,000 for the purpose of buying up stadiums at Stamford Bridge and King's Oak (formerly High Beech). Belle Vue took its place in the new League, but all the while Spence watched and waited for opportunities to damage it.

The League was too weak to deal with the general free-for-all that had arisen at tracks such as Audenshaw, and attempts to impose minimum standards were easily flouted. Yet, in spite of its outlaw status, Audenshaw continued to put on meetings, and blacklisted riders were able to earn more by operating on other tracks outside the League's jurisdiction. Many stadiums struggled to fulfil their fixtures and to meet their obligations to the League. Too many tracks had been built on unsuitable sites, such as that at Barnsley on a hilltop, or Wolverhampton, which, in order to economise on cinders, had utilised an old corporation tip. Here, according to Clem, it was all part of the spectacle for riders to be hit in the face by churned-up stones, broken bottles, tin cans, and even the odd dead cat. Before long, the League began to disintegrate, while, in Clem's words, owners were beginning a 'big offensive' against riders.

Chapter Eleven

Shirt-tails and Lamp-posts

'The Ministry of Transport has permitted to be unleashed
on the roads forces of destruction which it is beyond the
powers of the police to control.'
Comment of the newly-formed Pedestrian Society
on the rise in accidents involving motorcars
and motorcycles during the 1920s.

The relatively classless professional template of American and Australian speedway was not reflected in Britain's nascent dirt track business. On the contrary, British class-based distinctions were subtly incorporated so as to distinguish between sporting 'professionals' and 'amateurs'. A professional sportsman like Clem was a lesser breed, a worker, who required leadership and a good example to be set for him. In the nature of things, these qualities were provided by gentleman amateurs.

The focus of militant amateurism in the world of motorcycling was the network of ACU-affiliated clubs, such as the Stalybridge Motor Club, which Clem and Eli Anderson had been obliged to join in order to race at Audenshaw. Their regional centres had been the conduit for much bellicose opposition to the introduction of dirt track, but as the sport grew, diehards had to supplicate more humbly. They suggested that 'non-attached' riders (that is amateurs not under contract to promoters) should have ring-fenced opportunities to race at every track as well as practice facilities and, somewhat fancifully, they argued that successful gentleman riders who objected to cash prizes should receive trophies instead of money. The extent to which class bias informed the decisions of sport's ruling bodies at this time was well illustrated in two decisions of the Amateur Athletics Association, reached at the same meeting. While the AAA decided to ban 'any person competing as a dirt track rider for cash or prizes' from taking part in organised athletics, it was happy to confirm that athletes who earned money from journalism by writing about athletics would *not* lose their amateur status!

The peculiar distinction, which had long pervaded that most English of all sports, cricket, between 'gentlemen' and 'players', was ingrained in English society. It was typified in the armed services, where 'officers' and 'men' were differentiated unto, and even beyond, death, by statements of rank on war memorials. In speedway, owners and promoters invariably attracted a reverend 'Mr' when named in newspapers, and to avoid over-familiarity, only initials prefixed their surnames. In contrast, riders were identified by their first names or unprefixed surnames, or, like Clem, by daft nicknames. On the track, stewards wore that most symbolic token of English authority, the bowler hat, and were identified in the programmes by initials and surnames suffixed by 'Esquire', while ACU inspectors in the paddock were easily identified in tweedy plus-fours. Accordingly, in Sheffield, Clem's status as rider *and* director presented the local press with an identity problem. His title varied between 'C.H. Beckett' (gentleman), 'Mr Beckett' (director), 'Clem Beckett' (rider), and ultimately, when out of favour, just 'Beckett'. Given the pervasiveness of this class system, Hart's notion of involving riders in a sort of co-operative was revolutionary. Likewise, Clem's status as a director confounded journalists, whose knee-jerk reaction was to elevate him to gentleman in spite of his unimpeachable working-class credentials. Of twenty riders praised for their outstanding contribution to the success of speedway, 'C.H. Beckett' was among only three granted the gentleman's appellation – surnames preceded by initials.

However much the Auto-Cycle Union celebrated its commitment to sporting values, neither the veneer of gentility affected by middle-class officialdom, nor the efforts made by the Riders Association to secure track safety, could alter the fact that speedway had become the most dangerous sport in the land. Indeed, the risk posed to life and limb was undeniably part of the attraction for spectators – especially those more interested in human drama than the technical capabilities of motorcycles. Nowhere was this better illustrated than at Audenshaw, where, in spite of the tragic death of George Rowlands, the crowd roared their approval of Slider Shuttleworth, whose favourite trick when losing a big match was to stage a dramatic crash. Concealed in his pudding-basin helmet, typical of the inelegant protective headwear of the time, was a small balloon filled with red ink, which, whenever dismounted, he contrived to burst, giving the impression of gushing blood and superhuman bravery as he attempted to remount his machine.[1] Sometimes, though, riders could not remount, and had to be stretchered off the track. This prompted a journalist from the *Manchester Evening News* to plead with stadiums to ensure that before the end of a meeting spectators should be informed of the condition of injured riders by way of announcements over the public address system.

Shuttleworth's party-piece rather confirmed the point made by a correspondent to the *Motor Cycle* and signing himself 'Psychologist' that a proportion of spectators attended with the subconscious hope of 'seeing someone hurt, or best of all, killed,' and popular newspaper columnist Hannen Swaffer, with other concerns, was moved to censure speedway as a 'non-sport [...] followed by screaming girls and loutish youths in goggle-eyed witlessness.' Under this kind of pressure, *Speedway News* leapt to its defence: dirt track *was* a sport, and the main reason for its popularity was the 'sheer skill, high courage, physical fitness and mental alertness' shown by its participants. It was to become a repeated theme of *Speedway News* that most injuries on the dirt track occurred to lads who were unsuited to the game, and who, amongst other inadequacies, did not know how to fall from their machines 'safely'. Coming down in a slide done properly was 'the most harmless thing imaginable', far better than being thrown heavily trying to correct a misjudged manoeuvre.

But it was hardly that simple. Nobody was collecting statistics, especially regarding the cumulative effects of serial injuries. In his first season 'on the dirt', rising star Arthur Jervis was hospitalised for a total of nine weeks as a result of three separate crashes. Moreover, when a successful rider lost form, as was to happen to Clem, the trauma of recent injury was rarely given as the reason. It suited all concerned with promotion of the new sport to encourage a 'macho' culture, which also came to be embraced by a small number of determinedly brave women riders who broke into this largely male domain.[2]

Paradoxically, an almost flippant attitude to dirt track injuries was to become a feature of speedway journalism, glossing over the consequences when a rider 'bought a box of tacks' or 'came a purler'. Making light of 'coming down' became an editorial convention that journalists on *Speedway News*, answerable to International Speedways Ltd, observed infallibly. Such as when Noel Johnson, at an ISL Wimbledon meeting, 'received a nasty shock' when another rider's machine split his crash helmet. Naturally, Johnson 'escaped with a severe headache'. When Squib Burton 'came off badly' in a 'benefit' meeting for Coventry riders whose machines had been destroyed in a lorry fire, *Speedway News* complimented him on 'ignoring doctor's orders' by taking part in the next race. Newspaper accounts such as that in the *Sheffield Daily Independent,* describing how a falling rider came to rest on a trackside stretcher propagated the surreal notion that riders were like immortal cartoon characters to whom nothing really bad could ever happen. Yet, in his heart of hearts, every rider knew that serious injury or even death was waiting at the next bend. The number of riders disabled or enduring long-term injury as a result of accidents already warranted the establishment of the Speedway Riders Benevolent Fund.

All that said, in July 1929 *SN's* editor, Norman Pritchard, finally had the good sense to publish a defence of speedway, which would, then as now, find approval among the majority of the British public. Writing as 'Hon Sec' of the Ilford Motor Club and King's Oak Speedway, R.J. Hill-Bailey admitted that the days of Mr Toad were over. The 'open road' was the wrong place for a playground, and the dirt track was a necessary refuge for sporting motorcyclists to get off increasingly busy and regulated roads and 'out of the way of everybody'. Ah, how might this have chimed with the feelings of long-suffering residents along Oldham's main roads in the days of 'Road Louse' when Clem and the Andersons raced each other up to the moors. Now, dirt track was providing an opportunity for young men to indulge in speed bursts to their hearts' content, 'getting rid of their youthful energies, and ensuring complete safety for the onlooker.' It was a strong argument, which neatly sidestepped the obvious fact that there would be many energetic, daredevil youths who simply would not be inclined to expend their thrill-seeking energy anywhere other than on public roads.

Leather britches and jackets were, of course, an absolute requirement to protect riders in their frequent encounters with cinder surfaces.[3] They were expensive, however, and riders often shared their leathers. At an early meeting at Owlerton, an observant sports reporter for the *Sheffield Star Green'Un* described Clem's embarrassment after a joker 'borrowed' his trousers during a race. Attempting to recover his leathers from another rider, Clem dashed around the paddock, barefoot and trouserless, shirt-tails flapping.

In order to add to the League's difficulties, and in a typically cynical manoeuvre, EOS devised an agreement between Belle Vue and Audenshaw, enabling them to exchange riders, and on 6 July 1929 Belle Vue dealt the Northern League a mortal blow by deciding to withdraw from it. Before long Manchester White City were to ride their last League match.

Later that month Hart came up with the grand idea of staging a sort of Test match between Australian and British riders, which Gadfly did his best to publicise as, 'a friendly dust-up between the old country and one of our foremost colonies.' But Hart was up against the fact that nearly all the big-name Aussies were under contract to International Speedways, and in spite of Clem's billing as star man for England, the event seems to have fallen flat. Meanwhile, ISL was already planning to launch its own series of Test matches. Increasingly, the team to watch was Belle Vue, Manchester, as EOS, guided by his ISL paymasters, pursued a policy of attracting big names and even bigger attendances.

However, Clem made sure Belle Vue did not have everything its own way. At an evening meeting at the Manchester stadium the following week, he put in a brilliant performance, beating Australian Vic Huxley by two heats to one in a match race. Huxley, doyen of the Aussie 'invasion' the previous year, was at the peak of his form – and Belle Vue, with regular appearances of star men, and attendances of 30,000 or more, was well on the way to becoming the leading speedway venue of the north.

Alas, within a few days of his great triumph over Huxley, Clem Beckett lay in a hospital bed, fighting for his life. Before returning from a race meeting in Newcastle, which had earned him a handsome payment of £40 on the track, he had bought a second-hand motorbike and sidecar, intending it as a gift for a friend in Oldham – very likely one of the Anderson boys. His strategy for getting the 'outfit' back to Oldham was original and ambitious – motorbike and sidecar to be towed by a friend's motorcar, with Clem in the saddle on the bike. They did not get far. The sidecar 'lifted' rounding a corner, and in an effort to control it, Clem steered the bike outwards and into the path of an oncoming Corporation tramcar. He evaded the tram, as well as a motorcar coming up alongside it, but the car hit the tow rope, breaking it with such force that Clem's machine was hurled into a lamp-post. On impact, a broken foot-rest cut through Clem's boot into the ball of his foot. Although contemporary reports are silent on the point, it was almost certainly Clem's right foot which was thus impaled, being the unprotected outer foot for the rider of a motorcycle combination. Just as well, because although Clem was later to conform to the practice of his competitors by wearing a 'knee-hook' on his (left) broadsiding foot, he had no such protection on the streets of Newcastle.

It might have been another *Keystone Cops* episode were it not for the seriousness of Clem's injury. Had it been his left foot, that is to say his broadsiding foot, the wound would have been very serious indeed; but it was bad enough. Following first-aid in Newcastle, Clem returned home under his own steam, hoping for the best, rather as he had done after being bitten by the family Alsatian dog. Again, however, the wound turned septic, and this time it was worse than career-threatening. The Owlerton doctor intervened by opening up the wound to remove a piece of bone. With infection spreading up Clem's leg, Hart arranged for him to be admitted to a Manchester nursing home. This was more than a decade before antibiotics became available, and Clem was racked with pain, relieved at first by chewing towels, then by morphine.

Clem's sudden removal from the scene at Sheffield gave rise to worries that his leg had been amputated. Hart, anxious to quash such rumours, and quick to recognise a publicity opportunity, arranged for Gadfly to visit Clem in Manchester. Clem, putting on a brave face, got out of bed to prove he still had two legs. Gadfly made the most of his exclusive interview, relaying Clem's 'message' to the Sheffield fans to the effect he hoped to be back soon, and another one to colleagues in the team, lamenting that his nurses insisted on him drinking nothing stronger than milk. Tough-guy Clem, of course, survived to ride another day, but whatever the blessings of his natural healing power he never forgot the debt he owed Hart.

About the same time, Clem's best friend and deadly rival on the dirt track, Skid Skinner, had his own, less serious, encounters with street furniture. En route to a speedway event at Barnsley, he too collided with a lamp-post, an event that generated much local interest, and when summonsed to court Skinner's successful defence was that he had hit the lamp-post to avoid an oncoming vehicle. In another accident, which resulted in a County Court hearing, the judge accepted that Skinner's reason for his car colliding with a right-turning vehicle was that he dare not apply his brakes for fear of skidding. Naturally, the scenario was a gift for newspaper headline writers, and Skid's solicitor, Irwin Mitchell, achieved something of a 'Mr Loophole' reputation. Later still, Skinner's car collided with a post supporting tram wires – and this time it *was* a result of skidding.

The history of dangerous sports is littered with examples of men addicted to danger. Speedway riders accepted the risk of death or serious injury as an occupational hazard, and inevitably some became careless about less risky situations in everyday life, especially driving on public roads. Typically, both Clem and Smoky Stratton drove at speed, confident in their split-second judgment, oblivious to the dangers posed by misjudgments of lesser mortals. Soon after returning from the ISL tour of Argentina, enjoying his reputation as *el diablo roja*, and following a punishing meeting in London, Manchester rider Frank Varey sustained leg injuries when his car overturned during a 200-mile journey back from London.

Yet, while Mr Hill-Bailey realised that the game was up for riders and drivers who wanted to use public roads for sport, other influential voices resisted. *Motor Cycling* magazine was happy to encourage the notion of the open road as suitable terrain for the sporty rider: there would 'never be a finer sportsman on the King's highway' than the young man astride his sports model, and, of course, the same view was enthusiastically shared by sports car drivers. When the Nottingham coroner wrote an excoriating newspaper article blaming the popularity of dirt track for encouraging 'young men and boys' to risk their lives and the lives of others on public roads, he naturally provoked denials from the trade press, not to say ridicule. But the coroner was only expressing the same concerns that had issued from Oldham Watch Committee a few years earlier faced with the excesses of 'Daredevil' Beckett and the Anderson boys and their adoring pillion passengers.

Unfortunately, and in spite of Mr Hill-Bailey's strictures, the speedway press itself, habitually ready to massage the machismo image of riders, slipped easily into the practice of making light of the internal combustion engine's killing power on public roads. Best make it out to be a jolly jape – such as the time when a trailer being driven at speed by Varey's mechanic collided with a milk cart, with 'eggs and bottles flying through the air like cinders on a bend.' Or when Midland rider Colin Ford was injured in a near-fatal car crash, and was said to have 'bought a bad packet on the Coventry road'.

Only a few weeks after Clem's accident in Newcastle, the speedway world was in mourning for Bert Round of Barnsley. Round, the lucky victor of the challenge match with Clem a couple of months earlier, had been a regular competitor at Owlerton, as well as captain of the Barnsley team. In his last meeting, barely ten days before his death, twenty-three year-old Round had won three races to score maximum points. On 26 August, on his way to a dirt track engagement at Wombwell, Round sustained fatal injuries in a collision with another motorcyclist.

The ghost of Mr Toad was hard to lay to rest. By 1930 casualties on British roads had reached an annual rate of more than 185,000 injured, with more than 7,000 killed. Clem Beckett, also twenty-three, was extremely lucky not to be in the latter category.[4] Moreover, as events were to prove, neither the accident in Newcastle nor the tragic death of Round would be enough to cure Clem's addiction to risk-taking on track *and* road, either on a motorbike or at the wheel of a motorcar.

In the meantime, and while Clem was out of action, Hart, along with other promoters and stadium owners, was struggling to stay afloat. Alarmed at Clem's recurring problem of broken chains, an affliction brought on by his sudden and devastating bursts of speed, Hart approached seventy-eight-year-old Swiss-born Hans Renold, founder of a Manchester chain-makers, who reputedly responded by providing Clem with an unbreakable chain.[5]

League members, stricken by reduced gate income, were often unable to fulfil their fixtures. Even Sheffield was unable to raise a team for its League match with Halifax after suffering a string of rider casualties in three events held early in the same week. So, too, once-mighty Manchester White City was forced to cry off a fixture at Owlerton, ostensibly because it could not raise a team. Likewise, individual riders were reacting to the NDTOA cash limits by not fulfilling their engagements. Disappointed fans who expected to see a star man as advertised, were just as likely to be unforgiving of the stadium as of the rider himself – as when Clem's old adversary, Syd Jackson, failed to turn up at Owlerton for a Saturday night event. The issue came to a head when the ACU decided to make an example of Sprouts Elder, suspending his competition licence indefinitely for breaking several engagements. Elder then announced his intention to race in South America, even though Sheffield claimed to have first call on his services for forty rides, and Belle Vue claimed to have signed him up through their Dirt Tracks Booking Bureau.

The nascent sport of speedway, just over a year after its sensational introduction, was in a state of crisis. Apart from the ambiguous position of Belle Vue, which had set it on a collision course with the NDTOA and other stadium owners, riders' efforts to resist pay restrictions had reached a high tide. The Riders' Association threatened a strike (which the press described as a 'general strike' so as to alarm readers) and the NDTOA responded with a threat to shut down all tracks under its jurisdiction. At Rochdale, riders held up a meeting for half an hour until they got agreement on increased prize money.

Chapter Twelve

Slump

'Violence bred further violence, with the leader of the largest paramilitary army of all posing as a defender of law and order, even as he exculpated murders committed by his own followers.'
Michael Burleigh describing the rise of Hitler during the Depression.

By now Hart had appointed Smoky Stratton as manager of the Sheffield speedway. Fellow-director or not, Stratton's statement to the press regarding the threat of a riders' strike was in terms that guaranteed a complete rupture of relations between him and Clem. It amounted to strike-breaking by pre-emption. Suggesting that Sheffield was unlikely to be affected by a strike, Stratton insisted: 'The good riders are not complaining,' adding that it was 'second-class' men who were causing the trouble. Stratton pointed out that riders earning only two or three pounds a week before the dirt track boom were now making a good deal more. Stars like Squib Burton always made at least £35 when they rode at Sheffield, and commonly made £100 a week.

With a lack of sensitivity beggaring belief, Stratton cited 'the late Bert Round' who had earned £520 from the Sheffield track in the three months before his death. It would not be long before Clem himself would be ready to go public with his diametrically opposed view of speedway justice, but in any case, Hart's company was on its last legs; the directorships of both Clem and Stratton were virtually worthless, and as directors they were certainly powerless.

Barely eighteen months after the dramatic arrival of speedway in the United Kingdom, the nation stood on the brink of the Great Depression. Dislocation of the economies of America and Europe portended mass unemployment, and the nascent speedway business was not immune.

Men struggling to feed a family on meagre public assistance could not afford to pay entrance fees. Almost as rapidly as it had expanded, dirt track racing went into decline, and the inevitable consequence was that riders were less in demand. Moreover, unemployed men, desperate for cash, chancing a venture into professional sport such as speedway, were willing to undercut each other. Even established riders like Clem were soon to feel the harsh realities of the 'Slump' in the face of spiralling unemployment and distress.

In Britain the second minority Labour government had taken office in June 1929, powerless to resolve the economic crisis, riven by internal disagreement, and bitterly opposed by Communists, who had adopted the very un-British slogan: 'Class against Class'. Compared to more than eight million votes cast for the Labour Party, the total cast for Communist candidates was less than 48,000. A sense of helplessness in the face of change affected society as the economic depression deepened. Traditional industries such as steel-making and cutlery in Sheffield and textiles in Lancashire were in crisis, as steeply rising unemployment created joblessness and despair.

At the same time some of Clem's comrades in the Communist Party, including those he had known in the Young Communist League in Oldham, now had paid jobs within the Party, and their role was to agitate for revolution on a daily basis. Ernie Woolley, promoted to Northern Industrial Organiser for the CPGB, was busy supporting workers in disputes against pay cuts. On 8 August 1929 Woolley was one of two men fined 40s by Oldham magistrates for causing an obstruction outside the town's Coliseum Theatre while distributing Communist leaflets. Woolley was said to have been the cause of a fracas during a mass demonstration of textile workers, and police evidence was to the effect that many people objected to the Communist presence.

Woolley's career in politics was destined to converge with that of Comrade Beckett, but for the time being the two of them existed in parallel universes. While violent clashes with the police were being fermented by the Party in every industrial region where unemployment and distress were rife, there is no evidence that Clem was directly involved. That said, distrust and suspicion of Communists was by now so great that even an unguarded comment or declaration of allegiance carried the risk of retribution. Indeed, during the course of the 1920s hundreds of Party members were arrested for sedition or breach of the peace, many being sentenced to imprisonment with hard labour. No one ever accused Clem Beckett of being afraid to speak his mind, and having declared his allegiance to the Communist Party of Great Britain he was not going to recant.

Factory closures, falling industrial production and poverty put every aspect of speedway under pressure. While clubs were defaulting on League commitments, and riders were dishonouring agreements with promoters, the authority of the NDTOA was being irretrievably hobbled. Clem himself accepted engagements (presumably with the blessing of Hart) to race on tracks outside NDTOA control, a fact which surfaced at a meeting of the Belle Vue complaints department, and was no doubt noted by the omniscient EOS.

Against this background, the Dirt Track Riders Association, in which Clem was a prominent member, had little chance of improving terms for the majority of riders.[1] At a committee meeting of the NDTOA, held shortly after Belle Vue's decision to withdraw from the League, Mr Lees submitted a modest pay claim on behalf of his members. The claim was turned down flat, with A.S. Morgan, EOS's fellow committee member at the North Manchester Motor Club, bluntly informing riders that the owners could not afford it.

By September 1929, in the wake of Belle Vue's withdrawal, the Northern League was on the verge of collapse. Resignations followed from Warrington, Liverpool, Leeds, and even Manchester White City. Out of the chaos and desperation a new, unofficial body suddenly and mysteriously emerged to keep speedway afloat. Ostensibly, the aim of the Belle Vue Booking Bureau was to provide riders with engagements by matching them up with demands from non-League clubs. In a short period, Warrington, Gosforth (Newcastle), Nottingham and White City were, in effect, operating under the Belle Vue banner; in other words under the control of EOS. Rumours circulated that Sheffield would also be forced to join, but for the time being at least, Hart held out, maintaining Owlerton's independence.

While these events were unfolding, Clem was recovering from his lamp-post crash, still unsure if he would ever ride again. Back on his feet, but still not fit enough to rejoin the Sheffield team, he paid a leisurely visit to Belle Vue Gardens. Enterprising as ever, Manchester's multi-faceted venue had cottoned on to another entertaining and novel spectacle, the 'Wall of Death'. Motorcycle riders defying gravity by hurtling horizontally round a wooden bowl were packing in paying customers wherever they could find a venue. A version of the novelty had appeared at the British Empire Exhibition in 1924, and before that, amusements featuring death-defying motorcyclists revolving in a confined space had enjoyed popularity in Johannesburg and New Jersey. In England, after a Wall of Death show put on for holidaymakers in Southend-on-Sea, Belle Vue pleasure ground seized the initiative. Unlike speedway, recognised as an entertaining sport, the Wall of Death was sheer entertainment, more of a fairground attraction. Even so, as long as they could earn money from it, the distinction was of little significance to riders struggling to make a living. Clem observed Wall of Death proceedings at Belle Vue with a professional eye.

Before he could put his ideas into practice, however, another opportunity arose. Germany and Scandinavia were a tad behind England in rolling out speedway, but as they caught on, the shortage of able practitioners began to attract foreign riders. Clem had already ridden in Scandinavia, and word spread on the riders' grapevine about more opportunities in northern Europe. Enter Percy Platt, Oldham businessman and speedway boss at Rochdale, who now began to further diversify his business interests by becoming riders' agent and European tour manager. Both Clem and Skid Skinner put their trust in him.

In spite of his managerial status, globe-trotting Stratton seems to have been poised to leave Sheffield, already augmenting his income by taking part in beach races at New Brighton. The previous year Stratton had been among the pioneers of speedway in Paris and Cologne, and given the troubles of the Northern League, was already thinking about another trip to the United States. No doubt his unpopularity among both riders and fans played a part. Clem, still with strong ties in Oldham, and helping to support his mother, was unlikely to venture so far from home. But, in the autumn of 1929, hoping that his battered leg would stand the strain, Clem sailed for Germany, heading for Hamburg, where the first specially built dirt track had opened during the summer.

Whatever calls were made on Clem's loyalty to the Communist Party in the 1920s, they did not relieve him of the need to earn a living. Like all members he was called on to distribute Party literature, but the real focus of his life, the core of his being, was competitive motorcycling. This he pursued with the same uncompromising will to win he had shown when playing rugby league. That said, his fame as a speedway rider did not go unnoticed by the CPGB leadership. Although he was not yet on the Party payroll, his potential usefulness as a sportsman, especially a sportsman travelling in Europe, had already occurred to newly appointed General Secretary and fellow Lancastrian Harry Pollitt, and to those around him.

Since 1924 the Party's contact with the Russians had been made easier by the presence of the Soviet trade delegation in Britain. However, knowing that the British Secret Service was keeping a close eye on Russian delegates, and doing its best to intercept communications, the Party had gradually developed a sophisticated network of couriers. The obvious route to and from Russia was by sailings between Newcastle and St Petersburg (Leningrad), but secret messages passed on by couriers and agents operating in Germany and Denmark were much more difficult for the British Secret Service to monitor. As a professional sportsman, Clem would have had excellent cover for clandestine meetings with fellow Communists.

The knock-on effects of the Wall Street Crash in October 1929, with billions of dollars wiped off the stock market, led to unprecedented levels of unemployment in Europe. American banks called in their loans to Europe, with Germany especially hard hit. Things were bad enough in Oldham and England's industrial heartlands, but in Germany they were far worse. When Clem and Skid arrived, together with Percy Platt, and Eli Anderson travelling as mechanic, it was on the verge of political disintegration. There was a banking crisis; unemployment was to double within twelve months to 1.6 million, and within three years it would be more than six million. There was widespread homelessness, starvation and misery.[2] The democratically elected government in Berlin was losing control. Hitler's Brownshirts were fighting with Communist militias for control of towns and cities. But in Holstein and Hamburg, where Clem established speedway contacts, Communists still had the upper hand. When, in 1923, Hitler led a failed putsch in Munich, Ernst Thaelmann led a Communist rising in Hamburg. Although it, too, was a failure, Communists there remained well-organised with close links to the Comintern. Whether or not Clem was formally recruited for Party work abroad is an open question. That he made contact with fellow Communists whilst travelling in Germany and Denmark is likely. So might it have been on this trip that Clem first met his future wife, Eli Marie, also a Communist?

Born in Denmark, Eli Marie (known as Lida) Henriksen had returned to Europe after emigrating to Canada. If she and Clem did meet in

Denmark in the autumn of 1929, the circumstances remain as obscure as details of Clem's dirt track performances for the benefit of German speedway fans in the crisis-stricken Weimar Republic.

In spite of mass unemployment and the political maelstrom into which their country was descending, the German people still pursued their sporting passions. It was, after all, a German, Gottlieb Daimler, who had invented the motorcycle, and naturally enough the Germans were keen to make up lost ground in the art of cinder-shifting.

The tour took in the town of Vejle, in south-east Jutland, known as the 'Manchester of Denmark' on account of its cotton mills. Platt's contacts included a Yorkshire businessman with an interest in one of the mills. When Clem and Eli were invited to look round the mill, Clem was less than keen: 'Our bloody ears are full of it already,' he told Eli, recalling the noise of machinery in Oldham's mills.

Alas, in the autumn of 1929 Clem's tour came to a sudden end after an accident in which he broke his thigh during a race at the Hamburg stadium. Lying in hospital, Clem, who had a musician's ear and a penchant for learning languages, did his best to improve his German, and was perhaps a little over anxious to impress his nurses. The story goes that Clem was asked to assist with a blood 'transfusion' for a fellow patient, and thinking that he was being asked if he wanted food, replied with an unhesitating 'Ja'. He kept his word, however, thus becoming an early blood donor.[3]

Coming so soon after the serious injury to his foot, it is hard to resist the conclusion that Clem's return to the track was premature. Repeated injuries were taking their toll. From now on he would have to use a knee-hook. Following the accidents in Newcastle and Germany, Clem spent at least eight months in hospital in 1929. By December, he was back in England, but it was not the end of his business relationship with Platt.

Meanwhile, English speedway was in desperate straits, with further resignations from the Northern League by Burnley, Bolton, Hanley and Long Eaton – all towns feeling the pinch of unemployment and short-time working as the economy slumped. Struggling White City were taken over by Belle Vue. Late in October, even Northern League winners Leeds, reeling under the drop in gate receipts, went into voluntary liquidation.

There were rumours that a new League was being planned, especially when, in November, EOS attended a meeting of promoters in London, from which the NDTOA was excluded. EOS, as a representative of the ACU, was mandated to 'take any relevant action' – a strong indication of his growing influence in motorcycling's highest authority, and likewise of the omnipresence of International Speedways, one of whose representatives at the meeting was Johnnie Hoskins. Significantly, the venue was the offices of Wembley stadium, the ISL flagship, and all those present agreed they wanted to be rid of the NDTOA. Presciently, *Motor Cycling* magazine commented that Belle Vue was bound to be 'a great force' in the new order.

Other northern promoters responded to the crisis with a series of meetings, the first of which was held in the opulent surroundings of the Midland Hotel, Manchester, in December. Optimistic noises were picked up by the press. According to the *Auto Motor Journal* there were plans to form a new body, in alliance with southern promoters, with the putative name of the National Speedways Association, which would enable speedway 'to be put on a really business-like footing'. Yet another amalgam of interests coalesced into the National Dirt Track Association, which proceeded to pass a highfalutin resolution about promoting good feeling between riders and promoters, while more specifically determining to standardise riders' booking and payment terms.

Chapter Thirteen

The Mussolini of Speedway

'It is the greatest cycle show on earth.'
Land and water speed record-breaker Sir Malcolm
Campbell commenting on 'the Wall of Death'.

By the end of December 1929, Clem was back in Sheffield, helping Hart prepare the track at Owlerton for a special New Year's Day event. That is to say he was acting as groundsman. The *Sheffield Daily Independent* identified him respectfully as 'Mr Clem Beckett', informing its readers that he 'had made a good recovery from his accident in Germany,' and was hoping to take part in the forthcoming meeting. In somewhat contradictory terms, however, and mindful of the Newcastle accident, the *Independent*'s correspondent ventured a well-meant caution to Clem: 'It would be wise for him to rest his leg a little longer.'

However, in so far as Clem appears to have looked on Edgar Hart as something of a protector, even a father figure, there was bad news to come. By the end of the year, along with other northern speedway venues, the Sheffield stadium was in the hands of the official receiver. The chances of Clem and fellow-directors Smoky Stratton and Jimmy Hindle thereafter influencing the developments at Owlerton were nullified at a stroke; their shares in Provincial Dirt Tracks Ltd were worthless. Clem admitted, 'I lost all that I had invested', and although he felt no resentment towards Hart, he must have been more than disappointed. Events were being driven by harsh economic reality, and for the time being at least Clem was willing to maintain his links with the Sheffield club. Stratton, however, left for the USA early in the new year.

Given his helter-skelter lifestyle, the wonder is that Clem, still only twenty-three, had time or energy to follow wider events beyond the parameters of his speedway world, let alone politics. Similarly, given the free-wheeling entrepreneurship of his life, is it surprising that he kept faith with Communism, a creed increasingly disparaged in the media for its links to Soviet Russia. Yet keep faith he did, although beyond an occasional – and doubtless lively – expression of opinion, he would have had little time to attend meetings or demonstrations, or even to distribute copies of Party literature.

In the meantime, the CPGB's response to rocketing unemployment and despair in the industrial areas of Britain was to point up ever more gleefully the economic achievements of the Soviet Union. Glowing reports on the progress of the Soviet Five Year Plan appeared in the *Daily Worker,* mixed with paeans of praise for Joseph Stalin, who, according to an editorial published on 22 January 1930, was demonstrating an iron determination to crush 'Right deviationists'.

Still bearing the scars of two serious accidents within the previous six months, and after being appointed acting manager at Owlerton in succession to Stratton, Clem made the extraordinary decision to launch his career as a rider on the Wall of Death. By his own admission to the *Sheffield Daily Telegraph*, his injured foot was still giving him trouble, but by February 1930 the 'wall' had been erected within the two-shillings enclosure of the stadium, and Clem was practising, ready to open a nightly show in March. In all this he had teamed up with his old friend Hector 'Skid' Skinner. Skinner owned a garage in Tinsley, an industrial area of Sheffield, as well as having an interest in the struggling speedway venue at Hellaby, near Rotherham. Both men were hoping that the enterprise would raise enough money to see them through hard times. From the beginning, the Wall of Death project was managed by Percy Platt, straying beyond his native Oldham, and on the lookout as ever for an opportunity to exploit 'the newest thrill on the market' (Clem's own description). The odd thing was that Hart had allowed the 'drome' to be erected within the stadium; a situation that was bound to lead to conflict given the extra risk of injury to his star rider. In the event it was Skinner who sustained the first serious injury – a broken arm – when, on the eve of the opening of the 1930 speedway season, the show was being put on in Scunthorpe.

Yet even before his encounter with the reporter from the *Telegraph*, Clem had had another fall, bruising his head, when the footrest on his machine caught on the wires at the top of the wall that were designed to prevent machines flying into spectators. Bearing in mind that fairground and circus acts on the wall sometimes involved more than one rider, or featured riders blind-folded or hands-free, Clem appeared remarkably sanguine. It was hoped to put on the first public performance within a couple of weeks, 'If we last that long,' he added.

Although Clem and Skid were in the vanguard of Wall of Death performances in Britain, the market soon became swamped with new acts introducing a variety of stunts and gimmicks. In almost every case exponents of the art relied on American Indian machines. Good as it was on the dirt track, the Douglas was no good in the special circumstances of the Wall of Death. Accordingly, Clem and Skid purchased new, state-of-the-art, Indians. Their 'V' twin engines were similar to the Harley Davidson model that Clem had ridden as a tearaway teenager, but the Indians also had ground-breaking twist-grip controls and sprung forks. Above all they had 'rock-solid' handling, which in the mad, giddying world of the 'wall' was absolutely essential.

One of their rivals, who had likewise graduated from the Sheffield dirt track, was Billy Bellhouse, who revelled in the nickname 'Cyclone Billy' and whose speciality was driving an open-top motorcar round the wall. Other acts featured animals, such as lions, placed in the drome, or in the case of Bellhouse, alongside him in the passenger seat.[1] Women riders such as Lou 'Suicide' Cody and Winnie 'Fearless' Souter rapidly took to the wall, a sporting emancipation which chimed with the belated introduction of universal suffrage in Britain, as Parliament finally gave women the vote on the same terms as men. Winnie's act attracted the attention of the Prince of Wales, and even Labour's dour prime minister, Ramsay MacDonald, perhaps hoping to distract attention from his government's miserable failure to address the country's economic crisis. Echoing speedway's preoccupation with nicknames and hyperbole (posters claimed riders could reach speeds of 100mph, but the reality was more like 30-40), the *Daily Mail* helped boost attendances with a feature article, stressing that the wall was 'an astonishing exhibition of nerve and dare-devilry'. No wonder Clem was an early convert. The fact was, however, that performers on the wall were bereft of even basic safety protection. Spectators paid their money in order to witness fellow mortals taking extreme risks. Crash helmets, for example, would have been seen as almost cowardly; the greater the risk of injury the more spectators lapped it up. Moreover, the costs of setting up and dismantling the bowl (a procedure which took about ten hours), transporting it, arranging advanced bookings, advertising and ticket-sales were considerable;

Clem and Skid would have to come to an agreement with Platt as to how they were to be met.

They also faced extra competition for the hard-earned cash of thrill-seeking Sheffielders. The same edition of the *Telegraph* that carried the interview with Clem included adverts for the city's Cinema House, which, having installed 'a British Thompson-Houston reproducer' was due to introduce talking pictures in colour. While Clem and Skid were climbing the Wall of Death, patrons of the Cinema House would be watching a song and dance review entitled 'Climbing the Golden Stair', and in the warmth of nearby Central Picture House audiences would be able to see a Mickey Mouse cartoon with ground-breaking sound. For all that Clem and his fellow Communists looked to Russia for their political inspiration, their everyday lives were influenced far more by things American, especially so in Clem's life as a professional motorcyclist.

Quite apart from these apprehensions and distractions, there remained the over-arching issue of whether speedway would be able to reorganise itself in the face of the broken Northern League. The problem for speedway was to come up with a successful formula, such as professional football had managed to find by way of competitions run by the Football League. Clubs divided into a hierarchy of leagues, with all the excitement and tensions of promotion and relegation battles, were guaranteed to attract paying fans. However, there were difficulties in applying this template to speedway, given that ownership of stadiums was passing into fewer and fewer hands. This alone made it certain that one of the big attractions of speedway meetings – individual 'challenge' matches – would survive alongside team events and league fixtures. And in turn, dirt track's biggest promoter, International Speedways, through its publication *Speedway News*, fought its corner as *the* most dramatic spectator sport. A first-time attender at London's White City was quoted as saying that compared with the dirt track racing 'the Derby, the Cup Final and the Boat Race look like a mothers' meeting.'

On 25 February 1930, while Clem was practising on the Wall of Death, matters came to a head, and again the ubiquitous and seemingly omnipotent EOS was destined to play the decisive role. At a four-hour meeting in Manchester, with desperate NDTOA promoters deadlocked over the question of unassociated tracks, weary delegates conceded that any viable league would have to include Belle Vue. According to the *Daily Dispatch*, EOS was duly 'sent for'.

It is hard to imagine the scene as Spence entered the room without thinking of the hushed reverence shown to a king come to be crowned. There followed a humiliating surrender by NDTOA delegates in the face of EOS's ultimatum: that Belle Vue would only take part in a newly constituted league if the NDTOA played no part it in. Thus stripped of its *raison d'être*, the NDTOA was obliged to fall on its sword, its winding-up inevitable, and with administration of the sport defaulting directly back to the Auto-Cycle Union. It was a masterly *coup de grâce* by EOS which established Belle Vue as the premier speedway club, and his own authority beyond challenge. Having helped destroy NDTOA and the Northern League, he was now poised to create a new League in his own image. No wonder EOS was becoming known as 'the Mussolini of Speedway'.

The consequences of the Manchester meeting were soon felt by the sport. On 7 March, at another meeting in Manchester, the NDTOA duly passed out of existence, upon a proposal being put by a representative from Preston, and seconded by Mr MacDonald of Sheffield.

A National Speedways League was established, modelled along the lines of the English Football League, with Northern and Southern sections, alongside proposals for promotions and relegations between higher and lower divisions. Ominously for riders, however, it was agreed that teams would be limited to a maximum of four riders, compared with the former maximum of six. EOS was appointed chairman of the Northern League Committee, with all legal matters to be vested in it, including disciplinary powers relating to riders. Significantly, the venue of the first meeting of the committee on 18 March was Belle Vue. Early applications for membership were received from Glasgow, Preston, Liverpool, Edinburgh, Rochdale, Gosforth (Newcastle), Halifax, Leeds, Middlesbrough, and of course, the triumvirate of Belle Vue, White City and Sheffield.

However, E.B. Ware, renowned as an amateur three-wheel Morgan trials competitor, and representing the Auto-Cycle Union, made it clear that not all applications would be accepted. Nor were they: when the list was eventually announced, Leeds, Middlesbrough, and most notably, White City, failed to make the cut, although Barnsley, Wombwell, Leicester, and Warrington did. Spence also made a jubilant announcement to the press about his plans to involve Sheffield and the two Manchester venues in a three-cornered 'points league' in which the 'best men' from each track would race once a fortnight. In addition, EOS trumpeted big improvements to the track and stadium, in relation to which the reporter, grateful for his scoop, generously provided a list of contractors. There was no mention, however, of Amusement Caterers, set up to provide refreshment for hungry and thirsty fans, of which firm EOS happened to be a director. When riders complained that they had to pay for 'poor food at top prices' EOS graciously gave instructions that they should be provided for at concessionary rates.

Power being concentrated in the hands of EOS and Belle Vue created a feeling of exclusion among the further-flung stadiums in the North, and especially on the other side of the Pennines. While the *Sheffield Telegraph* blandly commented that the changes 'should lead to smoother working all round and the betterment of the sport generally,' riders like Clem and Skid Skinner, unrepresented in the secret cabals of owners and promoters, were becoming disillusioned with the autocratic organisation that was increasingly dictating the terms of their livelihoods. It was not just that power was concentrated in the hands of EOS: while the new arrangements enlarged the role of the Auto-Cycle Union to impose rules and regulations on stadiums and riders, they made no provision for riders to have their say. A journalist reporting on the new order in speedway, commented ominously, 'The fees of all dirt track riders will be on the decline in a short time.' And so it proved to be. The ACU set about imposing fixed rates of pay on riders according to their speeds. Because the rates were to be reviewed every month, Clem compared the new system to the hated 'means test' soon to be imposed on claimants for public assistance: if a man did not clock his grade time his pay was reduced in the same way that claimants, subject to periodic checks, would have their benefits cut. As times became faster, it became harder to break records, and even 'star' men were relegated to smaller fixed rates. Under this kind of pressure, there were efforts to reform the Riders' Association, but according to Clem they failed because riders on lower grades were not supported by the 'big men'.

Nor were they ever likely to be. Now it was truly every man for himself. With crack riders in the south not so harshly affected by the economic collapse, they deemed it wise to distance themselves from their northern colleagues. As the 1930 season approached, and with the approval of ISL, they broke away to form their own organisation, the British Dirt Track Riders' Association. Clem felt betrayed, but the *Motor*

Cycle crowed its approbation of a development which it thought would 'bring about real unity amongst the racing fraternity'. In their voiceless plight, the northern riders were typical victims of the times. As the Great Depression deepened and the economy went into free fall, working-class people all over the country were facing up to everyday humiliations of exploitation and unemployment. They had next-to-no money in their pockets, and without paying customers the future of speedway racing looked bleak. Like the traditional industries of the north, dirt track faced the harsh economic reality of 'rationalisation' – an emollient term for survival of the fittest. Captains of industry know that a precondition of profits is a stable or – better still – a rigged market. EOS had the nous to realise that in the troubled times of the Great Depression it would be easy to break the riders' bargaining position.

Chapter Fourteen

Capitalist Sport Bad, Workers Sport Good

*'Bourgeois sport has a single clear-cut purpose: to make
men more stupid than they are ... In bourgeois states sport
is employed to produce cannon fodder for imperialist wars.'*
From an article by Maxim Gorky, in *Pravda*,
the official Soviet newspaper.

The deepening Depression brought about fresh hopes in the Communist
Party that at last conditions were ripe for revolution. Yet its membership was
falling, and Harry Pollitt was left wondering why 'the transmission belts
were turning no wheels'. At the same time, in the excitable mood of the
moment, Pollitt helped to launch a new Party newspaper, *The Daily Worker.*
It was an expressive voice of Party policy, largely financed by money from
Moscow, a fact not known to the majority of Party members such as Clem,
encouraged to sell the paper at factory gates and left-wing gatherings.

The Daily Worker's content was heavily influenced by hardline
Party leaders such as Rajani Palme Dutt, a Marxist theorist living in a
world apart from members like Clem Beckett, and even further apart
from ordinary British workers and their families. Dutt wrote an article
condemning sport, or rather *'capitalist* sport' run 'under bourgeois
patronage'. Dutt singled out horse racing and football as 'profit-run
professional spectacles thick with corruption'. Stories carried by the paper
exposed the hypocrisy of what became to be known as 'shamateurism'
in football, with amateur players being suspended for receiving illegal
payments. When, however, the paper implemented Dutt's wish to cease
covering sport, there was a precipitous drop in circulation (from 45,000
to 39,000). Within a short time the episode prompted the Party to rethink
its view of sport, with results that changed the course of Clem's life.

CAPITALIST SPORT BAD, WORKERS SPORT GOOD

The British Workers Sports Federation owed its origins more to socialist-minded cyclists in the Clarion Club than to the Communist Party, but during the 1920s the Party became alarmed at the emphasis placed on sport as a means of recruiting young members by fascist organisations, especially in Mussolini's Italy and increasingly in Germany. Its response was to encourage 'workers sport' and the BWSF became a wing of the Party, affiliated to the Comintern-inspired Red Sport International. Accordingly, once Dutt's interdict about sport had been lifted, the *Daily Worker* focused on activities of the BWSF, finding also a *cause célèbre* in the refusal of the Labour government to provide entry visas for a Russian football team.

At the same time, however, evidence was emerging of Stalin's zealous persecution of two main groups. The largest was the 'kulaks', peasant smallholders obstructing the drive towards collectivisation of agriculture. The other was religious believers. Stalin was simply adapting the template of persecution of political enemies practised for centuries by his Czarist predecessors.[1] Clem, like the vast majority of Communist and socialist sympathisers, found reports of alleged atrocities beyond belief, wicked propaganda put out by the capitalist press, and indeed columns of the *Daily Worker* were regularly and generously given over to official denials from Soviet sources. But what if Clem had known the truth? What if Harry Pollitt had known the truth? Seventy years earlier, across an oak table in the library of Chetham's College, Manchester, Karl Marx and Friedrich Engels had plotted the downfall of capitalism. How unbearably troubled Clem and Pollitt might have been to realise that in Russia the noble theorising of their heroes, intended to save the human race, was partly fructifying in widespread abuse of human rights.

By now everyone in speedway knew that EOS was in the driving seat of dirt track racing in the North. In fairness to Spence, however, the changes he planned did improve the prospects of regular engagements for some riders, especially those who signed up with the Belle Vue Booking Agency. Likewise, the ACU raised its safety standards. Credit to EOS, also, for throwing his weight behind the campaign to block the introduction of organised betting into speedway. A move by Liverpool interests to get approval from the ACU for official 'totaliser' betting was denounced by Spence, and never got off the ground.[2]

However, except for a few 'star men', most of whom were scooped up by ISL in London, and by EOS at Belle Vue, the days when established riders could name their price were gone. In another canny move, EOS allowed his best riders to take part in an ISL-sponsored close-season tour of South America, preventing his protégés from being poached. Needless to say, Clem did not feature in EOS's plans.

In the spring of 1930, bruised and battered by injuries, overworking, and uncertain of his future, Clem was focused simply on survival, his own and that of his sisters and mother in Oldham. And so began the busiest period in his career, a speedway season in which his time was equally divided between riding for Sheffield, performing on the Wall of Death and recovering from one injury after another.

In the event, Clem, still billed as 'C.H. Beckett', was in for a rough patch on the cinders, attributable, according to Gadfly, to his use of unreliable 'fluffy' motors. This had prompted Clem to doubt the reliability of his beloved Douglas, and at Manchester White City's opening match of the 1930 season on 29 March, he appeared with a machine named after its designer, George Wallis.The Wallis Special incorporated revolutionary features such as hub-centre steering, housed within a pivoted fork, and had been taken up by several Australian riders. In fact, early in 1930 the must-have dirt track machine was the Rudge, fitted with Harley forks, preferably tuned by celebrated mechanic Johnny Leete.

The opening ceremony at White City, witnessed by 20,000 spectators, offered a curious glimpse of glamour and politics, with actress Mabel Philipson (née Russell) – a former music hall Gaiety Girl *and* a former Conservative Member of Parliament – officiating. Perhaps, just perhaps, Clem managed to join in the round of polite applause from the riders' paddock, as she wished all of them well. Ominously, with his old 'Doug' sitting in the trailer on standby, the Wallis resisted efforts to start, which was finally overcome by Clem having to run round the paddock with it. A reporter looking over the paddock fence observed Clem's annoyance, expressed in 'sergeant-major' language. No doubt the expletives deleted from the reporter's account were redolent of those let out by Clem a few years earlier when he had been kicked by a horse.

Indeed, it was an inauspicious start to the season on an unfamiliar revamped and widened track. Early in the third lap of his heat in the Golden Torch, Clem parted company with his machine going into the turn, forcing his withdrawal from later events. The *Sheffield Telegraph* lamented that he had been 'dogged by his usual ill luck' at Manchester White City. 'Unlucky' put it mildly. Still nursing bruises, Clem was unable to join the practice session at Owlerton the following Saturday, and when Sheffield riders competed in a return match with White City, he again turned in a disappointing performance.

The next day, before 10,000 spectators, Clem appeared at Trent Bridge in Nottingham's opening speedway event of the season. Promoters had worked up his rivalry with George Wigfield, and once again Clem had a torrid time. In match races he fell three times. A triumphant Wigfield, riding a new Rudge, was lauded for his brilliant comeback, while Clem had the indignity of being described by the *Nottingham Evening Post* as the 'one-time invincible rider who was no match for the Goldthorpe boy.' However, damage to Clem's standing was mitigated by what the *Post* reporter saw as 'one of the most sporting actions ever seen on the cinders'. An overcooked broadside had brought Wigfield off in front of Clem, who avoided running over his rival's spreadeagled profile by throwing himself from his own machine. Daredevil? Yes. Competitive? Yes. Determined to win? Yes. At all costs? No.

Clem always enjoyed the camaraderie of the dirt track. He might not have been a gentleman amateur, but with Clem speedway was always about fun, daring, and spectacle; about how you 'played the game', and respect between riders. Other competitors acquired reputations for foul play – typically cutting across the path of a rival ('boring') or trying to force a way past an opponent on the inside, while some were notorious for 'jumping'.[3] This involved accelerating away from the starting line before the starter waved his flag. The crime was especially prevalent in the case of 'rolling' starts where riders were allowed to ride a lap or two before reaching the starting line, supposedly dead-level.[4] Few, if any, allegations of this nature were ever made against Clem Beckett. He maintained an unblemished record as a 'clean' rider, a true sportsman – even when, as at Nottingham, he sorely needed a win. On 11 April, making his third appearance on the cinders in as many days, when Sheffield riders competed with Belle Vue men at Owlerton, Clem was 'decisively beaten' in a match race by Australian Jack Chapman. A few days later, before another home crowd, Clem was again defeated in a match race, this time against Australian Dickie Wise.

Clem was not on the starting grid at Doncaster speedway stadium the following week, because of another injury sustained on the Wall of Death, and was obliged to make a personal apology to disappointed fans for his inability to ride. Whether or not this gave rise to words with Owlerton colleagues, the situation pointed up an obvious and embarrassing truth: that between regular appearances in a highly dangerous fairground attraction, and team performances on the dirt track, there was an unavoidable conflict of interest. Henceforth Clem was under pressure, and there would be those who thought his troubles were of his own making.

He was, however, still a regular member of the Sheffield team, alongside Squib Burton, his old pal from the Marseille adventure, and newer recruits to Owlerton such as W.E. 'Gus' Platts and Jack 'Broncho' (sometimes 'Bronco') Dixon. Unfortunately, however, Burton and Dixon were among four riders suspended by the ACU in early April while investigations into alleged 'conduct prejudicial to the sport' were investigated. The essence of the charges against them was that they had entered into 'unofficial' contracts with stadiums which they would be unable to fulfil. It was a calculated demonstration of ACU power, which of course worked to the advantage of ISL.

Clem's disastrous start to the 1930 season inevitably triggered speculation that, at the tender age of twenty-four, he was already fading in the firmament of dirt track heroes; a burnt-out star. On 25 April, as if to emphasise Clem's difficulties, his record for the flying mile at Owlerton was broken by Arthur Jervis during a contest with White City riders. The *Motor Cycle* commented: 'Clem Beckett does not seem to have been able to get a motor to go yet.'

All these misfortunes and disappointments inevitably prompted armchair criticism. One commentator advised Clem that he might do better if he stopped showering spectators with cinders by riding nearer to the white line on the inside of the track. A photograph appeared in the *Auto,* featuring Clem standing side by side with Frank Varey in the paddock at Preston. Varey, relaxed, affects his usual Cheshire cat grin, but Clem looks worried, stern-faced, and overweight – barely recognisable from images of the trim, youthful, daredevil of happier times. It was even rumoured that Clem was thinking of taking up professional boxing. Gossip in the paddock had it that he was to be matched with former White City rider, turned boxer, Ian Ritchings, with the contest being staged at Belle Vue Boxing Stadium. It never happened.

To keep the show on the road at Owlerton, Hart was forced to allow his majority shareholding in Provincial Dirt Tracks to pass into the hands of Belle Vue. Overnight, Clem's boss had, in effect, become EOS, who lost no time in asserting his authority. Within weeks EOS announced himself as Sheffield's new 'Racing Manager'. His empire now included Owlerton, Belle Vue and White City. The Northern Bookings Agency gave him control over the appearances of more than 200 riders, and as Chairman of the Northern League Committee he was in position to exert a dominating influence on the fixture list. Riders at small tracks such as Thorne and Barnsley found themselves barred from competing at ISL tracks; they faced a 'closed shop' with EOS standing in the door.

Of course, the usual takeover assurances were given: that International Speedways would secure the future of the Owlerton stadium, and that Belle Vue and White City would share their star men with Sheffield. There would be a new 'private' league between the three stadiums, parcelling out ISL-contracted stars between them. Even Gadfly appears to have been taken in at first, bemoaning Clem's early season performances and suggesting to EOS that Sheffield needed 'another pair of star riders'.

But for insiders like Clem alarm bells were ringing. For a start he knew that EOS would have no truck with riders' pay claims, and that, as a founder member of the Dirt Track Riders Association, he and Spence were unlikely to see eye to eye on pay or riders' conditions generally. Given Spence's reputation for ruthlessness, Clem was bound to consider the possibility that he might be victimised. In any event, and no doubt arising from Spence's secret meeting with promoters in London, riders faced further pay restrictions. Ironically, one of the last acts of the NDTOA (by now reduced to a puppet of the ACU) was to announce that northern and southern owners had agreed to 'standardise' riders' appearance fees and prize money.

Spence's takeover of Sheffield had been accompanied by a volley of ISL propaganda purveyed through *Speedway News:* it claimed that the selection of teams for both Manchester clubs and Sheffield would ensure that 'the strongest riders available' would be 'carefully distributed' between the three of them. 'Tell it to the marines!' was Gadfly's response to the Sheffield club's official line that it was providing top-quality speedway. Cleverly, he damned EOS's running of the Sheffield team with faint praise. Acknowledgment of the arrival of rising star Chun Moore at Owlerton was tempered by mentioning that Moore had been a reserve rider at Belle Vue. Gadfly, incensed by the beating dished out to Sheffield the previous week by Belle Vue in the first of the much-vaunted triangular league matches, was in fact speaking up on behalf of Sheffield speedway fans being taken for mugs. Worse was to come: the next tourney in the series, at Owlerton, saw the home team 'totally eclipsed' 45-18 by White City, in front of 8,000 spectators. In addition, Clem, struggling with engine trouble, was obliged to witness a successful effort by Arthur Jervis on his British Mile record, with a time of 78.2 seconds, three-fifths (0.6) of a second inside Clem's time.

The obvious conflict of interest was of little or no concern to EOS. Yet for speedway fans it was as if the same manager was picking both teams for a derby game between their two rival football teams, Sheffield United and Sheffield Wednesday; hardly a serious sporting scenario. Gadfly's broadside continued at length. The Owlerton stadium was, he maintained, the best in the country, with high-standard floodlighting and safety fences, so why was the new regime neglecting to recruit top riders, and why was it that Sheffield's top men were not being given the opportunity to shine at Belle Vue? Why was it that the Owlerton track was not being maintained as it used to be, with a 'soft' surface favoured by the likes of Clem Beckett? In openly criticising the Sheffield management Gadfly was taking quite a career risk.

So too, there was little likelihood of direct criticism of the arrangement in the motorcycle press; certainly not in *Speedway News,* itself a creature of ISL, which announced its intention to extend coverage from London tracks to speedway countrywide, and predicted 'a wonderful season'. But more neutral observers in the press did not hesitate to wonder in print whether the Owlerton management was in effect the Belle Vue management. Moreover, the omnipotent EOS was unwise to rig the deck against his outpost of empire, given that Sheffield Wednesday, whose ground was less than a mile from Owlerton, were reigning League champions, and poised to win the title for the second consecutive season. With unemployment in the city at record levels, it was a no-brainer for working men on the breadline as to whether they would pay to see a second-rate speedway team or a top-of-the league football team.

In spite of setbacks, however, it was 'Daredevil Clem Beckett' who topped the bill at the reopening of the Leeds stadium at a night meeting on 3 May, in the illustrious company of White City riders Arthur Jervis and Sid Lewis, and Belle Vue's Max Grosskreutz, exalted as 'Champion of Australia'. A match race victory over local hero Harry Watson stopped the slide, and went some way to restoring Clem's reputation as a 'crack' rider. In an earlier heat the crowd thrilled to the sight of Clem and Watson passing and repassing each other four times.

By now Clem had been persuaded to ditch his trusty Douglas steed, and following his unhappy experience with the Wallis, had opted for the increasingly popular Rudge. Soon after his success at Leeds, he was in Leicester with the Sheffield team for a League match. Just before the second heat, Clem was seen to emerge from the paddock with his new machine in flames. His efforts to start the engine were in vain, and officials rushed to extinguish the blaze by smothering the machine with cinders. Like most riders, Clem was in the habit of concocting his own mix of fuel, his particular brand having come to be known as 'shoe polish', either on account of its appearance or smell. Perhaps the new-fangled Rudge was less tolerant of shoe polish than the Douglas, and a speedway journalist with the *Auto Motor Journal* was prompted to doubt Clem's ability to recover his old form.

However, Clem's recovery continued on 22 May with a storming performance in Glasgow at the city's new, but struggling, Carntyne stadium. Clem and Sheffield teammate Stan 'Dusty' Jenkins took most of the honours in races against local riders, but only 2,000 spectators turned up to watch them. Typically, Clem took a wide line, sweeping close to the outside of the track to establish a four-lap rolling start record. It was no coincidence that the Sheffield men were competing north of the border. There was a connection between the two enterprises, in that both tracks had been built by George 'Scotty' Cumming. The *Glasgow Evening Citizen* waxed lyrical: 'What a rider is Clem Beckett! I do not believe it is possible for a rider to lift his front wheel to a different course while travelling at 50mph. Yet I saw Beckett do it.' In spite of these thrills galore, the last speedway event at Carntyne took place two days later. In an era of austerity, the survival odds were on rival stadium Glasgow White City, with its team signed up to the new Northern League, and regularly hosting star riders from Manchester's Belle Vue.

Whatever the extent of Edgar Hart's interest in Carntyne, it was now in the hands of EOS and International Speedways. And in spite of the fact that the League was now controlled entirely by the ACU, stadiums were going out of business all over the country, with no room for sentiment. Reflecting the severity of the Depression in the north, meetings at Brough Park, Newcastle, and Cleveland Park, Middlesbrough, were suspended. The *Auto* predicted a wave of small town track closures, but while acknowledging the impact of 'industrial unrest and unemployment' it also blamed star riders for demanding bigger fees. Speedway was in the throes of the 'Great Shutdown', with abandoned tracks and stadiums adding to derelict landscapes of smokeless factory chimneys, silent shipyards and workless men standing on street corners.

Yet some stadiums fought to the last against this trend. On 24 May Clem appeared in a Saturday evening meeting at Rochdale, billed alongside Australians Max Grosskreutz and Bill 'Stippy' Sticpewich, the Rochdale team captain. An advert in the *Rochdale Observer* boasted 'The Usual Fleet of Motor Coaches will run direct to the Track,' and by all appearances speedway in the town was doing well. Clem beat Sticpewich in a match race, and went on to win the Golden Sash. Two injured riders were taken to the town's infirmary, one, typically, suffering from concussion, the other, untypically, from 'shock'. Clem was very much on his own 'midden', the scene of his early glory days, but he would have known all too well that as a cotton town in throes of the Depression, Rochdale was on its uppers.

Even Manchester's White City, in the power of EOS, was on its last legs, and Spence had no hesitation in justifying his ruthlessness: 'There is no more easy money in the speedway game either for riders or for promoters,' he instructed a journalist from the *Auto*. Given 'the present economic difficulties' it was no wonder tracks were going to the wall, Spence expanded: 'We are a business venture with no money for disposal as a dole. Our policy must necessarily be payment by result with the public as the judges.' However realistic EOS's analysis was of speedway as a business, the withdrawal of appearance money was having unintended consequences on dirt track as a sport. Spectators began muttering their suspicions that unsporting riders were retiring mid-race with purported engine failure when the real reason was that they had realised they were not going to win.[5] In the face of declining stadium attendances *Speedway News* went into wishful-thinking mode: all would be well if only there were enough first-rate riders to introduce a system of promotion and relegation.

Up on 'Red Clydeside' Clem would have sensed the tension, and seen the poverty, as mass lay-offs and wage cuts in the shipyards, together with reduced National Insurance benefits, took their toll. With unemployment averaging thirty per cent, Glasgow had become the most revolutionary-minded city in Britain.

CAPITALIST SPORT BAD, WORKERS SPORT GOOD

In the aftermath of Spence's takeover of Sheffield, Clem's loyalty to the Yorkshire fans was tested to the limit. At the beginning of the season he had assured a journalist from the *Auto* magazine that he would not allow Wall of Death commitments to come before dirt track appearances. But by the end of June he and Skid, managed by the ubiquitous Percy Platt, were putting on Wall of Death performances in a tour of Lancashire.

Clem would have noted in the *Daily Worker* a heightened expectation of economic disaster. All this went along with the Communist Party's new tack: capitalist sport bad, workers sport good. Guided by Pollitt's eloquence, the CPGB was preparing its readers for the revolution that it once again judged imminent.

Chapter Fifteen

Wall of Death

'If you have no work, do not wait for the clerk to ask.
Say: "No work".'
Notice prominently displayed at the Oldham
Labour Exchange in the early 1930s.

Mesmerised by Soviet propaganda glorifying the October Revolution, inspired by the storming of the Winter Palace in Petrograd, and by the revolt of Russian sailors at Kronstadt, the CPGB could not resist the parallel between the minority Labour government and the Provisional Government of Alexander Kerensky. In the *Daily Worker* Palme Dutt urged 'War on the Labour Government', dismissing it as 'the mask of capitalism', while Pollitt drummed up militant strike action below a headline proclaiming 'The New Spirit of Battle'. This was more than martial metaphor. One article after another focused on the role of the military. There was a history lesson on British troops who mutinied when ordered to attack Russian Bolsheviks, and regular court reports of comrades convicted of public order offences for distributing leaflets to soldiers. Comrades F.G. Spark and Edward Dorrell, of the Thames Valley Communist Party'Local' (branch) were reported to have been fined 40s and 20s respectively for using insulting words and behaviour outside Hounslow Barracks.

Truth be told, the Party had no interest in democracy at this time. Its intention was the seizing of power by whatever means were necessary. Its problem was, however, that in spite of Russian funding it lacked both the means to mount an insurrection, and the popular support needed for its success. Did Pollitt and Dutt really believe ordinary members were ready to take up arms and pitch themselves into a civil war? Ernie Woolley might have, true, but not Clem Beckett, nor even the majority of British Communists. Harry Pollitt, for all his sincerity, was left to peddle dreams and falsehoods about Russia relayed by the Comintern. Articles in the *Daily Worker* praised the 'iron determination' of Joseph Stalin to implement the 'Dictatorship of the Proletariat', the wonders of the Five Year Plan, and the role of collective farms in the Soviet struggle against 'Peasant Individualism'. They said nothing about emerging evidence that Stalin was steadily transforming Soviet Russia into a totalitarian state, controlling information, ordering show-trials, and directing the forced migration of hundreds of thousands of citizens.

Visitors to the Soviet Union – journalists and diplomats and apostate ex-Communists – were bringing back horror stories, but they were simply not believed by loyal CPGB members. Sincere in denials published in the *Daily Worker,* even Pollitt was fooled by campaigns of misinformation orchestrated by the Comintern. For many people the stark truth about Soviet totalitarianism was only confirmed beyond doubt following the collapse of European Communism in the 1990s.[1]

With superb irony, a regular advertiser in *Speedway News* was Russian Oil Products Ltd., established in 1924 following the Anglo-Soviet Trade Agreement. It quickly came under suspicion as a cover for Soviet subversion and intelligence gathering, providing links with underground elements of the CPGB. In so far as its facilities embraced a countrywide distribution network (much of it via canals), it had the potential to foster acts of sabotage. Ernie Woolley must have been aware of its importance, but Clem is unlikely to have had contact with the company – unless, that is, he favoured the ROP cut-price 'ZIP' petrol as a constituent in his own mix of fuel.[2]

No matter how downtrodden they were, the British working class endured the deprivations of the Slump believing that things would get better. Men moved southwards from the run-down areas of unemployment in the north and the Celtic fringes to southern England where things were not so bad, with new and growing industries, including motorcar and motorcycle manufacture. But in Lancashire, given the government's inability to revive the economy, job losses and closures continued to rise.

The world of speedway was not exempt from 'rationalisation'. Confirming suspicions at the time of the Belle Vue takeover, it would have come as no surprise to Clem that the future of the White City track was in doubt. Arthur Jervis had walked out of the club to race in Hamburg. Attendances were poor, and North Manchester Motor Club, controlled by EOS and unwilling to lose money, decided on closure.

The last home meeting featuring the senior team took place on 28 June 1930. The likes of Clem and Skid Skinner, catapulted to fame in the glory days of White City, could now see clearly that tough times were ahead, pushing them to find alternative ways of making a living from their mastery of the motorcycle. Their foray into the fairground world of stunts on the Wall of Death indicated their disillusionment with the dirt track. Out of favour with the big players such as Vivian Van Damm, general manager of IS, Clem was becoming an outsider. It was the end of the dream. Yet Clem could still work the old magic, and on 16 July he turned in an immaculate performance at Owlerton to the delight of his Sheffield fans by winning the *Star* Shield. According to the *Auto* he made old-stagers such as Gus Platts, Cliff Watson, Chun Moore, and Squib Burton 'look slow'.

Other reasons made it difficult for riders outside the magic circle of International Speedways to compete. Commercial interests, realising the advertising power of sponsorship, were putting money into technical developments, especially, when it came to speedway, by experimenting with new designs for frames and engines, and intricate variations in tyre tread. Until his dalliance with the Wallis, Clem's speedway mount had always been a Douglas. But times were changing, and Douglas were now facing a serious challenge from rival manufacturers Rudge-Whitworth, who were later to come up with the idea of marketing a kit of plates, bolts and spacers, which enabled teams with the wherewithal to fit lightweight, state-of-the-art DT (dirt track) JAP engines.[3] Clem had been on the wrong end of the result at Nottingham when George Wigfield had successfully demonstrated the new Rudge in action, and the event had prompted him to give it a try. Similar dynamics applied to tyres. At the outset of the speedway craze most bikes were shod with Hutchinson tyres, ribbed at the front, studded at the rear. But since 1929 big companies had been muscling in, including Avon and Firestone, experimenting with tread extending up the tyre wall as an alternative to the traditional beaded edge, which had a nasty tendency to come away from the rim. Tyre technology was a moving target, and only top riders with top clubs could be sure of benefiting from the latest developments.

So, too, with fuel technology. In 'pioneer' days most dirt track machines had been powered by petrol – although it is worth remembering that Clem's machine at Audenshaw had been fuelled by a mix containing ether. By now, however, many riders were experimenting with home-made fuels, and as Clem had discovered, his own particular cocktail of 'shoe-polish' could be somewhat volatile. It was not just a case of getting more bang for your bucks: men in top teams had access to 'rigs', upon which engines could be mounted to test various concoctions for horsepower output. Eventually, the standard fuel for speedway became methanol, favoured because of its comparatively low ignition temperature. But the fact was that Clem's speedway career was being outpaced by the twin factors of technology and market forces, not to mention the wear and tear of serial injuries.

In spite of safety improvements, casualties on the dirt track continued. On 24 July 1930 up-and-coming rider James Carnie died from head injuries after losing control of his machine in an event at Preston. The editor of *Speedway News*, mouthpiece of International Speedways, worried about criticism of the sport, blamed an increase in accidents on 'men, nearly all young who have neared the top class by an audacity and enthusiasm which have outrun their skill and discretion.' It was a point reiterated by rider Vic Huxley, one of ISL's original Aussie riders, who told magazine readers that he and fellow countryman Dickie Smythe had managed to avoid being badly hurt because they did not take 'unnecessary risks,' and that they had learned the skill of coming off their machines 'as gently as possible'. Clem too had learned this skill, although it was to prove manifestly more difficult to put into practice on the Wall of Death.

Prompted by the ongoing cricket Test match between England and Australia, the first in a series of five speedway Test matches between riders from both countries was put on at Plough Lane, Wimbledon, on 30 July 1930. Given his 'star' reputation, Clem Beckett was conspicuously absent from an English line-up which included Belle Vue rider Frank Varey.

Meanwhile, EOS confronted the broad picture of stadium closures and declining attendances at others with an uncanny chutzpah which baited speedway journalists to beat a path to his door. EOS put his cards on the table. There was no future for chancer promoters who thought all they had to do was to 'borrow a piece of waste ground', nor for riders who, having acquired a machine on hire purchase, thought all they had to do was 'sit on the bike, tour round the track and hire an accountant to check their income tax returns.' There was going to be 'no more easy money for riders or promoters.'

CLEM BECKETT: MOTORCYCLE LEGEND AND WAR HERO

The Aspley Lane Flower Show, Nottingham, early in August 1930, was an unlikely venue for 'Daredevil' Clem Beckett, contrasting markedly with the atmosphere at Wimbledon Test match, watched by over 30,000 spectators. Still, the appeal of the flower show had been widened by the addition of a funfair, with attendees being promised traditional entertainment by South Notts Silver Prize Band, as well as the highly novel 'Skid Platts Deathdrome'.

Given an admission charge of 3d (three old pennies) with otherwise free entry 'to the ground', additional charges must have been made for viewing the 'drome' – unless, that is, the stars of the show, Clem, Skid Skinner and an unknown 'Spider Anderson', were performing free for a hospital charity – most likely for their own benefit. The change from dome to drome had come about after representations from rival showmen claiming rights in the Wall of Death label. 'Skid Platts' was in fact W.E. 'Gus' Platts, newly recruited to the Sheffield speedway team. Spider Anderson was in fact Eli Anderson. The old firm from Roundthorn was back in business.

In the event, the Aspley Lane show passed off without mishap, and a week later both Clem and Platts excelled at Owlerton in a challenge match against a visiting team that included Smoky Stratton, now returned from America to ride for Nottingham.

Whatever the distractions of the 'drome', Clem soon bounced back onto the speedway grid. A meeting on 20 August at Owlerton took the form of another all-star challenge match between two teams: 'Clem Beckett's Team' took on 'The Visitors' led by Smoky Stratton, and the home team did well. Clem won his heat, and came second to Platts in the Golden Gauntlet. However, given the transient nature of these 'teams', and the fact that riders had no particular loyalty to entities contrived for a single evening's entertainment, it is difficult to imagine the Sheffield crowd responding with the same kind of passion and loyalty which they might have shown to the city's famous football clubs on match days at Hillsborough (Sheffield Wednesday) and Bramall Lane (Sheffield United). The new League had been another disappointment for promoters, and these ad hoc encounters were more akin to the occasional 'friendly' or 'benefit' match in football, with nothing much hanging on the result.

A few days after his Owlerton triumph Clem got in trouble at the wheel of his car. Having overtaken a long line of stationary vehicles at a crossroads near Rotherham he ignored directions from a policeman on point-duty, braking just in time to avoid a collision. The incident led to his third prosecution for dangerous driving, and he was lucky to escape with a fine of £18.

While Clem was going from dirt track to dirt track, from fairground to fairground, Ernest Woolley, on the Comintern payroll, was going from street corner to street corner, trying to incite revolution. Although the causes to which he lent the Party's official support were serious and justified, his personal contributions were sometimes comic. Woolley had a penchant for getting arrested and imprisoned, as he succeeded in doing following disorderly protests in Burnley and Bradford. Events described to readers of *The Scotsman*, concerning Woolley's arrest in Burnley on 27 August, read like a scene from *Laurel and Hardy*. Woolley, using a gramophone horn to address a crowd on the town hall steps, resisted the challenge from a police inspector by jamming the horn on the inspector's head. For his pains he got three months' hard labour. Hardly *Battleship Potemkin*. Even Pollitt found Woolley's antics exasperating, commenting that he had a 'police complex'.

In Rochdale, with half the town's workforce unemployed, promoters of the town's dirt track stadium made a desperate last-ditch effort to stay in business. In flagrant breach of ACU regulations, and bolstered by refugee riders from the now-banned Audenshaw track, they inadvisably relaxed the rule against betting. The ACU responded with its 'iron hand', and duly issued a list of eleven suspended riders and officials. The last meeting of the season, featuring a match race between Slider Shuttleworth and 'Dan de Lyon' (real name Ezra Deakin) took place on 16 August, and it was to be another forty years before dirt track racing returned to Rochdale.

Barnsley, at the heart of the stricken Yorkshire coalfield, was forced to drop out. Soon afterwards, at a meeting of creditors of the insolvent Preston speedway, the company's accountant blamed riders for demanding 'exorbitant' fees. But riders had been paid with cheques that had 'bounced', a disappointment increasingly common elsewhere.

Non-League stadiums like Audenshaw were still defying the regulators. On 31 August novice rider William Owen of Widnes died after being hit by another rider's machine on Audenshaw's pot-holed track. At an inquest, in spite of evidence that the track was in a dangerous condition, the coroner turned a deaf ear to calls for it to be closed. The tragedy was a stark reminder of just how raw life could be for dirt track riders, all the more poignant because Owen had been persuaded to give up racing by his parents, but wanted to honour a last booking with Audenshaw.

Clem persisted with his Wall of Death sideline. Early in September he and Skinner appeared in 'The Great Wall of Death' at the Gloops Carnival Gala, a fundraising occasion for Chesterfield Royal Hospital. The name 'Gloops' was derived from a cartoon cat, popularised by the *Sheffield Star*, and guaranteed to boost family attendances wherever it appeared as a cuddly costumed figure. The carnival was billed as a three-day event, but on the evening of the first day, to the consternation of the crowd, Clem fell off the 25-ft wall. Unconscious, he was rushed to the Royal Hospital, but discharged the following day after X-rays showed no broken bones. Thrill-seekers at Gloops Gala got their money's worth. The following day Skinner was thrown from his machine at the top of the wall. Badly shaken, he mounted another bike three minutes later and carried on with the show.

But Clem was soon back in the saddle. An advert placed in the *Sheffield Daily Telegraph* trumpeted 'The Finest Speedway for The Finest Sportsmen' in the hope of attracting crowds to see a series of match races between 'a wonderful array of stars'. It was, in fact more of the same, a contrived formula, with Belle Vue riders, including Eric Langton and Frank Arthur, top of the bill, and the Sheffield men, including Clem and Platts well down the list of riders.

The flavour of this event at Owlerton as an entertainment as opposed to a serious sporting occasion was emphasised by a 'last but by no means least' announcement that spectators would be able to witness 'a Really Sensational Feat by Wilf McClure, Who Will Ride Through Hoops of Fire.' Lest the credulous readers of the *Telegraph* deemed this insufficiently daring, they were reminded that 'The Blazing Rings Will Consist of Eighty Sacks Soaked in Petrol.'[4] They need not have worried. The whole event was cancelled, ostensibly due to rain. There was, however, scepticism about whether riders would show up as billed. Less than a week later the track was being used for horse racing – even though the same newspaper ad had promised readers future events 'every Thursday'. And so the 1930 speedway season ended prematurely for Clem, whose own experience was again complementing the doom and gloom of the Communist narrative. Sheffield, too, with its reliance on traditional industry such as cutlery, steel-making and heavy engineering, was among worst affected areas in England. Unemployed workers with empty pockets could not afford the luxury of paying to watch speedway.

Facing the onset of winter and the close-season, most riders, as ever, were left to their own devices. Clem and others had already popularised speedway in Europe and by the end of September Gus Platts was in Germany, along with Sheffield rider Jack 'Broncho' Dixon. With them in Germany was sixteen-years-old Sheffield girl Gladys Thornhill, and according to the *Sheffield Daily Telegraph* it was Clem and Skid Skinner who tutored her in motorcycle skills before helping her obtain an engagement in Hamburg.[5] By supporting Miss Thornhill, Clem and Skid were helping women break into a bastion of male chauvinism. London promoters, getting the nod from ISL, had barred women from their tracks, and Gladys had been denied insurance, but with the backing of Clem and Skid, who lent her their bikes, she managed to obtain an ACU licence. In fact, the advent of speedway, coinciding as it did with the successful campaign for equal voting rights, introduced several brilliant female riders to the public, notably in Yorkshire, where Miss Thornhill competed with Fay Taylour, Dot Cowley, and Babs 'Babe' Nield of Salford. There was even a Yorkshire Women's Motor Cycle Club. Neither, it seems, were women always prevented from competing against men, although this was often the case.

In due course, Clem joined the close-season exodus of riders seeking dirt track engagements on the Continent, while searching out opportunities to put on Wall of Death shows. By January 1931, however, he was lying in a hospital bed in Copenhagen, recovering from a fractured skull and concussion. Here, reflecting on poor prospects in a business controlled by omnipotent EOS, a change came over Clem. So dismal was the outlook for speedway that Clem, body bruised and battered by falls, appears to have reached a decision to quit the sport altogether, with the idea of earning a living on the Wall of Death. But he was also in touch with the leadership of the Communist Party of Great Britain, and in particular, William Rust, editor of the *Daily Worker*.

There was nothing secretive about Clem Beckett. Indeed, he was prone to indiscretions. Yet, the CPGB, to which he had pledged his allegiance at the tender age of eighteen, was a secretive entity, directed and financed by Soviet Russia, a circumstance understood and carefully monitored by British intelligence services, but little heeded by Party members such as Clem Beckett. Whether it was for the love of a girl or out of concern for family back in Oldham, or simply the wearying accrual of injuries, Clem never returned to the punishing circus of dirt track appearances. His status as a well-known speedway rider, however, continued to provide his bread and butter – just as it became the reason for his closer involvement in the Communist Party.

The dedication of British Communists to bring about revolution during the inter-war years was counterpoised by the fanaticism of the enemies of Bolshevism. Groups dedicated to the defence of the British Empire, and others influenced by the success of Benito Mussolini in Italy, known as *fascisti,* had co-operated with the authorities in breaking the General Strike, and were well connected to members of Stanley Baldwin's government. Even so, the CPGB remained convinced that its day would not be long in coming. Fanatical organisers like Ernie Woolley really believed that the accumulation of suffering brought about by the Depression would ignite revolution. They saw it as their job to light the fuse, and in the depths of the Depression, none seems to have gone about his work so confidently and recklessly as Woolley.

In Oldham, which had already endured a decade of economic decline, the Slump triggered by the Wall Street Crash added to the town's misery. Most of the working population struggled to cope on incomes savagely reduced by unemployment and wage cuts, as mill after mill closed down or went on short-time working. The Mayor, Elisha Bardsley, who himself had suffered losses in the flotation boom, declared that Oldham was 'financially smashed and pulverised'.

Chapter Sixteen

By Royal Appointment

*'The line between daring and recklessness can be a very
fine one. It is usually defined retrospectively, by the
action's success or failure.'*
From *'Jacobites'* by Jaqueline Riding.

In the depths of the Depression it was hardly necessary for the Communist
Party of Great Britain to foment unrest, because over large swathes of
British industry there was already a deep well of discontent among those
who had lost their jobs and those forced to accept lower wages.

This was especially so in the textile towns of Yorkshire and Lancashire,
including Clem's home town, Oldham, and by the beginning of 1931
unemployment in Britain had risen from about a million in 1929 to
2.5 million. Behind the figures in the worst affected areas lay destitution
for families of the unemployed. Hungry children suffered malnutrition.
The incidence of scurvy, rickets and tuberculosis increased. Against this
background, Communists remained optimistic that revolution was just
a matter of time – rather in the manner of First World War generals
who believed that 'one last push' would bring victory. Accordingly, the
Party stepped up its campaign to exploit industrial unrest, giving high-
profile support to workers striking against wage cuts. Notable in this was
Ernie Woolley's fanatical allegiance, as the Party's northern industrial
organiser, to the cause of Lancashire textile workers opposed to the
introduction of the 'Eight-Looms' scheme – an attempt by employers to
rationalise their beleaguered industry and bitterly opposed by workers.

The Communists were persistently hobbled, however, by the fact that
the overall situation in Britain was uneven. Motorcar and motorcycle
production had doubled during the 1920s, and however much business
confidence had taken a knock, car ownership carried on increasing.
Some areas, notably the Home Counties, were barely affected by

unemployment. Some industries, such as house-building, were actually enjoying a boom. New estates of semi-detached homes and 'ribbon' developments were changing the landscape. Even in hard-hit Oldham, builders, taking advantage of the falling costs of materials, were putting up new 'des-res' homes along main roads, especially those familiar to Clem on his boyhood outings to Bill o' Jack's, which climbed up the hillsides out of the town towards the villages of Saddleworth. Cinema-going workers, whose horizons had once been limited to terrace houses and tramlines, were already dreaming of better times, of living outside the town, with clean air and a view of the moors, new electrical gadgets, and a motorcar to drive to and from work.

Ever since Palme Dutt's denunciation of 'capitalist sport' the *Daily Worker* had been on the lookout for examples of exploitation, and although it is possible that Clem touted his exposé to the editorial department, it is far more likely that as a loyal and relatively famous member of the Party, Clem was invited to submit it. The 'Daredevil' was poised to accept a dare of a very different kind to those he readily accepted astride a motorcycle.

On 14 January 1931, an article appeared on the sports page of the *Daily Worker*, in the name of 'C.H. Beckett' below the headline 'Bleeding the Men Who Risk Their Lives on the Dirt Track'. Stadium closures were cited as 'failures of capitalism', followed by a comprehensive attack on promoters and their hand-in-glove relationship with the sport's administrators. Clem's no-holds-barred criticism focused on poor safety standards and the payments system which imposed a hand-to-mouth existence on the majority of competitors: riders like Donald 'Riskit' Riley, one-time winner of the Golden Helmet at Belle Vue, who, on being jailed by Hyde magistrates for obtaining five shillings by false pretences, told the court that in the absence of appearance payments his annual speedway earnings amounted to £32 prize money.

According to Clem, most riders had finished the 1930 season with 'nothing in hand', leaving them struggling to get through the winter, and faced with the necessity of buying two new machines, averaging £90 each, to start the next season. On top of that, their old bikes were likely to be worth no more than £15 at the end of the season, with weekly repair and maintenance costs averaging £5 pounds a week.

Yet, in the same article, Clem also lamented what he saw as the demise of 'the sporting side of the Dirt Track racing'. The art of broadsiding, which appealed to 'the sporting instincts of the public', was giving way to the importance of 'getting there first'. This may have been a reference to the new, faster Rudge machine, being used increasingly by successful riders such as Jim Kempster and Arthur Jervis, and a very different creature to the faithful, agile Douglas originally favoured by Clem.[1] Even so, Clem's reverence for the sporting spectacle of the dirt track expressed the true spirit of speedway and the reason why working-class fans, whatever hardships they were enduring, still wanted to see more of it.

But Clem reserved his biggest salvo for the Auto-Cycle Union, alleging that it exacerbated the financial problems of the sport by imposing an initial levy of £50 per track, as well as fees of two guineas per meeting.[2] In addition to fees for inspecting helmets, riders were likewise being taxed unfairly for the privilege of competing. A fee of 5s per meeting was being raised to a guinea, and if riders appeared on 'outlaw' tracks beyond the jurisdiction of the ACU they faced being suspended. Clem also accused the ACU of 'religious mania' in banning Sunday meetings, although the nub of the problem was vociferous lobbying and picketing of stadiums by members of the Lord's Day Observance Society. It was unfortunate, perhaps, in the light of what was to happen later, that Clem went on to express his admiration for riders at Audenshaw, who, in defiance of the ban, were carrying on riding there. For good measure, Clem accused the ACU of treachery by automatically suspending riders at the request of track owners. In a memorable phrase that found its way into conversation in every paddock and every pub frequented by riders and fans, Clem attacked the sport's governing body as 'composed of several old fogeys in various stages of Anno Domini, most of whom have forgotten what a motor-cycle is like.'

In the old days of 'hot metal' newspaper production, when lines of type were cast in molten alloy, the last opportunity to remove an inaccurate or potentially libellous statement before the paper went to press was simply to strip out the offending line or lines, or even to render offending words illegible by bashing the type with a heavy metal object. The result was to leave readers baffled by one or two unintelligible truncated sentences – but that was always judged a better option than the certainty of a writ. Just such a passage appeared halfway down the second article under Clem's name in the *Daily Worker* of 17 February 1931.

The article was the paper's response to an inevitable reaction to Clem's broadside on the speedway establishment and in particular the

Auto-Cycle Union. Its representative, E.B. Ware, a personification of the gentleman competitor, with a reputation as the leading exponent of racing three-wheeled Morgans, appears to have threatened legal action, categorically denying Clem's allegations. Clem was summoned back from his sickbed abroad to defend himself and the paper. 'Justification' being a defence to defamation, his second article purported to back up his claims with 'chapter and verse', beginning boldly by declaring, 'I can substantiate everything I said concerning the ACU. For most of my statements I can produce documentary evidence.' Indeed, the simple fact was that times were hard, and both promoters and riders were having to 'copper up' to survive – as when, after racing at Leeds, Glasgow team captain George Mackenzie was paid in coinage taken at the gate. Later, on the journey back north, he met other team members in a lay-by to divvy out the money.

However, it was not so much Clem's detailed attack on the ACU's exorbitant fees that sealed his fate, as the double-decker headline above which blamed 'Auto-Cycle Autocrats' for a 'Fine Sport Made Rotten With Financial Corruption'. Recalling the visit of the ACU representative to Owlerton shortly before its opening in 1929, Clem lamented their having to pay him £50 'for trundling a bicycle wheel round the track for one lap and counting its revolutions'. Then followed the mangled references to a contractor's dispute with the ACU before Clem went on to give examples of the ACU's mistreatment of riders. He then provided the names of two competitors who could back up his claim that the ACU had discriminated against them for entering early speedway events, and recycled the accusation that it acted against riders' interests, in cahoots with owners. As with the earlier article, it was spiced with abuse bound to touch raw nerves. Governing members of the ACU were 'Rip Van Winkles […] old, incompetent, out of date, and entirely out of touch with the men they profess to represent,' while lesser officials were largely pensioned-off army officers, many of whom had never ridden a motor-cycle.

In effect, Clem's foray into journalism amounted to a professional suicide note in two parts, and the ACU did not take long to exact retribution. Clem's licence to race on ACU-affiliated tracks was suspended. Moreover, Clem had been ill-advised to echo Palme Dutt's mantra that speedway, like other sport, was all a capitalist plot. By declaring that 'dirt track racing appears to have had its day in England,'

Right: *Clem 'Daredevil' Beckett:*
an irreverence for authority.
(Courtesy John Somerville Collection)

Below: *ruined remains of Clem's*
birthplace at Stone Rake, on the 'wrong
side of the Pennines' in Yorkshire's
West Riding. (author photo)

Swinton Street, Roundthorn, Clem's boyhood home near the centre of Oldham. (author photo)

Glodwick Lows, ideal for off-road capers on homemade motorbikes. In the distance, Saddleworth, where Clem and the Anderson boys raced over moorland roads. (author photo)

Above: *This lady motorcyclist advertising Percy Platt's Oldham showroom could not vote, but her male passenger, resembling Platt himself, was happy to take his seat in the sidecar.* (Courtesy of Oldham Local Studies Unit)

Right: *The Snipe, Audenshaw, a converted 'trotting' course, the setting for Clem Beckett's speedway debut. Bowler-hatted officials preside in the aftermath as pioneer rider Sid Meadowcroft gets to his feet having 'bought a box of tacks'.* (Courtesy of Speedway in Manchester)

Spectators run for cover behind flimsy fencing, as rider Jack Chapman comes to grief. Notoriously dangerous, speedway at Audenshaw was brought to an end by a combination of economic crisis and tragedy. (By Kind Permission of the Mary Evans Picture Library)

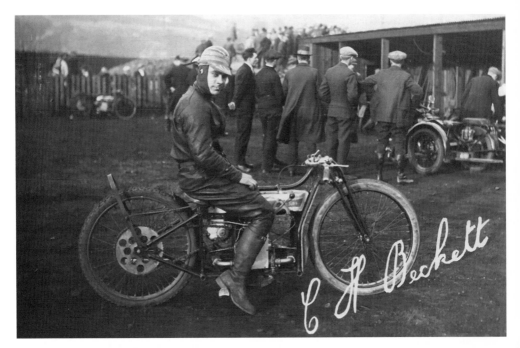

'The most dramatic figure of the tracks ... he rode as no-one had ever done.' By the end of 1928 Clem was living the high life, flying planes and racing speedboats. (Courtesy John Somerville Collection)

Clem achieved stardom in front of huge crowds behind the imposing facade of Manchester's nineteenth century White City pleasure gardens. (author photo)

Above left: *'Sprouts' Elder, dapper, genial, universally popular among fans and riders.*
(With Kind Permission of the ClassicMotorcycle/Mortons Archive)

Above right: *Eric Oswald Spence (EOS) 'the Mussolini of Speedway'.* (Courtesy John Somerville
Collection)

*Spencer 'Smoky' Stratton, rolling stone New Zealander, and Clem's co-director at Owlerton
Stadium. As with many dirt track adventurers the lives of Stratton and Elder ended in violent
tragedy. Elder committed suicide after the death of his wife; Stratton was killed at the wheel of
his car in a head-on collision.* (Courtesy Trevor James)

Marseille 1929. Clem, in pullover and crash helmet, is standing behind the line of riders. 'Skid' Skinner, extreme left, Burton third left, Arthur Franklyn fourth left. (Courtesy National Fairground and Circus Archive)

Speedway types: Track, A.C.U., and rider

The Motor Cycle *magazine's honest look at 'speedway types' in 1928: Clem resented slick promoters and 'old fogey' administrators - and got into serious trouble criticising them.* (With Kind Permission of The Classic Motorcycle/ Mortons Archive)

Above left: *Purpose-built Sheffield Owlerton speedway stadium was claimed to be the best in the land - but as with lesser, improvised tracks, pile-ups like this were plentiful in Clem Beckett's heyday, keeping the St John Ambulance Brigade busy.* (Courtesy Kenneth Chapman, Rossendale)

Above right: *Today, Sheffield Tigers speedway team shares the stadium with greyhound racing, its history writ large in murals on the stadium walls.* (Courtesy Students of The Sheffield College and Messrs Swann-Morton)

Denmark, c.1931: Clem on the Wall of Death. After his fall in front of the Danish King, Clem made fewer appearances on the wall, apparently persuaded of the wisdom of wearing head protection. (By Kind Permission of the Skinner Family through Alan Mercer)

Wall of Death performers Skid Skinner and Alma Morley pose for a publicity picture. Danish authorities banned spectators from throwing money into the bowl, leaving performers to sell postcards like this one to boost appearance money. (Courtesy Peter Morrish Collection and John Somerville Collection)

Clem, Skid Skinner and Percy Platt with Danish Wall of Death promoters, 1935. (By Kind Permission of the Skinner Family through Alan Mercer)

Two men in a boat, Denmark 1936. Oarsman Clem with a relaxed Percy Platt. But their politics were poles apart. (By Kind Permission of the Skinner Family through Alan Mercer)

Above left: *Harry Pollitt, British Communist leader, recruited Clem for Spain.* (Courtesy Marx Memorial Museum London)

Above right: *Benny Rothman, Mass Trespass leader, but rejected as a volunteer for Spain.* (Courtesy Working Class Movement Library)

Above left: *Clem's comrades in Spain, pictured at Albacete, wearing French First World War winter uniforms: (L-R) Eddie Swindells of Manchester, killed at Jarama, Syd Quinn, Glasgow, Maurice Levine, Manchester, and John Malcom, Glasgow. While the four were in action with the* Marseillaise *Battalion on the Madrid front, Clem was ordered to stay behind in charge of the auto-park.* (Courtesy Working Class Movement Library)

Above right: *Tommy Flynn, Clem's boon companion in Russia and Spain - until their friendship turned sour. Killed at Chimorra.* (Courtesy Kevin Buyers)

*Christopher St John Sprigg (*nom de plume *Christopher Caudwell) Clem's close friend at Madrigueras.* (Courtesy Marx Memorial Museum, London)

Manchester man Sam Wild, nursing four bullets wounds, helped evacuate wounded comrades from Suicide Hill, while Clem and Caudwell on the 'Shosser' gave them covering fire. (Courtesy International Brigade Memorial Trust)

Overlooking Suicide Hill and the Jarama valley from the 'Sunken Road'. A confusing topography of ridges and outlying hills hampered British dispositions. (author photo)

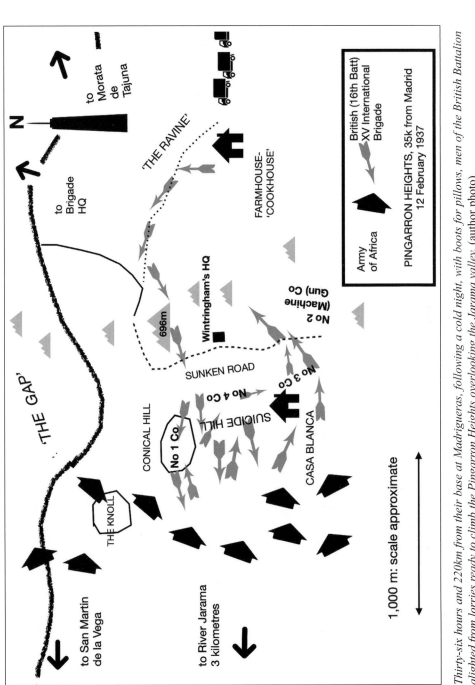

Thirty-six hours and 220km from their base at Madrigueras, following a cold night, with boots for pillows, men of the British Battalion alighted from lorries ready to climb the Pingarron Heights overlooking the Jarama valley. (author photo)

Within the map:

to Morata de Tajuna

N

to Brigade HQ

'THE RAVINE'

FARMHOUSE- 'COOKHOUSE'

696m

Wintringham's HQ

No 2 (Machine Gun) Co

SUNKEN ROAD

No 3 Co

No 4 Co

'THE GAP'

CONICAL HILL

SUICIDE HILL

No 1 Co

CASA BLANCA

THE KNOLL

to San Martin de la Vega

to River Jarama 3 kilometres

1,000 m: scale approximate

British (16th Batt) XV International Brigade

Army of Africa

PINGARRON HEIGHTS, 35k from Madrid 12 February 1937

SYBIL THORNDIKE

WILL SPEAK AT A

MEMORIAL MEETING

(under the auspices of the Manchester Spanish Aid Committee)

IN MEMORY OF

CLEM BECKETT

and other Manchester men, members of the International Brigade, who gave their lives in Spain fighting in the cause of Democracy.

In the COLISEUM, Ardwick Green,

(transferred from Co-op. Hall, Downing St.)

On SUNDAY, MAY 2nd, at 7-30 p.m.

OTHER SPEAKERS:

D. F. SPRINGHALL

One of the International Brigade Leaders—just back from Spain.

E. A. Gower
Chairman, Borough Labour Party

William Rust
Communist Party

Fred Bloor
International Brigade and Young Labour League.

Mrs. Lida Beckett

Rev. Stanley Mossop

Chairman: Councillor Harry Frankland
Labour Party

SALUTE THE HEROES OF SPAIN!
They have not died in vain, they have saved World Democracy from Fascist barbarism.

A memorial event for Clem was among the first of many for fallen Brigaders. In May 1937 the war in Spain was by no means lost, and meetings such as these helped to recruit more volunteers. After Harry Heap and Clem Beckett another four men from Oldham were to lose their lives. (Courtesy Working Class Movement Library)

JOE LEES
Oldham Volunteer in the International Brigade

Young Oldhamers, such as Joe Lees and Kenneth Bradbury, followed Clem Beckett to Spain – and did not return. (Courtesy Working Class Movement Library)

KILLED IN DEFENCE OF TERUEL
FOR PEACE AND DEMOCRACY
JANUARY 20th, 1938

KENNETH BRADBURY
Oldham Volunteer in the International Brigade ("Major Attlee" Company)

The gates of Alexandra Park, scene of Oldham's 'Park Parliament' where prime ministers addressed election meetings, and CPGB members, including Joe Lees, burned copies of the Daily Mail *in protest at its misreporting events in Spain.* (author photo)

Plus ca change ... *a young Oldhamer follows in the tracks of Mad Andy and Daredevil Beckett a hundred years after they too found off-road sanctuary on Glodwick Lows.* (author photo)

Madrid, February 2019: British demonstrators, including relatives of Brigaders whose bodies lie in unmarked graves, join Madrileños to demand investigation of Franco's crimes and recovery of victims' bodies. (author photo)

he was risking alienating fellow riders who still wanted to compete. He was also completely wrong.

What possessed him to do it? Why was Clem so reckless in his expression of contempt for the ACU, in full knowledge that their disciplinary powers would be used against him? Was he promised some sort of work with the Party to compensate for loss of livelihood? Was his judgment affected by concussion, a bang on the head sustained in Denmark? It was not as though his revelations had much effect. His was a voice crying in the wilderness. By comparison with other daily newspapers, the circulation of the *Daily Worker* was tiny, and its campaigns were merely sermons to the converted, never likely to be taken up by the mainstream press. There again, as a young man, not yet twenty-five, Clem may have been naive. Perhaps he did not understand the seriousness of his allegations, nor the likely consequences. He had assumed it would be easy to circumvent a ban on riding ACU tracks by going abroad. But later Clem was to claim that the ACU had ensured he was barred 'all the capitalist world over', specifically citing Germany and Denmark.

In contrast to Clem's indiscretions, and about the same time, Arthur Franklyn was tempted to air his views on speedway's woes. Billed as 'White City's Champion', Franklyn gave a press interview amounting to a master-class of constructive criticism, avoiding the temptation of personal abuse. His careful answers reflected the *savoir-faire* of an education denied to Clem. However, Franklyn himself was as disillusioned with the dirt track as was Clem, and was poised to quit the cinders to embark on a new career as a TT rider, before becoming a competitive aviator.

But Franklyn's views were different from Clem's. He did not think much of the riders' association, and wanted an exclusive all-star organisation to protect the interests of crack riders. Franklyn objected to the greater use of handicapping which had reduced his own earnings, also expressing reservations about star men such as himself being unable to pass slower men 'hugging the inside bend'. The problem arose from most courses having to fit inside dog tracks, and the answer was to build new ones, 'With a wider, more sweeping and banked track, the broadsider would find full scope for his skill.' Clem would at least have agreed with Franklyn as to the importance of broadsiding as a spectacle, but not necessarily as to the virtue of tracks being banked.[3]

There were still some dirt tracks, such as Audenshaw, intent on survival with or without the blessing of the ACU, but by now there was a big difference between the standard of racing at League tracks and unregulated ones. If Clem did return for the odd appearance at this lower level he would have adopted another name, but this seems an unlikely scenario. Accordingly, when the 1931 season got underway in April, Clem Beckett was a conspicuous absentee from the grid. Nor does his suspension appear to have prompted the slightest sign of protest or comradely support from fellow riders.

As it was, the 1931 speedway season went merrily ahead without Clem Beckett, and in no time he became a non-person in dirt track journals and local newspapers covering regular meetings. Apart from an aversion to revolutionary politics, their focus was on the day-to-day dramas of the track and the personalities of winning riders. London-based International Speedways were now in a position to dominate the sport in the North and the Midlands, resulting in a widening gap between their teams, centred in the great cities, and the struggling town-based 'also-rans' which had mushroomed into existence only two years earlier. Yet, when Harringay dropped out of the Southern League, EOS was able to raise another 'Manchester' team to take their place, while still fielding a Belle Vue side in the Northern League.

The ACU, however, did not concern itself with fairground attractions and by the summer of 1931, like an exiled outlaw, Clem was once again in Denmark, this time with Skid Skinner, as they toured towns and villages riding the Wall of Death. Oldham businessman Percy Platt was also there to make travel arrangements and bookings.

It is tempting to speculate that clattering around the wooden bowl may not have been the only purpose of his return to Denmark. Might he have met, or wished to renew his friendship with, Comrade Eli (Lida) Henriksen? Might he – and she – have had work to do for the Party, carrying messages, or as couriers of Russian money destined for London? For the purpose of the tour, and for whatever reason, Clem reverted to using the name 'Joe', which he had adopted as a teenager, embarrassed amongst friends by his relatively unusual given name.

Times were tough for stunt-riders. To attract paying customers the act had to be good, with the constant temptation to introduce novel and ever-more dangerous features on the bowl. Clem and Skid had by now developed a hair-raising sequence of acrobatic manoeuvres, weaving in and out of each other, riding in opposite directions, sitting on the handlebars, standing on the saddle, and preparing the audience for a final gasp of apprehension as the machines suddenly plummeted 4m to the base of the bowl.

Perhaps unsurprisingly, therefore, this latest adventure in Denmark got off to a bad start, with Clem falling from the Wall on the debut show at the Roskilde Road dirt track stadium near Copenhagen. Once again, after a crashing descent, he ended up unconscious and bleeding at the bottom of the bowl, mercifully spared from entanglement with the machine. Rushed by ambulance to Frederiksberg hospital, doctors confirmed his injuries were limited to concussion, cuts and bruises. During the next few days' bed rest, Clem's place on the Wall was taken by his old friend from the Marseille adventure, Arthur Sherlock. It was typical of Percy Platt to have ensured the availability of a substitute. This was, after all, show business, and the show must go on.

But the tour was soon to meet its nemesis in bizarre circumstances. On the last weekend of June 1931, at Braedstrup, about 240km from Copenhagen, and 50km from Lida's home in Horsens, Clem and Skid Skinner were preparing their show for the village fête when King Christian and Queen Alexandrine of Denmark paid a surprise visit. Platt would no doubt have recognised the marketing opportunities to be gained from a royal command performance, and much against their better judgement Clem and Skid agreed to put the show on early so as not to keep Their Majesties waiting. Some reports claim that, in the rush, the usual procedure of changing the engine oil was omitted. As Clem circled the bowl horizontally, the queen fled from the viewing gallery in horror. Accounts differ as to whether Clem's engine cut out, or whether a footrest snagged on the top wire. In any event, bike and Clem crashed to the bottom of the bowl. Only a personal appeal by the king prevented general panic. Clem was dragged out unconscious and taken to hospital. Diagnosis: concussion. Another lucky escape. It was little consolation to Clem that a bunch of flowers and a get-well wish from the queen arrived at the hospital.

'Not again!' was surely the reaction of *Sheffield Telegraph* readers when they learned of Clem's latest mishap, a day or two later. It was ironic that the accident was partly caused by the fact that Clem, a Communist, as well as manager Percy Platt, were overawed by the presence of royalty. Clem was to maintain a financial interest in the Wall of Death as an assistant to Platt, but the disaster at Braedstrup seems to have put paid to his career as a rider. After the royal debacle Clem's appearances on the Wall were few and far between, although this did not end his connections with Denmark, personally, professionally, or politically.

Clem's virtual retirement form the Wall left Skid Skinner to carry on, riding solo. Within a short time, keen to spice up his act, he travelled to Hamburg to buy a lion cub, with the idea of it being whizzed round the wall in a sidecar. In the meantime, the dirt track season in England carried on largely as Clem had described it to readers of the *Daily Worker,* although Test matches between English and Australian riders had added another dimension. Perhaps Clem glanced wistfully at newspaper reports of old friends and rivals on northern tracks such as Frank Varey, Squib Burton and Eric Langton playing their parts in winning the match, and series, for England, in the fourth Test at Belle Vue. Burton, however, suffered injuries which put him out of action for months, and the general opinion was that although the hype had attracted a crowd in excess of 40,000, it was nonetheless disappointing as a spectacle. For sure, the colourful presence of Clem and Skinner would have added entertainment value. Even so, all these men were Clem's pioneer contemporaries in the North and Midlands, who went on to enjoy many more seasons riding at top level, achieving national celebrity status alongside the Aussie invaders and home-grown London-based riders. In spite of all the plaudits he attracted – both contemporaneous and posthumous – the premature curtailment of Clem's career meant that he rarely appeared on London tracks such as Wembley and Wimbledon, and never really achieved lasting nationwide fame.

But at least this meant that he was spared exposure to International Speedway's efforts to present speedway as a 'respectable' sport, stamped with the imprimatur of the English class system, and graced by the beneficent approval of the 'right people'. William Forbes-Sempill, heir to the Scottish baronetcy of Craigevar, and glorying in the title of Colonel the Master of Sempill, was a good catch for ISL and was appointed as Chairman of Directors. When he or Lady Sempill were not presenting the prizes themselves at ISL's London stadiums, the mystique of their ancient nobility was relied on to attract other members of the great and good to do the honours. Royalty and aristocracy were natural choices: H.R.H Prince George, Princess Ingrid of Sweden, soon-to-be deposed King Alfonso of Spain, and Lady Dowager Swaythling. 'Speed king' Major Sir Henry Segrave, soon to die in an attempt on the world water speed record, and Captain Malcom Campbell, land and water speed record breaker, formed another branch of royalty in the eyes of ISL. Lady Eleanor Furneaux Smith personified the mix of glamour and nobility so beloved of ISL, but was hardly likely to impress Comrade Beckett. Moreover, a fair proportion of ISL's grandees had strong anti-democratic leanings: Sempill was being investigated by MI5 for passing sensitive military secrets to the Japanese, and had links with British fascist organisations, as did Malcolm Campbell, while Lady Eleanor, writer and 'Bright Young Thing' socialite, was to become a strong supporter of Spain's General Franco.[4]

However, as Clem had predicted, for surviving smaller tracks in the provinces, a world away from the glamour of ISL, prospects were bleak. Riders faced further pay cuts, especially those described by EOS as 'the weaker brethren', just the men Clem had been trying to protect from exploitation. At the beginning of the 1931 season 'new arrangements' had been announced whereby standard remuneration was to be £1 per rider for each race started. A spokesman for promoters dolefully insisted that they had devised the means whereby the smaller tracks 'have been given a chance of continued existence', adding rather gleefully that in any case 'few of the really successful men belong to the Riders' Association'. In reality, the system of riders' remuneration was shifting from one based on appearance and prize money to one emphasising team racing by contracted riders, all against a background of falling attendances. But whatever the system, Clem had been put out of it.

Safety remained a big issue, and nowhere were abuses so common as at Audenshaw. Excluded from the Northern League because it did not meet its track-safety standards, the Snipe stadium had come under the control of John Thomas Wolfenden, whose true vocation as chancer and entrepreneur was dignified as Clerk of the Course. With crowds of up to 6,000 there was still money to be made, but as it was an 'outlaw' track, riders frequently used false names. 'Dan de Lyon' was accordingly joined on the grid by 'The Thriller,' 'A. Douglas' and – with exquisite topicality – 'Red Terror'.

On 2 August, having negotiated 'Suicide Corner', James Kenny, riding as 'Jack Smith', was pitched in the air before being trapped under two machines. After being transported by car to the first aid room, he was dropped on a solid floor 'like a sack of spuds' by promoter Wolfenden, who then rushed out to get the next race underway. Volunteers who came forward to level out the surface were waved aside by Wolfenden. Nobody called an ambulance, and Kenny, suffering a fractured skull, was eventually taken to hospital by his brother, where he died two days later. Wolfenden then distinguished himself by arriving late for the inquest, and by interrupting other witnesses as they gave evidence of deep ruts in the track. The coroner's recommendations after the deaths of Rowlands and Owen had been ignored. To cap it all, Wolfenden was fined for contempt of court, and obliged to apologise for turning up uninvited at the coroner's home. Wolfenden got off lightly. The coroner was so incensed by his behaviour at the track and in connection with the inquest that he invited the jury to recommend a prosecution for manslaughter. Of the ten speedway fatalities in Britain up to that point, three had been at Audenshaw.[5] The brutal nature of Kenny's death was a sickening denouement, and the last dirt track meeting at Audenshaw took place two weeks later. Within a few years the track had disappeared under a new housing estate.

In truth, the new regime to which Clem took such great exception, was the creature of rationalisation carried out by ISL and EOS, but ultimately it ensured the survival of safer, albeit commercialized, speedway.

Chapter Seventeen

Dagenham Blacklist

'It matters not if rich or poor,
This is the future's great command:
Who does not work shall cease to eat.
Upon this rock I stand.'
From a poem by Max Ehrmann published
in the *Ford Times*, 1912.

Skid Skinner remained in Denmark during Clem's stay in hospital, eventually meeting up with Alma Morley, a glamorous Wall of Death rider from Hellaby, venue of the short-lived Barnsley speedway stadium, who helped herself to the now vacant title of 'Daredevil'. They went on to develop a spectacular double-act, and eventually married. Clem himself was soon back in England, but with speedway tracks barred to him, he was out of work, along with thousands of other jobless Oldhamers. Instinctively, he turned to the Communist Party for inspiration. Only two months after his spectacular fall in Denmark, Clem, riding the Wall of Death, was billed as the main attraction at a 'Lancashire Charter gala' put on by the British Workers Sports Federation in Haslingden.

In the depth of the Depression, many unemployed Oldhamers, despairing of the future of the textile industry, were joining the steady stream of migrants to London and southern England, hoping to find work in 'new' growing industries, producing electrical goods, tinned food, motorcars and motorcycles. The response of Ramsay MacDonald's minority government to the financial crisis of 1931, triggered by the collapse of the Austrian bank Credit-Anstalt, gave them little incentive to stay, hoping against hope. In the late summer of 1931, as MacDonald imposed a package of austerity measures including a controversial 'Means Test', Clem and Eli Anderson prepared to join the exodus.

The austerity programme split the Labour Cabinet, with MacDonald carrying on as prime minister of a 'National' government composed of Conservatives and Liberals and some Labour members. The bulk of the Labour movement accused him of treachery, of conspiring against the workers on the side of the capitalist class, and in September 1931 the National government introduced a package of measures which reduced unemployment pay by ten per cent.

By accepting nursing work, Clem's mother, Henrietta, may have qualified for unemployment benefit. Otherwise, she would have had to apply to the Oldham Public Assistance Committee and submit to the new, stricter, and much-hated means test. Crucially it involved a humiliating scrutiny of assets carried out by council officials, poking around people's homes, looking for items such as jewellery which would have to be sold to establish entitlement. Large items such as pianos were, of course, impossible to hide. As a deserted wife, the policy would have impacted directly on Henrietta. Sons of working age were deemed capable of contributing to family income, provided they shared the same address. The Means Test drove sons like Clem out of the family home to fend for themselves in lodgings, and many more families resorted to subterfuge. As a Communist, the episode perfectly vindicated his belief that parliamentary democracy would always be complicit in saving capitalism at the expense of the workers. In the event, MacDonald's failure to find other ways out of the crisis was grist to the mill of English Marxists. They correctly pointed out that MacDonald was allowing his policy to be dictated by London bankers, who insisted on a balanced budget as a means of stemming a run on the pound, and maintaining the 'Gold Standard'.[1] London's position as the world's financial centre was preserved at the expense of cutting unemployment relief, and many in the City hoped it would lead to a general reduction in wages. Unsurprisingly, the electors of Oldham turned against Labour and MacDonald. At the general election in October, they returned two Conservatives with massive majorities.

For Oldham's unemployed, who could not or would not leave, there was boredom and despair. There was not enough to live on. Crowds of men hung around street corners in idleness. Life was a constant struggle. Children went hungry to school. Yet even then, new industries and enterprises were bucking the trend. In and around the town the firm founded by brilliant inventor and electrical engineer Sebastian di Ferranti had invested in the nascent electrical industry, producing transformers as well as radios and consumer goods, and creating more than 5,000 jobs. Likewise, taking advantage of a ready supply of skilled labour, modern engineering works were being established in nearby Manchester, and men who had always walked to a workplace round the corner had to adjust by allowing for an hour's journey to and from work in the city.

Even so, far more opportunities were being created in the South, such as Henry Ford's new purpose-built automobile plant in Dagenham, east of London. And so it was, one autumn morning in 1931 that Clem and Eli turned up for work in Ford's citadel of capitalism on the edge of the Essex marshes.[2]

Henry Ford had broken into the European car market well before the First World War. In 1911 he had moved the centre of its operations in England from London to Trafford Park, Manchester, where a converted derelict building strategically close to the Ship Canal became the first operational assembly plant outside America. Moreover, workers in Manchester were the first outside the United States to be introduced to the methods and practices of mass production relied on by the Ford company, such as the 'production line'. Central to Henry Ford's philosophy was a detestation of trade unions and an absolute determination to prevent them organising in Ford plants – a policy which inevitably set his company on a collision course with the British trade union movement and the Communist Party of Great Britain. It was not a coincidence that among the first recruits at Dagenham were two card-carrying Communists from Oldham. They were part of a Communist 'cell' centred on the Ilford Local of the CPGB, directed by the Party's Central Committee, to which Ernie Woolley had been elected.

Clem and Eli were not the only Lancastrians in the Dagenham plant. Ford had been running down the Manchester plant throughout the late 1920s, and earlier in 1931 special trains had been chartered to move machinery from Trafford Park to Dagenham, as well as about a thousand men. Woolley, bloodied and bitter from his experience as the Party's industrial organiser in the textile areas of Lancashire and Yorkshire, was spoiling for another fight. He blamed the failure of Lancashire cotton workers to prevent wage cuts and the imposition of the eight-looms system on betrayal by official trade union leaders, and wanted to see a new form of industrial action led by 'Rank-and-File' members of the workforce who owed their allegiance to the Party. The strategy was integral to the aims of the National Minority Movement, another Communist front, whose aim was to achieve workers' control of industry through direct action. The CPGB was particularly strong in the East End of London, and Dagenham offered the possibly of a much-needed victory for workers. As disciplined and dedicated Party members, Clem Beckett and Eli Anderson were just the men to help achieve it.

Clem's experience as a blacksmith with the family firm of Bowmans was very different from the de-humanising regime imposed on Ford employees at Trafford Park, where men complained of being treated worse than prisoners at Alcatraz. Typically, Ford employed high-profile security officers to check the men were wearing numbered identity badges, and to enforce 'no-talking' on the shop floor. However tough conditions were at Bowmans, its owners did at least recognise the Blacksmiths Union, to which Clem and his workmates belonged. Furthermore, the shoeing of railway carthorses had very little in common with the production lines required in the manufacture of vehicles powered by internal combustion. The contrast was more than symbolic: in England, Ford at first concentrated on making commercial lorries, which, within in a couple of decades, would ensure the demise of railway carters.

Accordingly, during the crisis which obliged MacDonald to form an all-party 'National' government, the first 'AA' light trucks were rolling off production lines at Dagenham, alongside 'Model T' saloon cars, which came to symbolise suburban middle-class life in the 1930s. At the same time, Comrades Clem Beckett and Eli Anderson were embedded in the plant as part of an eight-man Communist cell, with instructions to attempt to unionise fellow workers. But the CPGB was not the only clandestine organisation operating at Fords. It had to contend with company 'spies' brought in to watch out for disruptive employees and briefed especially to counter activities of Communist Party members. The spies were thought to have been recruited by a sinister organisation called the Economic League, formed after the First World War to counter Soviet influence. Its leaders were retired Intelligence officers, who maintained links with the British secret service and had helped set up the International Entente Against the Third International to shadow Soviet sponsored activities. The League was believed to have access to police files, with the tacit consent of senior police officers. Typically, the result of an operation carried out by the Economic League was a 'blacklist' – naming workers who not only faced dismissal but who would then be unable to obtain alternative work when their names were circulated among other employers.

Some accounts claim that it was more than eight months before Clem and Eli were rumbled by company spies. If they did last that long it is surprising given that discovery was all the more certain in the light of Clem's temperamental inability to tolerate bullying. The story goes that a foreman spotted Clem with a packet of sandwiches to hand at the side of the production line. The foreman grabbed the packet and threw it into a nearby bin. Instantly, Clem Beckett made a stand, for himself, and for every man jack and woman ever described as a worker: 'Tek packet out now,' he instructed the foreman, 'or I'll put thee in t' bin wi' it!' The foreman, humiliated, complied, but the union, still precariously nascent, was unable to save him and Clem was sacked. In the spring of 1932 he returned to Oldham, while Eli kept his head down and worked on at Fords for some months.[3]

It could have been worse. A year later, In Dearborn, near Detroit, Ford security men and police opened fire with machine guns on 'hunger marchers' seeking union recognition. Five men died as a result of gunshot wounds; another sixty were wounded by shooting or by blows from clubs. Injured men were chained to their hospital beds by police. These were scenes far more violent than anything witnessed in England during the General Strike, but on both sides of the Atlantic the struggle of workers against ruthless employers was led by men, who, a few years later, would be moved to take up arms in defence of the Spanish Republic. Most notably, the battle against Ford in Detroit was led by America's first black trade union leader, Oliver Laws, who, like Clem, would become a volunteer soldier in the International Brigades.

And yet, however much the CPGB yearned for revolution, whatever suspicions existed between the haves and have-nots, there was a pervasive hope in 1930s Britain that extremes of violence such as those seen in Dearborn could be pre-empted by a residual bond of social cohesion. Moreover, the shoulder-work of Clem and Eli and other members of the 'Ilford Eight' was not in vain. Two years later, under a strike committee directed by Communists, there was a successful all-out three-day strike at Dagenham involving 5,000 workers. It paralysed the plant, and, faced with a determined workforce, Dagenham became the first Ford operation in the world to recognise trade unions.

But however dedicated to the cause they may have been, these two lads were a long way from their northern roots and may have been glad enough of an excuse to head back to the familiar landscape of their home town. The break from cinder shifting had probably helped heal old wounds. There were rumours that Clem's track ban might be lifted, and his career in the saddle was far from over. But back in Oldham, as winter drew on, times were hard. The mayor's 1931 appeal to provide poor children with a Christmas breakfast raised the meagre sum of £107, although with further donations from chapels and the Oldham Mission enough money was raised to feed 3,700 children, and to give each of them an apple, an orange, and a new penny.

Chapter Eighteen

Speed and Spondulicks

'I may be a wage-slave on Monday,
But I am a free man on Sunday.'
From the lyrics to *The Manchester Rambler*,
by Ewan MacColl.

When, on 26 March 1932, readers of the *Sheffield Daily Telegraph* learned that the ACU had lifted Clem's suspension, they were also informed that he had once again signed up with Sheffield Speedway. Given that he had missed an entire season's racing while under suspension, Clem's presence on the practice track was rather on sufferance, and the new manager at Owlerton, J.B.M. Sneath, probably appointed directly by EOS, was nervous about his presence. It would have been awkward for Clem too; once a co-owner of the stadium, returning from outlaw status, and, by common consent, not the rider he had been. Nor did it bode well that during the close season EOS had ensured the introduction of new ACU regulations on the registration and transfer of riders.

Clem may, however, have been cheered by the news that Sneath had also signed up his old friends and rivals Squib Burton, George Wigfield and Broncho Dixon. But what would they make of Clem, given his long absence from the cinders, and a growing reputation for left-wing politics?

The lifting of the suspension did not mean that Clem had repudiated his allegiance to the Communist Party. Moreover, the Party had work for him. Clem had been elected – more likely appointed – to the titular post of vice president of a newly formed front organisation, the British Workers' Sports Federation. And even while practising at Owlerton for the opening League matches of the season, he was preparing another broadside against the rulers of speedway. In touch with George Sinfield, editor of the Party's new monthly paper, *The Worker Sportsman,* Clem

129

had been commissioned to write a second article denouncing speedway shenanigans. It was all part of the Party's great campaign against capitalist sport.

British Communists had been slow to realise the potential of recruiting famous sporting names. Besides the thrills and spills of speedway racing and its novelty, the dashing, daredevil image of Beckett perfectly fitted the template of the Party's wish to exploit the working man's interest in popular sport. It was a strategy pursued by Hitler and Mussolini, with the intention of identifying sporting achievement with political belief, and making new recruits, especially amongst the young. The launch of the *Sportsman* was planned to chime with the Party's traditional May Day festivity, and Clem's fame as a speedway rider made him a natural choice to help the paper make a splash.

In search of a big-name sportsman, it was inevitable that CPGB General Secretary Harry Pollitt and Comrade Sinfield, also national secretary of the BWSF, would come knocking on Clem's door. The point they wanted Clem to help them make was that there were two kinds of sport. 'Capitalist sport,' according to Pollitt was where, 'only hired professionals participate ... sport is corrupted ... and bribery is rampant,' and which 'prostituted' true sporting principles to make profit for speculators. But now, thanks to the Party's rethink, there was 'workers' sport' helping to create 'a big fine upstanding race of young workers, healthy, strong, and of good physical stamina,' all the fitter to 'participate in the struggles of the workers.' It was, of course, a theoretical distinction which would never appeal to the ordinary working man willing to follow any sport that was sufficiently exciting to distract him from the toils and tribulations of daily life. In fairness, away from political theorising the BWSF took up cudgels on issues that really did affect the lives of worker sportsmen. It was voluble in the campaign to lift restrictions on pitches and other facilities owned by straight-laced local authorities who would not allow them to be used on Sundays – the only day of the week when many workers *could* use them. Likewise, it exposed the hypocrisy of rule-makers who persecuted working men in 'amateur' sports for receiving payments that enabled them to take part. It was an argument which, in sports such as tennis and rugby union, was to rumble on for another fifty years or so. In its championing of access to the countryside, the BWSF seized the initiative while other 'respectable' campaigners went on doffing their caps to landowners. Moreover, in its castigation of preparations for the Olympic Games that year, to be held in Los Angeles, the *Worker Sportsman* rightly drew attention to the fact that only a select few middle-class competitors could hope to qualify for the national team. Most workers were excluded because the cost of 'apparatus, javelins, shots, and hurdles' was beyond their means.

Gadfly of the *Sheffield Star* was a skilful journalist. He had an engaging, avuncular style, which gave the impression that the great and good of motorcycle sport beat a path to his door to confide their innermost thoughts. His authority was enhanced by telling stories in the first person, as when, making the most of a brief encounter with EOS before Sheffield's match with Wimbledon on 20 April in the new National League: 'I had a word with E.O. Spence this week, and he is very anxious to see the Sheffield team make good. Naturally it will be better for Belle Vue.' Of course, Gadfly did not follow up by asking the obvious questions: perhaps there was an ever so slight conflict of interest, given EOS's financial stake in *both* clubs, and, therefore, how could he expect the fans to take the competition seriously? The seventy or so members of the Sheffield Speedway Supporters Club would certainly have appreciated answers, and were already pushing for a meeting with Sneath to put their concerns to him. The club had not yet won a match, and was bottom of the League. In the event, in the columns of the *Green'Un*, Sheffield's Saturday sports paper, Gadfly reported the Wimbledon match as a thrilling spectacle, while conceding that the attendance had been disappointing. Clem, however, played no part in it, although he won a heat in another event, before falling and sustaining facial bruises. A week earlier he had come off in the team's first home League match, injuring his neck.

Clem had other things on his mind, and an event planned by the British Workers' Sport Federation for the following Sunday was one of them. The Federation, urged on by Clem's fellow BWSF vice president, Bernard 'Benny' Rothman, and the Manchester branch of the Young Communist League, was at the forefront of a campaign to gain access for walkers to the vast moorland estates of the Duke of Devonshire. Rothman, assisted by Clem, was also working on sending a team of British cyclists to visit the Soviet Union.

The exclusion of walkers from the massif of Kinder Scout, in the Derbyshire Peak District, so as not to disturb the grouse on his lordship's moors, had long been resented by ramblers, but it was the BWSF that resolved to take direct action on their behalf. Clem had become familiar with Kinder's wild, alluring landscape on countless Pennine crossings between Manchester and Sheffield, and it was a natural target for protest.

On Sunday, 24 April, 400 or so mainly young men and young women gathered at Bowden Bridge Quarry, Hayfield. From there they set off climbing onto the moor, determined to reach the summit, in spite of resistance from police and gamekeepers. In addition to protesters setting off on the Manchester side, another group from Sheffield was able to reach the Kinder plateau from the eastern side. Among the Manchester contingent was Young Communist League member Maurice Levine, destined to serve alongside Clem in the Spanish Civil War. The two groups met in triumph on the watershed at Ashop Head. A third group reached the plateau from Edale. If Clem was among the trespassers he kept his head down, and was not among the six men arrested at Hayfield. The police picked out men of Jewish appearance, and if found to have anglicised their names, made a point of charging them in their original Jewish names.

If Ernest Woolley was on the Trespass he would have been proud of his troops. Some would have been graduates of his YCL Cycle Corps, trained to use code and carry messages, ready for the day when the revolutionary balloon went up. In the thick of the 'action' at William Clough, they easily outsmarted the line of gamekeepers armed with clubs. Younger and fitter, the trespassers carried out a masterly outflanking movement up the steep sides of the clough, with Maurice Levine in the vanguard. The trespassers were condemned by 'respectable', law-abiding ramblers, including Edwin Royce, president of the Manchester Ramblers Federation, who wanted to negotiate access agreements, and co-operate with gamekeepers. In the event, and partly because of the prison sentences meted out to the leaders, including Rothman, the Mass Trespass on Kinder proved to be one of the most successful acts of civil disobedience in British history.[1]

A week after the Mass Trespass, Clem was in a quandary. The ACU was indicating that the lifting of his suspension came with strings. Forms were required to be signed, and according to the *Sheffield Star Green'Un* 'some little difficulty was in the way'. Chances are that the ACU wanted him to sign either an apology for past misdeeds or a promise of indemnity for future lapses from the straight and narrow; a gagging order in other words. All this came on the eve of publication of his article in the *Worker Sportsman*.

The Mass Trespass provided good copy for the *Worker Sportsman,* as the first issue of the paper was being put together for publication on 1 May. Clem's article had already been typeset, as had Benny Rothman's tub-thumping denunciation of 'big-bellied bosses' for keeping the Derbyshire countryside to themselves. In fact, there were many other areas, including swathes of moorland above Bill's o'Jack's, reserved for grouse-shooting, from which the public remained excluded.

Clem's piece, entitled 'Speed and Spondulicks', carried over to the second issue on 1 June, was ostensibly an exposé of rider exploitation, intended to dovetail with Palme Dutt's railings against capitalist sport, and to support the Party's plans to develop workers' sport. Top of Clem's target list were 'promoters', whose intervention in what had been a largely amateur sport had corrupted its noble amateur origins, and who had formed a cabal to limit riders' remuneration. Once again, Clem took the opportunity to decry the decline of speedway as a spectacle, repeating his assertion that faster machines 'intended to get there first' were reducing the amount of spectacular broadsiding.[2]

If Clem had been absolutely determined to get back into speedway he would have been more cautious. He knew the risks. This time, in the light of his attack on the speedway establishment a year earlier, he was inviting reaction which would be terminal to his hopes of returning to the cinders. Least wise of all might have been to name names, especially that of Eric Oswald Spence. But Clem threw caution to the winds. Mention of the ACU and the owners 'having established a dictatorship over the whole dirt track business' was followed by a reference to EOS 'regularly and openly referred to in the press as the Mussolini of dirt tracks'.

The reference to Mussolini was a provocation, seemingly certain to lead to a reimposition of the suspension. Yet there were many in England, including council members of the ACU, and even Winston Churchill, who admired the Italian dictator for his suppression of Communism, and 'making the trains run on time'. Such a comparison was by no means the libellous insult it would become – on a par with comparisons to Adolf Hitler. Indeed, the careful phrasing by which EOS's name was hedged about, in particular by the assertion that the 'dictator' badge had already been pinned on him by other publications, was a clever lawyer's defence against a libel writ. There were other signs of legal proof-reading. The name of the maverick promoter from Rochdale who cheated riders in Marseille appears to have been removed from the text at the last minute, hastily replaced by the words in the wrong font which read: 'whose name was, shall we say, Black'.

Just as he had done a year earlier, Clem went on to predict a bleak future for speedway. The twenty or so tracks within a thirty-mile radius of Manchester in 1929 were now down to one – EOS's Belle Vue. White City, Rochdale, Warrington, Barnsley and Huddersfield had joined Audenshaw as speedway graveyards. Roaring broadsides and showering cinders had given way to eerie silence, overgrown tracks, and visits from builders looking for development sites. The bankruptcy court was busy with the affairs of promoters who had got in too deep. Some, it was reputed, were so desperate for cash that they were melting down trophies to weigh in the metal. Hundreds of riders were out of work, unable to dispose of their costly machines. Speedway, Clem bemoaned, had been 'crushed by capitalism'. And yet, as if it pained him too much to abandon hope, Clem refrained from pronouncing the last rites. Dirt track might still survive, but only if it could be rescued from its present sad state to become 'a spectacular show for the public'.

In the event, Clem provided an account of a sport that was more mad than bad, with participants and promoters alike constantly coming up with hare-brained schemes to attract paying customers, and nearly always coming to grief. Take, for example, the account of his adventures in Marseille. His description of the conflict between English riders and French authorities comes across as a comic adventure rather than an indictment of capitalism. Moreover, Clem appears to have been entirely at home in this demi-monde of chancers, proud of his experiences, and glad of an opportunity to relate them, no matter how off-message. Nor could Clem resist the temptation – while the editor was unwilling to resist his inclination – to sprinkle an attack on 'capitalist track owners' with amusing asides about his love-life and chronic air-sickness. Moreover, in his newly launched Wall of Death career Clem had not demurred from the growing practice of product sponsorship. For wearing pullovers bearing the boldly knitted motif 'Castrol', he and Skid Skinner received discount on the purchase of the oil required in copious quantities for red-hot engines revving round the wall.[3]

The articles evinced another side to Clem's character: his loyalty. Just as he maintained his friendship with the Anderson boys in Oldham, never allowing idolatry to affect his affability and approachability, he remained loyal to his one-time patron, Edgar Hart. This in spite of the fact that Hart had been forced to transfer his interest in the Sheffield stadium to Belle Vue's backers, thereby consigning Clem's dirt track future to the manipulative EOS. Moreover, to all appearances, Hart was a typical capitalist, an entrepreneur, a company director, a boss, a trader in stocks and shares, whose class excluded him from any commonalty with mere workers and wage-slaves. The wonder is that Clem's special pleading for Hart, along with a 'Mr Lees of Bury' – both of whom had helped him form the Dirt Track Riders Association –was able to get past the editor of the *Worker Sportsman*.[4] This was, after all, at a time when, pursuant to a Comintern directive, the basis of CPGB strategy was 'Class Against Class', a policy that deemed any dalliance with non-Party people tantamount to consorting with the enemy. However, Clem was unlikely to forget that it was Hart's generous and timely intervention following his sidecar accident which saved his leg from amputation. He was also eternally grateful to Lees, a gentleman-amateur dirt track rider, who, time and again, negotiated with hostile stadium owners in an effort to negotiate better pay for the professionals.

As for his ill-fated career as company director, Clem felt bound to recant: 'I should like to state that at no period of my career as a dirt track director or shareholder have I ever drawn profits, fees, expenses or any monies in any shape,' adding, guiltily, 'My financial career served me right.' This is a very wide claim indeed, and begs the question: what exactly was Clem's source of income from speedway? Obviously both prize money and appearance money were paid at all tracks, including Owlerton, however unremunerative his investment in Provincial Dirt Tracks Ltd. There is always the suspicion when Clem is writing about the woes of dirt track riding that he was very much at pains not to stir up interest from H.M. tax inspector.

On Wednesday, 4 May 1932, three days after publication of the 'Spondulicks' piece, Clem Beckett rode his last speedway race in England, at Southampton, in the new National Association Trophy competition. It was only his second appearance as a member of Sneath's team, and even then he was originally selected as 'reserve'. Clem had not improved his chances of healing the rift with Sneath by telling Gadfly 'something about Russia', which was duly reported in the *Star Green'Un*. The report lamented that Clem was having 'to take a back seat on the list after being so brilliant,' with a heavy hint that the writing was on the wall for his hopes of a comeback: 'We still think a lot of him in Sheffield, however, and I hope he will stay with us long enough to improve his form. He could not be employed better than making that track as it should be.' Clem Beckett, only recently acclaimed as the greatest dirt track star, had well and truly fallen from the speedway firmament.

It was fitting that on Clem's farewell ride at Southampton his old friends George Wigfield and Squib Burton, competitors in many a dirt track dual, were among his teammates, and that, according to the *Star Green'Un*, Clem 'did well'. Of course, Clem, who had once been a company director, had no intention of following Gadfly's advice by becoming a groundsman. In any case, desperate to generate income to compensate for falling attendances in the depth of the Depression, the Owlerton stadium was diversifying. A new track was being built round the edge of the speedway course, and from now on dirt track in Sheffield would have to compete with the very different attraction of greyhound racing – together with its inevitable concomitant, on-course betting. Moreover, when later in the year a new National Speedway League was launched for top clubs, Sheffield was conspicuously absent. Five of the League's nine members were London clubs, the only northern team being Belle Vue.

Chapter Nineteen

The People's Broadsider

*'We were struck by signs of activity all along the
dockside. It seemed strange after seeing idleness
on every hand in Glasgow.'*
Glasgow cyclist Tommy Flynn, in Russia
with Clem, comparing sights on the
River Neva with those on the Clyde.

The explanation of Clem's extraordinary May Day salvo against the
speedway industry was simple: he already had another engagement
lined up, well beyond the jurisdiction of the ACU or the omnipotent
EOS. Buried at the bottom of an inside page on the *Sheffield Telegraph*
of 21 May 1932 was a brief announcement that Clem Beckett 'once the
Daredevil of the Owlerton Speedway' was off to Russia.

Indeed he was. Clem had been selected as a member of a British
party of sportsmen on the flagship BWSF project, a tour of a country
they all believed was a workers' paradise. His place might just have
come at a price, and 'Speedway and Spondulicks' might have been it.
Selected on the basis of his Communist Party membership for an all-
expenses-paid boondoggle of comradely competition, it promised to be
just about the softest job Clem had ever had. In the company of athletes,
boxers, swimmers and footballers (not all of whom were CP members)
Clem sailed for Russia at the end of May. Given that 'Spondulicks' had
questioned whether dirt track could any longer claim to be a sport, there
was a certain irony in Clem's selection. Benny Rothman, mass trespasser
and Clem's fellow-contributor in the *Worker Sportsman,* was omitted.

As the Russian ship *Alexei Rykov* nosed through the choppy waters
of the North Sea bound for Leningrad via the Kiel Canal, Clem was
the life and soul of the party among the motley collection of worker
sportsmen on board. Accompanied by Clem, an accomplished player of

the concertina, these ambassadors of British sport were encouraged to sing socialist hymns and anthems as they neared the promised land. It would have been better, though, in view of what was to befall him in the Soviet Union, if Clem had left the instrument at home.

Among the voyagers was Joe Norman, a Manchester boxer, engineer by trade, trade unionist, but not yet a member of the Communist Party. Like Clem, Norman had already done some travelling, having joined the Royal Naval Volunteer Reserve, and visited the West Indies, where he had been appalled at the level of poverty in the black community compared with the luxurious lifestyle of colonial whites. The travellers enjoyed a stopover in 'Red' Hamburg, where the footballers beat the locals 11-2, and, naturally, comradely hospitality was provided.

Clem and the rest of the thirty-five strong delegation arrived in Leningrad on 3 June, travelling directly to Moscow, where a grand welcome had been prepared. While these itinerant ambassadors for British workers' sport were almost smothered in hospitality wherever they went, Clem was picked out for special attention. Being the only dirt track rider in the party, and in the total absence of dirt tracks in Russia, his role was to present demonstrations of broadsiding on whatever makeshift surfaces could be found. Clem's greatest moment of adulation came at the Moscow Dynamo stadium where, in spite of a makeshift track surface, he earned the rapturous cheers of thousands of Muscovites with a master class in broadsiding. Afterwards, Clem was surrounded by adoring fans with a worrying enthusiasm for removing parts of the Douglas as 'souvenirs'. The threat of his machine being completely cannibalised by comrades starved of consumer goods such as motorbikes and spare parts became a constant problem.

The July issue of the *Worker Sportsman* waxed lyrical and milked the tour for propaganda. Bands played, banners waved, fraternal greetings were exchanged and effusive speeches of welcome were given wherever the Brits went. 'Rousing' events such as the 1-1 draw between Moscow Dynamo and BWSF were woven into a narrative which every day revealed fresh evidence of 'the spirit which achieved the revolution is making colossal strides in socialist construction under the Five-Year Plan.' Comrade Vic Farrant, chairman of the BWSF, was impressed by a unit of Red Army troops 'singing their rousing songs', and by accommodation provided at The Central House of Physical Culture. Cyclist Tommy Flynn from Glasgow was struck by bustling activity in the docks along the River Neva, compared with the silent dockyards on Clydeside. Flynn, who would later meet up with Clem in Spain, was said to be much impressed by his Russian comrades' high standards in running, jumping and swimming, and also in their proficient 'shooting, grenade-throwing, and gas-mask wearing,' given that 'war on the Soviet Union may not be far off.' By all reports, the British delegation were overwhelmed by hospitality, and especially, so readers of the *Worker Sportsman* were told, by 'the magnificence and abundance of the food'.

What none of the tourists knew was that as their visit progressed the Soviet government was once again facing the threat of famine. It responded by pursuing its policy of collectivisation of the land with renewed vigour. Uncooperative peasants ('kulaks') continued to be deported en masse to northern areas, such as Murmansk, to work in lumber camps or to excavate apatite deposits for fertiliser. At the same time prisoners were being set to work building a canal to join the White Sea to Lake Onega. Exiled families were living twenty to thirty groups to a tent, with hundreds dying of exposure, typhus and smallpox. But prisoners were never employed in lumber work within 200km of large centres of population, a policy designed to prevent visitors such as those in the BWSF party from being disabused of their preconceptions.

Even so, evidence of outrages was gradually seeping out. English diplomats in Moscow had their own sources, and Malcolm Muggeridge, Moscow correspondent of the *Manchester Guardian* was slipping his minders to observe the realities of life in Soviet Russia. In the grain-growing region of Kuban, from which whole villages had been exiled, he noted well-fed troops garrisoning starving peasants. Concerned not to offend its left-wing readership, the *Guardian* expurgated Muggeridge's reports, and resolved to depart company with him.

As for Clem, his later contribution to the fraternity-fest is somewhat mysterious. After Moscow, the party divided into two, with soccer players and athletes remaining in the west of the country, while Clem and Norman appear to have been members of a smaller group which travelled east and south, with Clem giving exhibition rides in towns along the Volga, and in Georgia and Armenia. Surely there would have been a tangible boredom factor for any gathering assembled solely for the purpose of watching one man and his motorbike circling a makeshift track, however much cinder-shifting Clem was able to generate?

The greater mystery, however, lies in the reason why, after his fellow tourists had returned to England, Clem remained behind for a further four months. There are two mutually exclusive accounts, both of which were given by Clem to different audiences.

Firstly, there is the explanation which became absorbed into the posthumous hero-worship heaped upon Clem by Party historians and propagandists. According to them, Clem was persuaded by his Russian hosts to extend his broadsiding extravaganza, with a series of further displays interspersed with lessons and instruction to Russian comrades. Then, towards the end of November, mission accomplished, Clem sailed home to England. But apart from the onset of the Russian winter which would have limited outdoor performances, there are several reasons to doubt this 'official' version of events.

According to Clem, the Russians were most interested in his Douglas motorbike: so interested in fact, that one way or another, by the time Clem came to leave Russia, it had disappeared altogether, stripped by souvenir hunters or cannibalised for spares (the nascent Russian motorcycle industry would have had no difficulty getting its hands on a showroom model, so state-sponsored industrial espionage as a motive for theft can be ruled out). Clem more or less confirmed this version of events when he met up with Joe Norman, saying that the Russians had sent him home 'on a fishing boat, minus my bike'. A variant on this, better explaining the length of stay, is that Clem followed in the footsteps of other British Communists by enrolling at the Lenin School in Moscow to learn all about political economy and agitation. This is unlikely, however, especially in the context of Clem's later relationship with CPGB members in Spain.

The problem with any version of events which puts Clem inside Soviet Russia throughout the autumn of 1932 is that he contradicted it himself, by giving a totally different account to the Sheffield *Daily Independent,* published on 9 March 1933. Interviewed by an unnamed journalist, he lamented that he had recently arrived back in the country 'broke', after throwing himself on the mercy of the British consul in an unnamed European city for the price of the homeward voyage from an unnamed port. Later, Eli Anderson was to relate how, on Clem's disembarkation at Hay's Wharf on the Thames, they had ridden home to Oldham, on a motorbike collected by Eli from George Sinfield's address in London.

So if Clem had not come from Russia, where had he come from? Almost certainly he sailed back to England from Hamburg. Not only was that city mentioned by name in the *Independent's* story, it was well-known to Clem from earlier trips to Germany, and where he had contacts in the speedway world, and friends in the Communist Party. But before that? How did he get to Hamburg? Crucially, the *Independent* mentions Clem being an 'instructor to the Balkan Motor Club' following 'a civic reception in Russia'. There were of course, many civic receptions for the BWSF delegation in Russia, including the usual exchange of fraternal greetings, and in Georgia and Armenia. Might it have been that Clem became bored by endless formalities in these far-flung Soviet outposts in the Caucuses, where, according to him, the locals had never even seen a motorbike? Or might he have begun to suspect that he was only being presented with a selective picture of Soviet society, and that below the veneer lay the brutal truth of human rights violations on an unimaginable scale?

Taken together, and bearing in mind that in the extensive contemporary coverage of the BWSF trip in the *Worker Sportsman* there is not a single mention of Clem, the likely explanation is that, either on the way there or the return leg of the journey, he 'jumped ship', crossing the border into neighbouring Romania. There, only two years earlier, he had enjoyed a memorable whistle-stop speedway tour. Was the relative proximity of his happy Balkan hunting ground just too much to resist? After all, whatever the joys of the Russian boondoggle, once back in England he faced a bleak future as a dirt track outlaw. Sure enough, following the publication of 'Spondulicks' the ACU had moved to suspend him from their tracks a second time. Moreover, Clem was well aware that, thanks to EOS, there was now next to no chance of engagements at non-ACU meetings. Of the twenty or so dirt tracks that had mushroomed within a thirty-mile radius of Manchester, only Belle Vue remained.

Evocations of *The Great Escape* with Clem roaring over the Soviet border to freedom are somewhat fanciful, but they are more consonant with the facts than any other explanation of his sojourn in Europe during the autumn of 1932. Romania, with its large minority of motorbike-mad *Rumaniendeutchse* (ethnic Germans) had featured in Clem's European travels in the 1920s, and it would have been natural for Clem, who had already picked up conversational German, to look up contacts in familiar and more prosperous venues. Why else would he become an 'instructor' to the Balkan Motor Club? Unless, that is, he wished to distance himself from the Communist BWSF mission by keeping quiet about it.

There were, however, other things on Clem's mind, which may help explain his reluctance to return to England: his love life had landed him in trouble. Just before his departure for Russia, or while he was there, an Oldham woman applied to magistrates for an affiliation order, in respect of a child allegedly fathered by Clem. He had unsuccessfully opposed the order, and (no DNA tests in those days, of course) appealed to Quarter Sessions. The mother's case was upheld.[2]

As for his sojourn in eastern Europe, what might have seemed to be a good idea at the time turned out to be a disastrous miscalculation. Clem explained that he got paid in local currency, probably the Romanian leu, rendered virtually worthless by the knock-on effects of the banking crisis in Germany.

However he got as far as Hamburg, by bike or train, it seems there was a short stay in Czechoslovakia, where Clem boasted to the credulous reporter that he had established two world records, and earned the equivalent of £200 which helped him on the last leg of his journey. Clem could always tell a good yarn. Some of the money that got him home was advanced by the British consul; some was remitted from either family or friends, likely as not the Anderson boys.

Clem's route to Hamburg lay through the German-speaking area of Czechoslovakia, known as Sudetenland. Although Adolf Hitler had not yet become German Chancellor, his National Socialist 'Brownshirts' were already agitating to bring about reunification of German minorities within the 'Fatherland'. Slowly but surely the Nazis were subverting German democracy by violence. In 1922 the accession of Mussolini as fascist dictator of Italy had been put down to mercurial Italian temperament, but now events in Germany, with Hitler on the brink of power, presented a more serious challenge. This was hammered home to Harry Pollitt and the CPGB by first-hand accounts brought back by BWSF delegates who, like Clem, had stopped off in Hamburg en route to and from Russia. Yiddish-speaking Jewish members of the delegation found no difficulty in communicating with German comrades. The experiences of members of a BWSF football team who had taken part in a 'Spartakiade' in the German Ruhr, just as Clem was making a dash for the Balkans, left no doubt about the dangers of Nazism. At a stadium in Essen, on 3 July 1932, Hitler's toughs, encouraged by police, had opened fire on the crowd, killing five and wounding many more. In the aftermath, English players were roughed up by the police.

Clem's personal story of distress matched the sombre mood of the times as related by the *Independent*. It shared the front page with a report of Neville Chamberlain, Chancellor of the Exchequer in Britain's new National Government, blaming the depressed state of British industry on the downturn in world trade, and a brief reference to the doomed attempts of Ramsay MacDonald, Labour prime minister, to pursue international disarmament talks. Even so, through his experiences in Europe, east and west, Clem Beckett already had a greater understanding of the Nazi threat than Neville Chamberlain and Ramsay MacDonald had between them. At the same time, the average British newspaper reader had none at all.

Chapter Twenty

On Mosley's Manor

'Spain is the World at the Crossroads.'
Harry Pollitt, General Secretary of the Communist
Party of Great Britain, writing about British
volunteers in the early days of
the Spanish Civil War.

Clem's days as a dirt track adventurer were over. Riding back to Oldham with Eli Anderson, the two of them discussed opening their own motorcycle business, and within a matter of weeks they had made it happen. This in spite of a misleading announcement in the *Sheffield Independent* at the beginning of the speedway season that Clem would once again be on the grid at Owlerton.

On arrival in Oldham, however, Clem's immediate concern was the possibility of arrest for non-payment of child maintenance. He went to some lengths to avoid being recognised, hiding his motorcycle at his mother's home, and boarding with Eli. The following day, for fear of being identified on the tram, the pair walked half way to Manchester, where Clem had arranged to meet Albert Oldham, owner of a motorcycle business.

Clem duly bought 'Nick's Motorcycle Depot' at 169 Oldham Road – presumably on easy terms. By March 1933 he had moved out of his mother's home in Swinton Street to live 'over the shop', being joined there by Eli. The business premises lay at the heart of the working-class district in the north of the city, on the border of New Cross and Miles Platting, and close to Collyhurst and Ancoats. A century earlier this had been the stamping ground of radical agitators such as Elijah Dixon and James Wroe as they battled for reform in the aftermath of Peterloo.

Irving Anderson was also called on to lend a hand with the business. For the three friends reunited it was just like the old days, with back-slapping remembrances of police chases round Bill o'Jack's. Older and wiser, setting up in business was a natural progression for a sportsman coming to the end of his career, especially where the end was hastened by injury or simply by age-related weariness. Yet, in the spring of 1933, Clem was only twenty-six, an age when in some sports, including speedway, he might have had plenty more to offer. It was ironic that just as Clem was turning his back on the dirt track, dismayed by its rulers and battered by injuries, British cinema audiences were being treated to a dramatic but disturbing fictional account of the speedway scene, echoing some of the episodes in Clem's career.[1]

By now the Slump had bottomed out. In America President Franklin Roosevelt's 'New Deal' programme of public works was reducing unemployment, gradually impacting on the economies of Europe. Although signs of recovery were not entirely welcomed by Marxist prophets of armageddon, slowly returning business confidence went hand in hand with increased demand for motorcars and motorbikes. True, Miles Platting and New Cross were among the poorer districts of Manchester, favoured by Irish and Italian immigrants, and few in the nearby slums of Ancoats and Collyhurst had the money for a new motorbike. However, situated beside the main road to Oldham, Nick's Motorcycles was well placed for passing trade, and the business did well. Clem acquired an additional building close to the junction of Oldham Road and Butler Street for use as a workshop, and purchased a stylish *Crossley* motorcar.

Once again, Clem faced an identity crisis. How could membership of the Communist Party be reconciled with his role as employer and, heaven forfend, businessman? In 1933, however, the Communist Party of Great Britain was undergoing a fundamental policy shift. From its inception in 1920, the Party had ridiculed the inability of democracies, and democratic socialists, to bring about change. Party policies had been directed at hobbling democratically elected governments of the left, never more ferociously than when the minority governments of Ramsay MacDonald were in office. Day after day, the *Daily Worker* had poured scorn on Labour politicians, characterising them as feeble lackies of capitalism, and friends of business. Now, however, with falling unemployment, the CPGB was coming to terms with the fact that the country had declined its offer of a revolution, and that the idea of renewing the offer was, at least for the time being, out of the question.

It was entering a new phase of accommodating and co-operating with those who did not share the purity of its ideals.

The nation had not forgotten the two great national crises of the General Strike and the Great Depression, but increasingly characterised in the mainstream press as a party of demagogues and ideologues, backed by a foreign power, the CPGB was struggling to maintain its support in all but the most distressed areas, such as South Wales and Clydeside. In fact, although overall numbers of unemployed were falling, the number of long-term unemployed in areas like these was actually increasing. Moreover, an entirely new political party, with populist appeal, had emerged on the scene, and for a time it threatened to poach the allegiance of those who were weary of 'do-nothing' politics.

Less than a mile from Nick's Motorcycle Depot stood Ancoats Hall, ancestral home of Sir Oswald Mosley, sixth Baronet of Ancoats, a minister in Ramsay MacDonald's Labour government. Mosley, charismatic and tipped as a future prime minister, had resigned when his revolutionary proposals to cure unemployment (copying Roosevelt's programme of public investment) were rejected by the Cabinet. Courting support from leading Labour Party figures, he formed the 'New Party'. Impatient, messianic and egotistical, Mosley was seduced by the dazzling success of Mussolini and Hitler, and in October 1932 he had formed the British Union of Fascists. It met with limited success, notably in working-class areas in the East End of London. In speeches up and down the land, including several in Manchester, and at least one in Oldham, Mosley aped the mannerisms of Hitler. Anti-semitism crept into his repertoire, and his black-shirted disciples, acting like Hitler's paramilitary henchmen, acquired a reputation for violence.

The success of fascism set alarm bells ringing in the Communist Party of Great Britain. It had outflanked them. By pitching for working-class support, and defining his policy as 'revolutionary', Mosley was desecrating sacred ground. Moreover, the experiences of BWSF footballers at the sharp end of Nazi violence left little doubt about the fate in store for comrades in Germany. Jews were prominent in the leadership of the CPGB nationally as well as in the BWSF, and, more significantly to Clem, in working-class areas of Manchester and Salford, such as Cheetham Hill, home of his BWSF comrades Benny Rothman and Maurice Levine.

Clem's Communist friends in *Rotes (Red) Hamburg,* now faced assassination, knocks on the door at midnight, imprisonment without trial, and concentration camps. By the end of the year, with Hitler installed as German Chancellor, there were more than 100,000 political prisoners, democratic rights had been suspended, and 50,000 Nazis had been recruited as police 'auxiliaries'. Yet shocking evidence of Hitler's actions in Germany did not alter the fact that human rights abuses in Russia continued. Facing the prospect of famine and the collapse of its Five-Year Plan, Stalin fell back on scapegoating. Whereas Hitler scapegoated the Jews, Stalin picked on nebulous 'enemies of the people'.

In contrast with those who had real inside knowledge of Stalin's ruthlessness, the vast majority of left-leaning people, such as Clem, wanted to think well of Russia. They shared Harry Pollitt's pride in a working-class that had thrown off the shackles of oppression and smashed the power of the 'bosses'. Accordingly, when in March 1933 the Soviets made allegations of industrial sabotage against five British engineers working in Russia, there was an inevitable polarisation of opinion. The men were employees of Metropolitan-Vickers, a company with strong links to Manchester and Lancashire. After a show trial, two were convicted with the help of false or forced confessions at the hands of the secret police. There was a widespread view that the whole episode was a stunt to distract attention from economic problems, but loyal readers of the *Daily Worker* like Clem were allowed nowhere near the facts. Any criticism of the Soviet Union was simply discredited by a pre-emptive claim that the capitalist press was irredeemably biased, as well as by misinformation carefully fed to Communist sympathisers by agents of the Comintern. The truth, however, was that Stalin's Russia had by now become as absolutist as the Tsarist State.

Even so, the threat of fascism prompted the Comintern to revise the 'Class Against Class' policy imposed on British Communists. In its place the Party ushered in a strategy allowing greater co-operation with non-Communist bodies across a broad front. Its rallying cry became 'Fight the Fascists!' Anyone – intellectuals, academics, social democrats, liberals, conservatives, and even businessmen – was welcome to join them in a 'Popular Front' against fascism. Henceforth, as Hitler consolidated his grip on Germany, anti-fascist agitation shared the Communist Party's agenda with the usual issues of unemployment, exploitation and poverty.

Not that these shifts in Party policy meant much to Clem or the Anderson boys, who were trying to build up their growing motorbike business in Miles Platting. Apart from sales, they kept busy on repairs, and it would be hard to imagine any enterprise in Manchester with more motorbike expertise. At some point Clem's Party membership was transferred from Oldham to the Platting branch.

Clem could never have detached himself from the frenetic political consciousness of working-class Manchester in the early 1930s. A decade earlier, a fifty-strong group of young Mancunians studying *Das Kapital* had dwindled to three within a month. Now the city echoed to the sound of left-wing oratory. Less than a mile from Clem's shop was Stevenson Square, hallowed venue of Chartist gatherings a century earlier. Now it was a breeding ground for socialism and agitation against fascism, a threat all the more alarming to the city's large Jewish population. In this the CPGB took a leading role. As well as Harry Pollitt, Manchester Communist leaders such as Mick Jenkins and George Brown were addressing crowds of up to 400 people in the 'Queen's Park Parliament', also close to Clem's home, where they made well-argued speeches full of passion and humour. Adept at disrupting opponents by heckling and interjections, their mastery of Marxist theory was expressed in well-turned phrases in everyday language. To earn their spurs, less experienced Young Communist orators regularly mounted soapboxes at Marshall Croft, High Town, close to Cheetham Hill, and Albert Croft, Collyhurst. In a development that anticipated the cross-class solidarity of volunteers in the Spanish Civil War, Oxbridge graduates Robin Page Arnot and his wife, Olive, gave lectures on Marxism to eager working-class youths at Manchester's YMCA.

However, though Clem's belief in Communism has never been questioned, there is no evidence that he took part in major demonstrations organised by the Manchester Party. These included the protest against the appearance of Oswald Mosley in 1933 at a Blackshirts rally at Belle Vue, close to the sacred turf of the stadium where Clem had scored many a victory.

The stark truth, which CPGB members were slow to recognise, was that in spite of high unemployment the chances of a Russian-style revolution were ebbing away. Assisted by building societies such as the Halifax, a product of the campaign for enfranchisement a century before, parts of the country, especially southern England, were enjoying the availability of cheap mortgages and a boom in house-building. Thanks to trade agreements between the Labour government and the Soviets, this was assisted by imports of cheap timber, much of it sourced from slave-labour camps in northern Russia. By the mid-1930s British industrial output was twenty per cent higher than it had been in 1929. The setting up of the National Grid, which cut the cost of electricity by half, led to millions more consumers, generating demand for new consumer goods such as radios, irons, cookers and vacuum cleaners. Even speedway, after wholesale closure of venues in the depth of the Slump, was enjoying a revival. The reopening of stadiums and opening of new ones reflected the public's insatiable appetite for cinder-shifting, confounding the view, partly shared by Clem himself, that the boom of the late 1920s had been a flash in the pan.

Likewise, the mood of panic shown by the authorities towards the CPGB was abating. When in July 1934 Harry Pollitt and Tom Mann stood trial for sedition they were unexpectedly acquitted. Mann jokingly commented: 'It almost makes us say there is something in British capitalist justice after all.' It was an admission that the perennial tensions between capital and labour were, for the moment, less important than the threat of another European war. Yet, in the depressed areas of the North, South Wales and Central Scotland, political discontent remained, with the CPGB still proclaiming that only Communism could provide a solution to unemployment and poverty.

Clem may have been back in Denmark as early as 1934, helping Platt and Skinner with their Wall of Death show, and possibly assisting the Party as a courier. In any event, politics led to romance. In January 1935 he married Lida, the girl he had met in Denmark, who shared his commitment to Communism, and who had joined him in Manchester some months earlier. Clem and Lida set up home together 'over the shop' in Miles Platting. Lida *who?* There were at least three versions of her surname before she became Mrs Beckett, as well as two other given names. Known in the Party as Leda Tynsen, information provided to the North Manchester Register Office identified her as Eli Marie Henrikson or Johnson. Lida Beckett was a divorcee, having lived in Canada as well as Denmark. Back in Oldham, among Clem's adoring fans, there were disappointed aspirants for the title of Mrs 'Daredevil' Beckett, while the union with Lida seems to have surprised friends and family alike. Mysteriously, the marriage certificate records the occupation of Clem's absent father as 'farmer', while Clem's description as 'motorcycle expert' suggests that by now he had branched out beyond sales and repairs at the shop in Oldham Road. Quite apart from his mechanical knowledge, insurance companies and loss adjusters had need of reliable valuations.

The marriage to Lida also reinforced Clem's identity as a citizen of the world. He had acquired first-hand knowledge of events in Europe at a time when most people in Britain were averting their eyes from the rise of Hitler and German rearmament. The notorious declaration of the Oxford Union that it was unwilling to fight for King and Country, matched by a home-spun 'Peace Ballot' perfectly expressed the prevailing mood of appeasement. Talk of standing up to aggressors prompted accusations of warmongering, but British Communists were among the first to identify such complacency as a dangerous fallacy.

In spite of non-stop globe-trotting over a period of four years, Clem had maintained his contact with Oldham. Naturally, his first concern was the welfare of his mother, and there was also the long-standing friendship with Eli Anderson, on which Clem had relied a good deal through thick and thin during his speedway career.

Clem made further trips to Denmark in 1935 and 1936, assisting with the Wall of Death and possibly, so as to combine business with pleasure, accompanying Lida on holiday and visiting her family.[2] Surviving photographs show him with Platt and Skinner (but not Lida) in various Danish towns, seemingly as a member of the Wall of Death team starring Skinner and Alma Morley. Sometimes he is shown in the company of besuited Danish fairground entrepreneurs. Clem himself is dressed in smart tweedy clothing, including a fashionable version of his trademark cloth cap, and plus-fours! On other occasions, he is shown with the whole Wall of Death support team, consisting of half a dozen 'roadies' together with promoters and VIP guests. However, Clem's likely role as Platt's mechanic and 'go-for' in Denmark is most strongly suggested by a surviving photograph from the collection of Alma Skinner. Clem, described as 'Beckett', is shown at the oars of a rowing boat with 'Platt' reclining in the seat at the back of the boat. At this time Platt was acting as agent for 'Daredevil' Alma and probably, also, Skid Skinner.

As with Edgar Hart, Clem seems to have trusted Platt, who appears to have been considerate and fair in his dealings with riders, and whose letterhead now boasted of him being Oldham's sole agent for Humber, Jowett and Triumph cars. Alas, during a promotional tour of the Middle East, including Baghdad and Palestine, Platt had acquired strongly anti-semitic views, even expressing admiration for Hitler. It is tempting to wonder, therefore, if, perhaps alone among the whispering reed beds fringing a placid Danish lake (see plate section) Clem Beckett and Percy

Platt ever discussed politics. Did they wonder out loud about the march of European fascism and the threat of war? Did either of them have any notion of the impending conflict soon to shatter both their lives?

Another photograph, apparently taken during the same trip, shows Clem riding the Wall of Death, but almost certainly for fun, and with no sign of paying spectators. There he is, somewhere in Denmark, *hors de combat,* whizzing horizontally round the wooden bowl on a sunny spring day, wearing short-sleeve pullover plus trademark flat cap. And as a final flourish, in an essay of fearless bravado, Clem smiles at the camera, cigarette dangling from mouth. It is an image to savour: the episode was the last in which Clem Beckett was able to relax in his favourite milieu of motorbikes and foreign travel.

But where was Lida? Back in Manchester minding the shop, or in Denmark visiting relatives – or perhaps acting as a courier for the Comintern? From the accession of Hitler to the German Chancellorship after 1933, it would have been too dangerous for messages between King Street and Moscow to go through northern Germany. The route through Denmark would be all the more vital.

Fascist takeovers in Italy and Germany had damaged the credibility of the Marxist assertion that a proletarian victory over capitalism was inevitable. Now, however, events in Spain were moving rapidly in the direction of an opportunity to correct the course of history. If fascism could be stopped in Spain, it might also be defeated throughout Europe, and if Communists were seen as the instrument of that defeat, then world revolution could be achieved after all. Clem, the internationalist, well understood the threat from Italy and Germany, but like most people outside the simmering cauldron of the country's politics, the outbreak of civil war in Spain in July 1936 would have taken him by surprise.

The isolated nature of Spain's geography, its backward economy, and the fact that it had not participated in the First World War, meant that its troubles had been paid scant attention by other European nations. Indeed, the overthrow of the Spanish monarchy in 1930 had appeared to suggest that the country was on the road to reform.

Only four years earlier, writing in the *Worker Sportsman*, vice president of the BWSF Benny Rothman had managed to weave into his tirade against 'parasitic landowners' an incongruous reference to 'war preparations going on in boss-controlled rambling organisations'. Now, however, 'Down with Warmongers' was no longer the slogan of the day.

Under the banner of the Moscow-orchestrated Popular Front, the CPGB presented itself as the saviour of democracy, albeit under the unifying slogan of 'anti-fascism'. No longer was there talk of socialist allies being 'useful idiots', as Lenin had called them, or 'friends of the bosses' as the invective of the *Daily Worker* had so often lampooned them. Increasingly, CPGB rhetoric called for a united front against fascism, welcoming backing from Labour and socialist groups it had condemned for years as enemies of the people. It was a case of all hands to the pump, and for self-employed members of the Party like Clem Beckett, the shift of emphasis away from villainous bosses was welcome. Even so, it required contortions of logic for the CPGB to explain why it supported the fight against fascism in Spain, but was still opposed to 'warmongering'. To its eternal credit, however, the Party soon realised that force had to be met with force. Unprecedentedly, the Communist Party of Great Britain was transforming itself into the one single political party prepared to fight in the name of democracy.

It was a fight in which the majority of the British people showed little interest. In July 1936, as Spanish Army officers launched their rebellion against the lawfully elected Republican government, Oldham was enjoying its annual Wakes Week holiday. The town's newspapers reported on plans for a new fire station and a new maternity block at Boundary Park Hospital, and when, with the failure of the generals' *coup d'état*, war broke out, only members of the Communist Party and the Independent Labour Party showed the slightest interest in it.

Chapter Twenty-one

Look After Mother

'The great majority are here for the sake of an ideal,
no matter what motive prompted them to seek one.'
Miles Tomalin, British volunteer in Spain.

Travelling through Republican Spain by train, on their way to war, British volunteers were fêted as liberators by the townsfolk and villagers of Catalonia, Alicante, Castile and Murcia. Mayors made speeches of welcome, and at every station bands played the *Internationale* as the Communist anthem was sung in half a dozen languages. Young men who had never even held a rifle gave the clenched fist salute and were overcome with emotion.

Five months before these euphoric scenes, on 11 July 1936, a Dragon Rapide light aircraft chartered by a Spanish monarchist journalist, had taken off from Croydon airport, piloted by an Englishman, Captain Charles Henry 'Cecil' Bebb. Also on board were a retired English major and two English women. All of them subsequently claimed to have been duped over the true purpose of their journey, which was to transport General Francisco Franco from the Canary Islands to Morocco to seize command of the Army of Africa, and to rise against the Republican government of Spain.[1] Before the month was out, both Hitler and Mussolini had authorised the sending of transport aircraft to Morocco, for the purpose of air-lifting Franco's troops to mainland Spain. Hitler's provision of Junkers 52s was crucial.

Some well-off Oldhamers, among the holidaymakers in Spain, were caught up in the early days of the rebellion. Solicitor Harold Fort and his wife were discomfited as workers seized their hotel in San Sebastián to prevent it being occupied by rebels. The Forts were quickly evacuated to safety in France, and Harold Fort, typical of the vast majority of his townsmen, who held no particular view on the conflict, enjoyed telling the tale to the *Oldham Evening News*. 'Looking back ... it seems in a way, very funny. If there was a window unbroken something had to be done about it.' Fort's jocular attitude perfectly matched the indifference of the British government to the rights and wrongs of the Spanish conflict, and his affectation of neutrality complemented priestly prayers for the success of the Nationalist crusade against the 'godless Republic' soon to be heard in many a Lancashire Catholic church. In their support for the Spanish Republic, ordinary Communist Party members like Clem Beckett were at first in a distinct and despised minority.

As arms, men and materials poured unto Nationalist Spain from Germany and Italy, pleas for help from the besieged Spanish Republic were ignored by every European government except Soviet Russia. The two countries from which the Republic might have hoped for salvation – the democracies of Britain and France – proved to be their abject betrayers. France had its own considerable fascist following, while in Britain the so-called Nationalist cause, led by Franco, was supported by sinister City interests, fascist sympathisers in the Civil Service (especially those in the Secret Service who had been keeping an eye on CPGB activists such as Pollitt and Ernest Woolley) and the Roman Catholic Church. For the duration of the war the governments of Britain and France refused help the Republic, choosing instead to hide behind the farcical policy of 'non-intervention'. The policy, supported by the official Labour opposition in Parliament, and the Left generally, was riddled with pacifist fuzzy logic and muddled thinking. Even the Labour leader, George Lansbury, preached pacifism. Rather like the 'respectable' ramblers who were not prepared to muddy their boots in mass trespassing, they were letting others do the fighting for them. This widely publicised element gave direct encouragement to Hitler to carry on sending help to Franco, most notably arms and aircraft, which were to prove decisive in the military defeat of the Republic.

Lancashire Communists, however, set about the uphill task of mobilising working-class support for the Republic. In Oldham and Manchester collections of foodstuffs were organised, and at a big public meeting outside the gates of Oldham's Alexandra Park, Clem's friends burned copies of the pro-Nationalist *Daily Mail*. In August, after a protest march in Manchester, Harry Pollitt delivered a full-blooded denunciation of non-intervention to enthusiastic supporters in Stevenson Square. Pollitt, one of the greatest public speakers outside Parliament, was at the peak of his powers. It was said his speeches could 'bring tears to a glass eye'. Thoroughly prepared, carefully argued, resonant with integrity and gravitas, Pollitt lambasted the British government, and appealed for help on behalf of the Spanish people. Clem Beckett was among 130 or so young men from Greater Manchester, convinced by the strength of Pollitt's impassioned arguments, and soon to become soldiers in Spain. Some burned with righteous idealism, some were spoiling for adventure. When the call to arms came, men like Clem would answer it, not in defence of King and Country, not as mercenaries in a foreign war, but as soldiers for freedom and democracy. Some propagandists – but not Pollitt – made romantic comparisons with the poet Byron fighting for Greek independence – a parallel with ominous portents.

At last, after a good deal of hesitation on Stalin's part, the Politburo of the Soviet Communist Party instructed the Comintern to begin the systematic but clandestine supply of materials to Spain, as well as taking steps to organise recruitment of international volunteers. But this was not until October, three months after the rising began, during which the rapidly advancing Nationalists had taken delivery of a steady stream of arms, planes and military men from Germany and Italy.

Pollitt came under great pressure. Through the Executive Committee of the Communist International he was informed of the need to recruit a thousand volunteers 'at any price'. By secret cable he replied that it would be difficult to raise even 500, but gave a promise to find at least 200. The word went out from King Street, and Party members, especially past and present comrades of the Young Communist League, like Clem Beckett, came forward. At first, many were passed over, which is odd given the Comintern's urgent request for 500 'postcards' (code for recruits).[2] Pollitt was hesitant about sending naive, idealistic, and mostly unfit volunteers into mortal danger. He was well-placed to know about the early successes of the Nationalists as well as the atrocities and reprisals being carried out by both sides. The fall of Toledo in September, with its iconic Acazar fortress, had handed Franco a massive propaganda victory, and for a time Pollitt shared the view that the fall of Madrid was only a matter of time.

The CPGB remained what it always had been, a semi-secret body, under orders from Moscow, operating through cadres of dedicated members such as Ernie Woolley, with an organisation that was hierarchical rather than democratic. Now it even had a secret radio link with the Comintern. The Party had always appealed to energetic young men like Clem Beckett, who were attracted precisely because it emphasised action and discipline rather than debate and endless discussion. Now the war in Spain presented them with an opportunity to take action. Once the CPGB had given Clem a platform to attack the 'old fogeys' presiding over injustice in speedway. What was on offer now was far more challenging: the hour had come to show shilly-shallying politicians and hand-wringing pessimists what could really be done.

It mattered not to Clem Beckett and other naturally adventurous members of the CPGB that the Spanish cause did not fit neatly into the Marxist gospel of capitalism being brought down by a militant industrial proletariat. Spain remained an essentially feudal country, its peasant population abominably oppressed by a corrupt and self-serving aristocracy. There were other paradoxes: workers in Catalonia and the Basque country, in favour of regional autonomy, were more influenced by the Anarchist philosophy of Bakunin than Communism as preached by Karl Marx.

Equally, for long-standing Party members like Clem, schooled in the idea of seizing power from the British government on behalf of the people, the notion of fighting in a foreign war must have required a reorientation of political thinking. And for him, as for many of the young men and women who went to Spain, the call to assist the democratically elected government of the Republic came more or less out of the blue. Up till then the Party's emphasis had been on injustice at home such as unemployment and the Means Test. Even the threat from Nazi Germany had prompted a campaign against 'warmongers', and an equally ambivalent alliance with pacifist groups who were anti-war in principle. However, in some areas of the country, especially those where Jewish men and women were well-represented in the ranks of the CPGB, there was an immediate encouragement for them to take up arms. On 3 October 1936 supporters of Sir Oswald Mosley's British Union of Fascists marched through the East End of London, provoking a massive counter-demonstration. In what became known as the Battle of Cable Street, around 170 people were injured, and 150 arrested. For many men who volunteered to fight in Spain, and for the many women who volunteered as nurses, Cable Street was the catalyst.

Clem's contacts with the Party in Europe, to say nothing of his reputation as a mechanic, aviator, and one-time member of the Territorial

Army, meant that when Pollitt visited Manchester to interview would-be volunteers at the Party offices in Swan Street, he had no difficulty in making the cut.[3] According to Maurice Levine, who was rejected by Pollitt on first volunteering for Spain in October, Clem was accepted because of his experience in the TA, and because he knew about machine guns. Eli Anderson and Benny Rothman were also among early volunteers rejected by Pollitt. Whether or not it was raised by Pollitt, while he was interviewing Clem at an address in Fountain Street, the slight matter of him having deserted from the BWSF delegation in Russia was overlooked. The man selected to travel with him was a mysterious figure. Arnold Jeans came from White Russian émigré stock, a circumstance that could hardly have been more calculated to excite suspicion. Jeans's connections even extended to English royalty, having been a tutor to the Bowes-Lyon family, but along with his cosmopolitan background, came fluency in several European languages, including German and Russian. At this stage usefulness rather than idealogical soundness was uppermost in selection criteria. Indeed, there are now grounds to suggest that both Clem and Jeans were selected for work in Spain as a result of a direct approach from Pollitt, under great pressure from the Comintern to send qualified men.[4]

There was, too, an irony in the pairing of Clem Beckett and Arnold Jeans that was to weave through the unfolding story of British volunteers in Spain. There, under the leadership of the Soviet Comintern, came men from polar opposite corners of society, brought together as comrades in arms, and in a common cause. They went for different reasons, and each had his own beliefs, but their egalitarianism transcended politics. Clem Beckett, the lad from Oldham who could not afford to take up a scholarship, lived out the last chapter of his life as the acknowledged equal of other volunteers who, in their younger lives, had enjoyed upper-class privileges and the best education money could buy. In their camaraderie these men were to live and die together in a selfless nobility which not only put the English class system to shame but implicitly challenged the notion that class warfare alone determined the course of history. What their unity and loyalty to each other was to demonstrate in blood was that men and women from all walks of life could fight together for the overarching ideal of vanquishing evil.

An additional and most bitter irony lay in the fact that just as these men were volunteering to risk their lives for democracy, Joseph Stalin was orchestrating the first in a series of 'show trials' in the Soviet Union to purge the followers of his rival, Leon Trotsky. Within a few weeks during the summer of 1936 sixteen senior Party officials had been charged with conspiracy. False confessions were extracted by secret police, and the day after guilty verdicts were pronounced, they were shot. Similar 'trials' followed as Stalin descended into paranoia, and before the end of the war in Spain the long list of *apparatchiks* executed for alleged treason included Alexei Rykov, whose name had once graced the prow of the ship on which Clem had sailed to Russia.

For Clem's family back in Oldham, news that he was going off to war in Spain was a shock. 'Look after Mother,' he told his sister, Mary, along with an instruction to inform Percy Platt. As with a large number of later volunteers, nothing much was said to family or friends about going to 'fight' in Spain. The usual cover story was that of going to drive an ambulance or to assist with medical aid. This not only alleviated family concerns, but also kept the authorities from obstructing the journey to Spain. Clem's last words to Lida were (she claimed), 'So long, kid, don't worry.' According to Party sources, however, soon after leaving for Spain, Clem wrote to her saying, 'I am sure you'll realise that I should never have been satisfied had I not assisted.' What a curiously formal statement, so dissonant with his movie-speak farewell. Lida was planning to visit family and friends in Denmark, so Clem's dog, an Alsatian like the one he had fought and subdued for Cousin Elsie, was taken up to Oldham to be looked after by Henrietta. Other Manchester men already on the way to Spain, or soon to follow, such as Sam Wild, were more emotional about their reasons for going. Mourning the death of fellow Mancunian George Brown, Wild eulogised him as 'a true son of the working class' who maintained 'the great traditions of the Manchester people from Peterloo onwards.'

At the same time, probably in pursuance of unwritten CPGB standing orders, Clem appeared to have submitted a false address, in Chadderton, Oldham, to which the Party was happy to turn a blind eye, or – more likely – had provided for him.

Once committed to the Spanish Republic, the international network of the Comintern was well placed to outwit the authorities in Britain and France who were anxious to keep their citizens, as well as their armies, out of the conflict. After all, the network had been up and running for the best part of twenty years, chiefly to facilitate the movement of Party members, of different nationalities, in their secret travels around the world. Even before the Revolution of 1917, Russian dissidents had become accomplished at smuggling men, money and materials across international borders, and the British Communists had learned from the Russian hierarchy.

At the end of October 1936 Clem crossed the Channel with Arnold Jeans as part of a British Medical Aid convoy, funded and organised by the CPGB. Another driver recruit was Christopher St John Sprigg, a writer with the *nom de plume* of Christopher Caudwell, whom Clem met in London as the convoy was being prepared. Geography dictated that the French Communist Party was bound to play a crucial role in getting volunteers into Spain. Crucially it was the only organisation capable of providing a network of safe-houses, together with guides who knew how to outflank French bureaucracy along clandestine routes between Paris and Spain.

Well before that, however, both the CPGB and the Comintern had boots on the ground in Madrid and Barcelona, while some British volunteers managed to reach Spain by their own devices. Foreigners were fighting, and a great many were dying, in the cause of the Spanish Republic from the moment the rising began. During a raid to blow up a Nationalist ammunition train in Aragon, Felicia Browne, a sculptress, became the first British volunteer to be killed. In the early days of the war the border with France remained open, with hundreds of men and some women crossing into Catalonia, ostensibly to provide humanitarian aid to the civil population. Although volunteers also arrived in Barcelona and Alicante by sea, Clem and Jeans, as part of a British Medical Aid unit, crossed into Spain driving ambulances to the Mediterranean frontier town of Port Bou, just south of Perpignan.

At about the same time, in response to the Republic's need of aircraft mechanics, Ernest Woolley reached Spain, also via Port Bou. It would be another couple of months before the French government, wobbling in its support for the Republic, and under pressure from Britain to adopt a 'non-intervention' policy, closed the Spanish frontier. Later, volunteers had to reach Spain by walking over the Pyrenees.

In the early days of the war most British volunteers who got to Barcelona under their own steam, such as George Orwell, joined Catalan militias fighting in Catalonia and Aragon. Tom Wintringham, ostensibly in Barcelona as a correspondent of the *Daily Worker,* was part of a small group of top Party members reporting back to Pollitt in London.

In the meantime, groups of Europeans, notably German and French Communists, had already established fighting units. Wintringham was involved in forming a small group of British arrivals into a curious unit known as the Tom Mann Centuria, which heralded the formation of the British Battalion. An iconic photograph of these men, holding ancient rifles and gathered round their banner, shows them looking more like a troop of senior scouts than soldiers – hardly likely to strike fear into the Nationalists who were receiving ever more quantities of modern weaponry from Germany and Italy. Neither was the evocation of Tom Mann, who had recruited Clem for Communism, without irony. Even Frederick Engels had doubted Mann's revolutionary commitment, mocking his 'fondness for mentioning that he will be dining with the Lord Mayor'. And although a Communist, Mann was first and foremost a 'syndicalist' believing in a workers' state organised by trade unions, having more in common with the Trotskyists and Anarchists of Catalonia. The greatest and saddest irony was that Mann himself was to outlive so many young men, who, like Clem Beckett, had been drawn into politics by his messianic appeal.

Now the greatest threat lay in Franco's rapid advance on Madrid, and volunteers like Clem and Jeans, shepherded into Spain by French Communists, were sent post haste towards the capital. Early on, most likely in mid-November, at Albacete, a drab town, renowned for manufacturing knives, in the Spanish hinterland of La Mancha, Jeans and Clem were separated on the basis of the qualities for which they had been selected.

New arrivals at Albacete were paraded in the bullring, to be addressed, in French, by Andre Marty, a trade union leader whom the Comintern had put in charge of the thousands of men arriving from all over the world. Marty, sporting a thick walrus moustache and wearing a large black beret, was an intimidating figure, but neither Jeans nor Clem – who had picked up a smattering of French in Marseille – would have had difficulty understanding his growling orders. According to Clem's sister, Mary, Clem had an innate ability to learn languages, and by the time he arrived in Spain he had also picked up conversational German, Danish, and Russian. This contrasted with most British volunteers soon to arrive at Albacete, such as Maurice Levine, who found themselves struggling to understand orders in French.

160

Jeans, the linguist, was immediately attached to the mainly German Thaelmann Battalion, in which a number of other nationalities, including British volunteers, were already serving on the Madrid front. However, Marty, a bully to say the least, had other plans for Clem. For the thousands of volunteers arriving at Albacete, some 250km from Madrid, lorries would be needed to reach the front, as well as ambulances at the front. Hardly surprising, therefore, given the glowing CV that had commended him to Pollitt, Clem was immediately ordered to take charge of the motor depot.

Chapter Twenty-two

Rotten Dissident

'I suppose there is no one who spent more
than a few weeks in Spain
without being in some degree disillusioned.'
George Orwell, *Homage to Catalonia.*

Volunteers who were elated by joyous scenes along the railway line from the coast were in for a rude awakening to the reality of war when they reached Albacete. The ground floor of their billet, a former barracks, was stained with the blood of *Guardia Civil* members who had declared for Franco. Averting their eyes, British volunteers crowded into the upstairs rooms to sleep. Meanwhile in Britain, the bloody struggle in Spain had been knocked off the front pages of newspapers by the antics of King Edward VIII and Mrs Wallace Simpson. For the majority of the British public, the abdication crisis was an all-consuming distraction at a time when their attentions should have been focused on Franco's atrocities against the Spanish people.

For all the talk about democracy in Spain, the International Brigades were creatures of the Communist Party, operating in a command structure accountable to the Soviet Comintern. Marty, their senior representative in Spain, had the ear of Stalin himself, and enjoyed throwing his weight about. He reputedly ordered the execution of hundreds of men, and those who thought he shared the psychopathic tendencies of his Russian master, described him as '*Le Boucher d'Albacete*'. Marty sat at the apex of a system of 'political commissars', based on Soviet revolutionary army structures, reflecting the simple fact that, although non-Communists were welcomed into the brigades, they were strictly organised and controlled by Communists.

Whether or not Clem really expected a garage job when he got to Spain remains a mystery. Early in November British volunteers who had arrived at Albacete were moved to an overflow training base for English-speaking recruits, 20km away at Madrigueras. Although linked by rail to Albacete, Madrigueras was an isolated village, many of whose poor inhabitants made a living harvesting saffron in surrounding crocus fields. Its streets were unpaved, most of its simple houses clustered round a partly-cobbled square, with a fountain and water-trough. The whole village lay in the shadow of the church with its cement-stuccoed wall and crowned by an imposing, balconied bell-tower.

Clem, missing the camaraderie of fellow countrymen, kicked up a fuss, announcing that attachment to the autopark was not at all what he had in mind when he volunteered. In a letter written in late November, he declared: 'I came here to fight fascism,' and demanded transfer to a fighting unit. It was not the first, nor would it be the last, occasion on which Clem Beckett ruffled the feathers of those in authority. However, in the letters he wrote to his mother Clem maintained the fiction that he was not a member of a fighting unit, but rather part of the ambulance service. As if to reassure her of his eventual safe return, letters to Henrietta usually contained a plea for her to 'look after the dog'.

Perhaps the issue was referred back to Pollitt, who, with a soft spot for his fellow Lancastrian and alumnus of the Boilermakers Union, was able to point out that Clem's technical expertise went far beyond knowledge of the internal combustion engine. A grasp of the workings of anything mechanical would be qualities readily appreciated by a British command short on technical expertise. Indeed, Clem claimed that he had been sent as an unpaid expert on machinery, including aviation, not specifically to maintain motor vehicles, and that anyway there was no work for him at the Albacete motor depot.

However, in the same letter in which he asked for a move to a fighting unit, Clem also requested leave to return to Manchester for two weeks. Convinced that the British government would use its powers under the Foreign Enlistment Act to liquidate his business, he wanted time to pre-empt this by selling it, and making provision for his mother and Lida from the proceeds.[1] This was an issue which had not been raised at the time of Clem's departure from England, but had now surfaced, probably in letters reaching him from Lida. Clem's requests clearly gave rise to concern on the part of Marty, who, on 26 November, referred back to his Comintern masters in Moscow. In spite of the fact that the first fully equipped field ambulance sent out by the CPGB arrived at

Albacete on 12 December 1936, with five more on the way, Clem's transfer to Madrigueras was approved. But the request for leave was not – reasonably enough, in view of the desperate military situation in Madrid, and, perhaps, the unresolved issue of Clem's departure from the BWSF Soviet tour in 1932.

At any rate, when Clem eventually arrived at Madrigeuras in mid-December, as moves were afoot to form the British Battalion, it was in the company of two comrades: Tommy 'Jock' Flynn, an outspoken Glaswegian draftsman, and Joe Holland, an equally forthright steelworker. At Albacete they formed a noisy and noticeable trio, and notwithstanding different backgrounds, had already established a reputation as the 'Three Musketeers'. Clem and Flynn had first met on board ship as part of the BWSF delegation bound for Russia in 1932, for which Flynn had been selected as a member of the small cycling team. Even so, the refusal of leave continued to rankle with Clem. Always a plain speaker, he made his feelings known. His indiscretions reached the ear of the British command.

Clem was arrested, taken to Albacete, and detained for interrogation on suspicion of disaffection. According to comrades who spoke up for him, the arrest was made on the basis of 'an inaccurate report'. They testified to the effect that insofar as Clem had been critical of anything or anybody, it was of the 'too-casual approach to military proficiency'. Allowing for sanitised official records, the likelihood is that Clem got into trouble for general irreverence towards the political commissars and Party propaganda, as much as his disgruntlement about being refused leave. It was as natural for straight-talking Clem to criticise battalion command as it had been to ridicule the 'old fogeys' of the Auto-Cycle Union. For some men who had volunteered for fighting, there was a typically British aversion to lectures from commissars on Marxist philosophy, and Clem was among their number.

Clem's arrest could only have been by order of one or both of the two commissars for the British volunteers, Peter Kerrigan, and his deputy, Dave Springhall, both long-serving CPGB officials and confidantes of Harry Pollitt. Both were 'old school', staunchly pro-Moscow, and firm believers in Party discipline. It was even said of Kerrigan, only half-jokingly, that he regretted the absence of a handy gulag in England for the punishment of reprobate Party members. Clem's antics with the BWSF were sure to be on file; hardly a recommendation, and a reason to watch him carefully. But the arrest backfired. Clem's popularity was such that fellow brigaders protested so loudly that he was released and returned to Madrigueras, probably as much a result of Pollitt's intervention. Even so, the episode came as a shock to Clem, and although he accepted rejection of his application for leave, he remained understandably bitter. No doubt, also, it was intended to discourage similar applications in the uneasy, volatile atmosphere that prevailed at Madrigueras. Not all recruits were idealists. Some had answered the call to escape trouble at home, or gone off to Spain simply in a spirit of adventure. Grumbling about one thing or another was rife, and as with any army, there were those with a great liking for drink and shirking.

Writing to Pollitt soon after Clem's release, Kerrigan and Springhall sought to justify their action, anticipating 'more trouble with your friend Clem Beckett'. This was a prelude to a thorough-going character assassination, in which Clem was described as 'a dolt as honest as he is big, but confused and muddled as it is possible to be.' The report made clear the real reason for their concern: 'He (Clem) is setting himself up against the Party leadership and become the voice of all the rotten dissident elements.' It was ironic that about this time the *Daily Worker* carried a front page photograph of Clem, taken two months earlier in London, among a group of volunteer ambulance drivers. Kerrigan evidently still had hopes of directing Clem (who, although muscular, was in fact slightly below average height) towards political re-education of the kind encouraged in Soviet Russia. Clem's boon companion in Madrigueras, Joe Holland, an early arrival in Spain who had already seen action with a militia unit in Aragon, was eventually repatriated to England, 'needing further political education,' but 'with the highest possible credentials'. Within weeks, the CPGB resolved to ensure that Clem Beckett would also be accorded the highest possible credentials.

Prior to the formation of the British Battalion, men from the United Kingdom and Ireland were being attached to brigades and units made up of volunteers from other European nations. As a valued weapons instructor, however, Clem had to bear the disappointment of being left behind as friends and comrades went off to fight in the desperate battles to save Madrid. This was the time when, faced with imminent Nationalist occupation of the capital, and buoyed up by arrival of volunteers from abroad, *Madrilenos* summoned up the courage to hold up Franco's advance. The cry of '*!No Pasaran!*' (They shall not pass!), a phrase recycled from the French Army's resistance to the Germans at Verdun, echoed through working-class districts close to the fighting on the northern edge of the city, and appeared as graffiti all over Republican Spain. Meanwhile, according to the *Daily Worker's* Frank Pitcairn (*nom de plume* of Claud Cockburn), companies of British soldiers were marching to the front singing 'It's a Long Way to Tipperary'.

Clem's companion on the journey to Spain, Arnold Jeans, was one of eighteen Englishmen in the Thaelmann Battalion who fought at University City, close to the centre of the capital, in early November. He was among the ten who survived, alongside Esmond Romilly, a nephew of Winston Churchill. When, however, in mid-December, the battalion was ordered to defend the *pueblo* of Boadilla del Monte, 50km from Madrid, Jeans was once again in the thick of the fighting. Of the original English contingent, only Romilly and Bert Ovenden, a Communist from Stockport, survived. Asked why the English casualties were so high, a German officer replied: 'Because every one of them was a hero.' Writing soon after the battle, however, Romilly said: 'If there was one who deserved the appellation of hero it must have been Arnold Jeans.' In words presaging the fate of many later volunteers, Romilly added that Jeans's death had 'passed quite unnoticed in England'.

On Christmas Eve the first British No.1 Company, 145 strong, among them Maurice Levine, was entrained to fight with the XIV Brigade on the Córdoba front, At about the same time, Tommy Flynn was posted to the Dimitrov (Chapiaev) Battalion of the XIII International Brigade, composed mainly of East Europeans. By then, possibly because Flynn had disagreed with Clem applying for leave, and possibly because of his links with fellow-Glaswegian Kerrigan, he and Clem were no longer on speaking terms, and when Flynn left for the Madrid front, Clem refused to shake his hand. Hopefully, there was no such reticence shown towards Harry Heap, an Oldham CP member who reached Spain at about the same time as Maurice Levine. Heap, who had changed his name to Rawson, was the oldest of the town's ten volunteers for Spain, and as a result of service in the First World War (in which he was decorated for gallantry) became a Lewis gun instructor. He was killed in action at Lopera.

When, early in January 1937 No.1 Company returned to Madrigueras, only forty-five men remained, including Maurice Levine.[2] Clem was among the 500 or so British volunteers who met the survivors as they marched into the village under the command of Captain George Nathan. Memorably, Nathan gave the following order: 'Waiting to greet you will be many of your friends who have followed you to Spain. They will call out your names. Ignore them. You will march into the village like guardsmen. Each man will look at the neck of the man in front. No turning to the left or right. Show them you are battle-hardened soldiers.'[3] They were.

The order was carried out to the letter, with Nathan leading the men in. The survivors of Lopera brought back first-hand evidence of war's brutality. Moorish troops, with a feared reputation for knife work, regarded castration as a rite of battle. A Spanish comrade, struggling to evacuate British wounded, had matter-of-factly told a volunteer that rather than be captured he had saved two bullets – one for each them.

Chapter Twenty-three

Friends and Flunkers

'We pretended to shoot at things and we pretended to be evading the enemy. We learned one or two things about camouflage. And we played at soldiers.'
Manchester volunteer, Maurice Levine,
recalling his training at Madrigueras.

Of all the volunteers from every imaginable background who melded into the British Battalion of the International Brigade at Madrigueras, no two might have seemed to have less in common than Clem Beckett and Christopher St John Sprigg: Beckett, the working-class speedway star, educated at council schools, too poor to take up a grammar school scholarship, conditioned by trade union politics amid the fire and clangour of a blacksmith's shop; Sprigg, an emblematic representative of the English intelligentsia, a privately educated polymath and published author, who had used the name Caudwell (his mother's surname) as a *nom de plume.* Before his conversion to Marxism, Sprigg had acted as a volunteer strike-breaker in the General Strike. Comrades in training were immediately struck by the incongruity of conversations in which Beckett's blunt Lancashire accent contrasted with Sprigg's rounded southern vowels. So, too, were they of very different appearance: Clem, cigar-stub clenched in mouth, looking as if he'd just come out of a garage; Sprigg, a non-smoker, neat and tidy.

Yet Clem and Sprigg had more in common than met the eye. They were about the same age. Both, in boyhood, had suffered parental loss. Sprigg's mother had died when he was eight, while, as a boy of twelve, Clem had waited in vain for his father to return from the war. Neither man had led a sheltered existence: Clem's globe-trotting as a speedway rider compared to Sprigg's butterfly existence as a journalist and writer; both men had experienced failure in business. Clem's setbacks in

Sheffield and Marseille compared with Sprigg's bankruptcy in the early thirties, and both men might reasonably have blamed the vagaries of capitalism for their misfortune. Though in very different endeavours, both had demonstrated exceptional talent. Each, by the age of thirty, could boast spectacular achievements. Daredevil Beckett, a record-breaking sporting hero; Sprigg, excelling as journalist and author, whose works ranged from philosophical treatises to detective novels. Sprigg was also an expert on aviation, and like Clem, capable of flying a plane. Above all, and by whatever route, these two men went to Spain because they believed in the CPGB's credo that fascism in all its violent manifestations should be opposed by armed force.

Clem and Sprigg had first met in London, recruited by the CPGB for their knowledge of all things mechanical, but ostensibly to drive ambulances to Spain. Later, recollections of surviving volunteers suggest that whereas most men from the Manchester area formed close friendships with each other, Clem remained more aloof, partly because he was an Oldhamer, not a Mancunian, and partly, perhaps, because his diverse travels and exotic experiences in speedway meant he had more in common with Christopher Sprigg than he had with them.[1] So, too, did other middle-class volunteers such as Frank Graham, a classics master, and Noel Carritt, an Oxford academic, formed close friendships with Clem, in spite of his disdain for Party dogma.

Arriving at Madrigueras a few weeks later than Clem, Sprigg was elected second in command of his section, and both were billeted in the former home of the priest, one of the better properties in the impoverished village, distinguished by having its own well, and near to the church which acted as the battalion mess. Even so, none of the volunteers had the luxury of a bed; they slept on straw-filled palliasses. One volunteer was told that on the outbreak of war the priest had shot at villagers from the church tower, before being killed himself, and his body hung from a hook in the window of the butcher's shop. Such incidents as this, and at the bloodied barracks at Albacete would have left volunteers in no doubt about the bitterness of the conflict in which they were now participants.

The British Battalion, attached to the XV International Brigade, was under the command of Wilfred Macartney, a former British Army officer, who had made money from writing, and had served a term of imprisonment for spying for Russia. His adjutant was Tom Wintringham, still very much a confidante of Harry Pollitt.

Clem and Sprigg developed a remarkable rapport. They volunteered for extra guard duties so that they could be together. Quite apart from a mutual interest in aviation, Sprigg, the designer of an early automatic gearbox, and Clem, the architect and constructor of Road Louse, were never going to be stuck for conversation. Perhaps, too, the mutual fascination arose because neither had ever before made friends across the chasm of the English class system. In spite of membership of the Communist Party in the East End of London, Sprigg had struggled to throw off the image of the 'toff', while Clem, the daredevil, was rarely credited with qualities beyond those required to survive in the world of motorcycle sport. Knowledge of engines and all things mechanical brought them together, but in their friendship each of them was plugging a gap in his education, escaping from typecasting imposed at birth.

To Clem, the war in Spain evoked the world of couriers and coded messages, introduced to him by Woolley and Pollitt, offering a challenge which transcended the excitement of the dirt track. To Sprigg, life as a volunteer offered adventure, as well as the opportunity to complement eloquent theorising with action. Ostensibly, neither man had originally gone to Spain to fight (Sprigg, like Clem, had been sent by the CPGB to deliver an ambulance), but both men came to accept it as their destiny. In subsequent correspondence between Harry Pollitt and Sprigg's brother, Theo, there is a suggestion that Clem was influential in Sprigg's determination to stay on.[2] In any event, both men's beliefs were shared by the vast majority of volunteers who joined the International Brigades. And whether they were card-carrying Communists or not, all were obliged to accept Party discipline as a fact of life.

As weapons instructors, the manifest technical ability of Clem and Sprigg was vital. What few weapons arrived at Madrigueras came in all shapes and sizes, needing careful handling and demonstration. It was a big responsibility for two novice soldiers. They were good instructors, popular with their comrades, and the superior accommodation allocated to them reflected the importance attached to their skills by the battalion command.

A large room in the priest's house was used for weapons instruction and as a lecture theatre by Wintringham, who, in addition to weapons training, put on lessons in map-reading and compass work. Training also included route marches, rifle practice, and machine gun instruction. When Professor J.B.S. Haldane, an intellectual Party guru, arrived at the base to lecture on the use of the Mills bomb, a British Army hand grenade, Clem as his volunteer student seems to have resented the intrusion. With the pin removed, Clem held onto the grenade just long enough for beads of sweat to appear on Haldane's brow. Yet again, Daredevil Beckett got away with it, and the learned professor was relieved to move on to a more theoretical discourse on gas and chemical warfare.

Inevitably, the idealism which had brought most of the 600 men of the British Battalion to Madrigueras came under strain. Incessant rain upon the treeless plain of La Mancha surrounding the town did not help. Clem's dignity suffered a further blow when his volunteering for motorcycle duties met with a peremptory rejection. He was naturally unhappy about being turned down by 'some tester' – probably Springhall, himself a motorcyclist. What Clem, with his love of horses, did not know was that some consideration was being given to the establishment of a battalion unit, but horses, and even donkeys, were in short supply.

Older recruits at Madrigueras, with experience of the First World War, brought with them a typical soldierly determination to hang on to familiar values and to prick pomposity. In its wisdom, the Party named the battalion after Shapurji Saklatvala the first Communist to sit in the House of Commons. This was never going to catch on with the sort of men who had pronounced Ypres as 'Wipers' and Ploegsteert as 'Plug Street', and who had already begun rendering 'commissar' as 'comic star'. Nor did it go down well with the Irish, Scots and Welsh volunteers to find that the Spaniards, equally unable to pronounce Saklatvala, had settled for '*el Battalion Ingles*'.[3] In correspondence with Pollitt, Wintringham complained: 'About ten percent of the men are drunks and flunkers. I can't understand why you've sent out such useless material'.

Whereas individualists like Joe Holland and Clem Beckett chafed against authority, differences in political allegiance and background gave rise to more serious schisms. Irish volunteers resented taking orders from Englishmen as much as they resented the fact that the *Daily Worker* had described the heroic deeds of the British No.1 Company at Lopera, without mentioning their own considerable sacrifices. Matters were made worse when George Nathan, the dapper hero of Lopera, came under suspicion of having been a spy for the notorious Black and Tans, Crown forces whose ruthless conduct in Ireland had earned them particular loathing. Specifically, Nathan was accused by ex-IRA interrogators of personally carrying out doorstep assassinations, including that of the

Mayor of Limerick. His eloquent loyalty to the Republic's cause saved him from summary execution, but later the Irish, whose number included about thirty ex-IRA men, expressed their complaints volubly at a boozy Burns supper organised by Scottish volunteers.

Ironically, and not without a degree of poignancy, Sprigg had written a moving poem for the event, expressing anti-fascist comradeship between Scots and English, only to have the mood of amity overwhelmed by Irish dissension. Amid the ruckus, Sprigg could barely have made himself heard. In the end, pursuant to a controversial decision by Macartney, the rebellious Irish were allowed to leave to join the American Abraham Lincoln Battalion based at nearby Villaneuva de la Jara. However, a good many decided to stay, including Kit Conway, another hero of Lopera, and Frank Ryan, who were to play important roles in future actions with the British Battalion. Others, according to future commander of the battalion, Fred Copeman, soon returned to the British camp.

For Clem and Sprigg, together with the great majority of volunteers in training at Madrigueras, the episode was unwonted and worrying. Against the background of heavy casualties already suffered by both British and Irish contingents, with Franco's troops poised to encircle Madrid, and the battalion about to go into action, it should have been a time for unity. Even so, from a motley pool of men largely without military experience, Macartney and Wintringham had not done badly. It was not their fault that – thanks to the British and French governments' policy of non-intervention - their armoury included out-of-date rifles and machine guns, some of them of pre-First World War vintage, and no artillery. Ancient Austrian rifles were eventually replaced by more up-to-date ones received from Russia, but old soldiers immediately dismissed them as inferior to standard British Army Lee-Enfields. At least, however, Marty had obtained better uniforms for the men – apparently procured from French army stores.

There was, however, another crucial element present in the British Battalion of the XV International Brigade as it faced its baptism of fire in the defence of Madrid. Men of all the constituent nations of class-divided Britain, now sharing the same privations and living side by side far away from home, had developed a comradeship that overcame their differences. Academics such as Christopher St John Sprigg, Frank Graham, and Noel Carritt, as well as aristocrats such as Lewis Clive, a descendant of Clive of India, found themselves in the same team

172

as shipyard workers, mill-hands, unemployed miners, renegade ex-servicemen and mavericks such as Clem Beckett. In their idealism, and in their camaraderie and loyalty to each other, there was a purity of spirit worthy of King Henry's band of brothers at Agincourt.

Writing to Pollitt, Macartney told him: 'I've commanded the Battalion for nearly a month by kicking, yelling, nagging, swearing … but I've made something of them.' On the eve of the Battalion's first battle, in another report back to Pollitt, and pleading that all new recruits should be imbued with a hatred of fascism, Kerrigan echoed Wintringham's concerns about the commitment of volunteers: 'Tell them this is war, and many will be killed.'

Chapter Twenty-four

The Worst Machine Gun Ever

'While irresponsible politicians, financiers and civil servants showed no care for the safety of our Commonwealth of Nations, this gallant handful of men gave freely of their blood, and very many of their lives, in an effort to keep it safe.'
Said of British volunteers at the Battle of Jarama, by American journalist Henry Buckley.

As the hour of battle loomed, morale in the British Battalion could hardly have been helped by tensions at the top. Macartney, a non-Communist, had to endure a campaign of carping criticism from Kerrigan and others. Astonishingly, with the Nationalists at the gates of Madrid, arrangements were made for Macartney to take a period of leave in England, in order, so it was said, to fulfil parole conditions arising from his early release from prison. Meanwhile, Nathan, although popular with the majority of volunteers, was faced with an outbreak of antisemitism, and possibly one of homophobia. His assiduously cultivated upper-class accent might also have triggered resentment among working-class volunteers, especially the remaining Irish contingent. But most of the men, who, like Clem, knew that their fate would depend on leadership and discipline, were in fact impressed by Nathan's military bearing. Surrounded by improvisation and muddle, there was something reassuring about Nathan's affected air of authority, complemented by his immaculate British Army uniform, Sam Browne belt and swagger-stick.

On Saturday, 6 February 1937 Franco ordered a new attack to the south-east of Madrid. Key to his plans was the role of the Army of Africa, consisting of units of the Spanish Foreign Legion and Moroccan *regulares*, Moorish soldiers recruited from Spain's Moroccan colony. On the same day, at or after a 'farewell' dinner in Albacete, in what was claimed to be an accident, Macartney was shot in the arm by Kerrigan, thereby ensuring that he never returned to the battalion. In his place, Clem's fellow instructor, the loyal but irascible Party man Tom Wintringham was promoted from *Capitaine Adjoint-Majeur* to *Commandant de Bataillant.*

Andre Marty's insistence, wherever possible, on the use of his native language as Brigade *lingua franca* did not cut much ice with working-class lads like Clem or even middle-class recruits like Christopher Sprigg. Officers were a military necessity, but while the Comintern tried to conceal its absolute control of the International Brigades, its camouflage did not extend to abolishing revolutionary nomenclature. Beckett and Sprigg addressed each other *and* their commanding officer as 'comrade'. As between officers, commissars and soldiers, only saluting by clenched fist was permissible. But for many, there was little time left for saluting.

On the evening of Wednesday, 10 February the British Battalion began moving towards the front under cover of darkness. As they did so, readers of the *Daily Worker*, who, more than subscribers to any other British newspaper, were aware of the desperate situation in Spain, had their diet of desperation leavened by a preview of the coming dirt track season. 'Speedway Thrills Will Soon Be Here Again,' announced the sports editor, 'The boys will soon be dashing round the track again, to the roars of thousands of voices.' It was ironic that his style was indistinguishable from that of Sheffield's Gadfly half a decade earlier, stressing close contacts with the great and good of the sport such as Johnnie Hoskins. It was doubly ironic that the official organ of the CPGB was now celebrating the healthy state of a sport whose demise had been confidently predicted by Clem Beckett, its celebrity contributor, barely five years earlier.

In Madrigueras there was speech-making, and villagers with whom volunteers had been billeted turned out, some weeping, to wave them goodbye. Only as the battalion waited to clamber into lorries did the men realise that Wintringham was in command. Amid rumours about Macartney's shooting it was a shock to find that their fate was now the responsibility of 'a kind of instructor'. Others, such as Clem's Mancunian comrade, Maurice Levine, thought the appointment should have gone to Nathan, with his proven record of command in action. By this time word had got round amongst the men that Macartney had been wounded 'accidentally on purpose'. Volunteer Charles Bloom later reflected: 'Wintringham was not the type of commander we wanted. He was not a mixer. He was a bit of a snob.' Nor did Wintringham do much to inspire his nervous troops by bluntly informing them that one in ten of them were likely to be killed in the impending action.

The greater part of the battalion's journey northwards was in packed, open lorries. It was an uncomfortable, bumpy ride, much of it over pot-holed unmade surfaces. Most of the men had still not been issued with rifles. Some, the most recent arrivals, had not even held one. The battalion was ordered to take up position in the Sierra Pingarrón, low-lying hills which divided valleys formed by the rivers Manzanares and Tajuna. As part of the Republican Army's XV Division their task was to engage Nationalist forces in the Jarama valley, thereby blocking the way to Madrid and preventing them cutting road and rail links between the capital and Valencia (now home to the evacuated government of the Republic).

Whatever the problems of the International Brigades, the arrival of arms and ammunition from Russia, procured through underworld arms dealers so as to disguise Soviet involvement, had boosted civilian morale. Now the Republic had fighter planes and tanks every bit as good as those supplied to the Nationalists by Germany and Italy – even though it had cost the Republic the greater part of the country's gold reserves.[1] But they were in short supply, and as the volunteer soldiers of the British Battalion were about to discover, when it came to arms and munitions, their enemies always seemed to have more and better.

Likewise, by the time the British reached Chinchón, 220km from Albacete and 45km from Madrid, units of the Army of Africa had made dramatic progress. They had been advancing steadily since 5 February, with Moorish troops carrying out a series of audacious and stealthy attacks that caught Republican defenders napping. At Arganda and Pindoque sentries guarding key bridges were knifed, allowing Nationalist forces to pour across onto the eastern bank of the Manzanares river, and bringing the Madrid-Valenica road within shelling distance. Thus established, the bridgehead wrong-footed the Republican units, who had been preparing for an offensive. Next, an entire Nationalist brigade advanced with astonishing rapidity into the Tajuna valley to the south of a government defensive line along the Pingarrón Heights. In the north, near the confluence of the Jarama and Manzanares, another brigade had crossed the river, to capture the 697m peak, La Maranosa, in spite of the resistance of two Republican battalions who fought to the last man. Later in the day, at Chinchón, rifles were issued to the battalion, with time for firing practice.

In their billets at Chinchón, the men spent a tense night, struggling to sleep against the cold, with only boots for pillows, listening to the sound of distant gunfire. They were completely unaware that crack enemy troops had already stolen a march on them. One or two volunteers unable to sleep, and feeling the need of Dutch courage went out looking for wine. Not Clem, who 'seemed his usual self', cradling his Chauchat machine gun, occasionally smoking a cigar, and clenching the stub in his mouth long after it had gone out. Friday, 12 February dawned bright and beautiful, suggesting a warm winter's day and hinting of spring. Across the valley the men could see the Sierra Pingarrón, its lower slopes fleeced with olive groves, a pleasant contrast with dreary and rainy Madrigueras; as was Chinchón itself, nestling on the plain of Tajuna, below a medieval castle, its Plaza Mayor surrounded by picturesque galleried houses, and its avenues lined with cypress trees. Spirits rose.

At home, readers of the *Daily Worker* were waking up to an account by Frank Pitcairn, infused with inside knowledge of the critical situation now faced by the hard-pressed Republic, as well as propaganda. Pitcairn did his best to boost morale, and to stress the importance of Communist resistance. The paper's front page headline ran: 'Victory Will Be Ours – Spain Communists' Counter-Attack Call'. Alone among British newspaper readers that morning, *Daily Worker* subscribers got the facts about the seriousness of the situation, though its other front page story was an exercise in wishful thinking: 'Attack on Madrid Checked, Rebels Driven Back on Valencia Road'.

In contrast with the latest equipment supplied to the Nationalists, and in spite of more shipments from Russia, everyone knew that the battalions' weapons were either elderly or cumbersome. Moreover, most of the men were unfamiliar with the standard-issue Russian rifle. With fixed bayonet it seemed awkward to carry *a port* (with both hands) so many men would discard their bayonets at the first opportunity. With more time and better instruction they would have realised that because the entire weapon had been designed to be in balance when shouldered, it was more easily carried over a distance with bayonets fixed.

Clem and Sprigg, with their Chauchat machine gun and ammunition belts, had a different problem. With its tendency to jam, its vulnerability to heat, rain, and flying earth, it was notoriously unreliable. The 'Shosser' or 'Shossi' as it became known to British volunteers had been the standard French army machine rifle. Its shortcomings, which had been exposed in the First World War, were only too well known to the survivors of Lopera. It had an incurable tendency to jam, which meant that had to be crewed by two men instead of one; one to fire and the other to change the quadrant-shaped magazine at the first sign of jamming. In addition, the Shosser was prone to punch a man in the eye if improperly held, it had flimsy bipod legs which were so long that they exposed the shooter to enemy fire, and its poorly designed metal aiming sights tended to shoot low and off centre. No wonder that Tom Wintringham, like Clem and Sprigg, a weapons instructor, but now their commanding officer, believed the Chauchat to be 'the worst light machine gun ever devised'.

Once more the men of the British Battalion climbed into open lorries, this time with their weapons, travelling northwards, over the River Tajuna towards the road between the whitewashed pueblo of Morata de Tajuna, and the village of San Martín de la Vega, to the west, which had been stormed by the Nationalists at dawn on the previous day. A 15-km stretch of dirt road brought the battalion to a crossroads within sight of Morata, where, at about 5.30am, the column appears to have halted for an hour or so, as Wintringham confirmed his orders. At first he was optimistically informed that the British Battalion would be held in reserve.

Alas the Republican high command was barely able to keep pace with the speed of the Nationalist advance, and in spite of attempts to reorganise a defence line along the Pingarrón Heights, the XIV Andre Marty Battalion had already suffered catastrophic losses to the north, in and around Arganda. Together with Nationalist success at San Martín, this boded ill for the XV Brigade, including the British Battalion, which was now being directed to the central part of the front as the enemy pushed forward to threaten its flanks. Desperate to stem the tide, Wintringham's orders – from the commander of the XV Brigade, Colonel Gal – were to deploy his battalion in a defensive line along the Pingarrón Heights to block the main thrust of the Nationalist attack.

Accordingly, the convoy of lorries turned westwards onto the hilly road between Morata and San Martín, and then southwards onto a track which ran back towards Chinchón. By 7.00am the battalion had reached an imposing roadside farmhouse. Here the volunteers were provided with breakfast and given a rousing speech by political commissar George Aitken, a tough Scottish Communist, who reminded them that they were fighting not just for Spain, but 'for all the peoples of the world'. Yet even as these stirring words were being spoken the extent of Communist involvement in the defence of the Republic was causing alarm in Madrid. Largo Caballero, Socialist head of a coalition government, was attempting to have the International Brigades absorbed into the regular army.

Before the arrival of the British volunteers, the farmhouse could claim a poignant connection with the unfolding tragedy of the Spanish Civil War. Its tranquil situation and bodega had provided a summer retreat for one of Spain's most famous matadors, Ignacio Sánchez Mejías, whose death by goring had been immortalised by poet, Federico García Lorca. Himself an early victim of the war, Lorca had been murdered by Nationalist thugs in Granada. Soon, for obvious reasons, to be renamed 'the Cookhouse', the farm's history would have meant little to the men drinking coffee and anxiously scanning the hillside above them. It was from here that the men of the British Battalion began their climb up the gentle slopes of the Tajuna valley. At the same time, on the other side of the heights, *tabors* (Moorish infantry units) of the Army of Africa were already moving stealthily towards them, through the olive groves of the Jarama valley.

Chapter Twenty-five

Suicide Hill

'Death stalked the olive trees
Picking his men;
His leaden finger beckoned
Again and Again.'
Lines written by British volunteer, John Lepper,
recalling his experience at the
Battle of Jarama.

From the farmhouse the men began moving forward in the direction
of the fighting, carrying weapons and full packs, and wearing good
quality, heavy, ex-French army winter uniforms. They encountered a
steady climb, through olive groves at first, then along a treeless, dried-
up watercourse. Some men were to recall it as a 'ravine', but it was
more like a steep-sided gully, typical of the Pennine moors above Bill o'
Jack's, which Clem would have called a clough. The scent of wild thyme
hung in the air as the volunteers slogged uphill. Years later, survivors
would tell how sudden exposure to the pungency of thyme was enough
to trigger memories of the horrors that followed.

To limit the damage from enemy shells or aircraft, the men were
supposed to spread out in standard 'artillery formation'. Given the
several parallel gullies leading up from the road, each of the four
companies might have taken a different route to the ridge at the top,
about 4km from the farmhouse, so as to minimise the target presented
by their moving columns. However, none of the company commanders
had been issued with maps (so much for map-training at Madrigueras)
and it seems that to avoid getting lost the companies followed the same
track, simply spreading out as best they could. The overall impression
made on Fred Copeman, a future commander of the battalion, was not
encouraging. It seemed to him 'just a huge crowd. It looked like a bloody

summer's outing.' Infantryman Patrick Curry recalled the moment in similar terms: 'Off we marched like boy scouts,' adding that many of the men were given to understand the object of their mission was to defend the farm track alongside the Cookhouse, whereas their real purpose was to prevent facist forces cutting the main road between Madrid and Valencia, several kilometres to the north and east of their position.

For men like Copeman, who had served in the Royal Navy (when he had been a leader of the Invergordon Mutiny) there were other troubling factors affecting the fighting capacity of the battalion. The machine gun company was understrength, and so was No.1 Company, which lacked the battle-hardened survivors of Lopera (including Maurice Levine) who had been assigned to guard brigade headquarters, and was without its respected commander, Jock Cunningham, laid low by influenza. It did not help that the commanding officer, Colonel Gal (real name Janos Galicz), a naturalised Russian of Hungarian birth, was judged by many to be incompetent. In addition to the 650 men of the British Battalion, the brigade comprised 800 men from various Balkan countries in the Dimitrov Battalion, 800 men of the Franco-Belgian Battalion, and 550 Americans, including the dissident Irish who had rioted at the Burns supper.

As the rest of Clem's fifteen-man section struggled under the weight of their packs and unwieldy Russian rifles, he and Sprigg were left to haul their Chauchat machine gun and ammunition belts over the rough terrain. Halfway up the gully they were attacked by a single Italian fighter-bomber. Clem, who spotted its approach through binoculars, gave the order to take cover, and when it returned, he got off a round of machine gun fire aimed at the plane's belly. There were no casualties, and by 10.00am all four companies were intact when they emerged onto high ground, about 600m above sea level. In spite of being scored by steep dips and gentle undulations, this became known as 'the plateau'.

However, the climb had taken its toll in other ways. Troubled by the awkwardness of carrying their heavy rifles, volunteers had left a trail of dumped belongings. Naturally enough, weighty tomes on Marxist theory and poetry anthologies were the first to go as the climb stiffened and the sun rose. But further on men had abandoned greatcoats, blankets and spare clothes, and most incredibly of all, ammunition, machine gun spare parts and hand grenades. Some items were neatly piled, with a view to being collected later; others were discarded one by one. What could have provoked such recklessness beyond a mixture of chronic unfitness, wild-eyed optimism and rank indiscipline? Given that the majority of men had got into Spain by climbing the mighty Pyrenees, and that these hills were only slightly higher than the English Pennines, the effects on them of a relatively gentle climb, albeit with full packs, are even more surprising. What on earth were company commanders and section leaders thinking of not to have intervened? Given Clem's known aversion to slackness it is difficult to imagine him allowing such conduct from members of his own section.

Once on the plateau, Wintringham deployed two of his three infantry companies – No.3 Company, which included Clem's section, and No.4 Company – along a west-facing ridge, a hundred metres or so below the highest point of the plateau, overlooking the Jarama valley, supported by No.2 Machine Gun Company. To reach it they had to descend from the rim of the plateau, cutting across a rough farm track coming in from the road between Morata and San Martín de la Vega, which was to become known as the 'Sunken Road', and which afforded cover for Wintringham's headquarters. No.1 Company, commanded by Kit Conway, a veteran of Lopera, and one of the Irish volunteers who had not departed to the Americans, was held in reserve, out of sight of the enemy behind Wintringham's headquarters, much to Conway's chagrin.

The British (16th) Battalion of the XV Brigade of the 35th Division of the Army of the Spanish Republic was now poised to do battle with the Army of Africa. While the enemy was undeniably better trained, better armed and more experienced, the British nevertheless occupied an excellent position, with a clear line of fire on the hillside below, from where the attack was anticipated. The Franco-Belge Battalion, it was hoped, was in position further north along the heights, and would protect the British right flank.

However, almost before Clem and Sprigg had a chance to set up the Shosser, a squadron of German bombers appeared, flying low towards them. Once again, as the veterans of Lopera had learned to do, volunteers dropped to the ground, preparing to fire when the bombers passed overhead. But a moment later, to the satisfaction of the British, Republican fighter planes appeared, and after a short dog-fight the bombers were chased back across the valley. For the foot soldiers of the British Battalion, the aerial curtain-raiser was an encouraging, if surreal, beginning to the Battle of Jarama.[1] But there would soon follow a sequence of events in which almost everything else was to go tragically wrong.

It seemed obvious that the abortive Nationalist air raid was intended to soften up the battalion's defensive positions prior to imminent ground attack. But soon afterwards survivors remember the arrival of a 'messenger', probably a Russian engineers' officer, who had also been sent to lay a telephone link to brigade headquarters. Wintringham was told to advance there and then. Unsurprisingly, and no doubt miffed to receive orders in this off-hand way, Wintringham raised objections, probably wondering if Gal's orders had been mangled in translation. However, the orders were eventually confirmed personally to Wintringham by Captain George Nathan, now promoted to Gal's adjutant, who passed on the assurance that the advance would be supported by a Spanish cavalry unit on the left, and a reinforced Franco-Belge Battalion to the right. At about 11.00am, against his better judgement, and probably Nathan's as well, Wintringham was obliged to witness his three infantry companies moving precariously forward.

Why and how this happened remains a subject of bitter debate. At some point in the morning when brigade forces were massing in the area of Morata, Gal had told him, 'You will advance at once in this direction,' pointing his finger at a blue pencil line on a map. If this was the entirety of the orders received by Wintringham at that time it did not pre-empt his discretion as a battalion commander as to *how* the advance should proceed. It was obviously not Gal's intention to put the British Battalion into a position that would risk its survival, but that was the inevitable consequence of his later order. The die was cast. Oddly, Wintringham's biographer insists that some of his men disobeyed orders in proceeding beyond the ridge, and indeed Wintringham's report following the battle appears to confirm this. Even so, it would have been a big ask for a newly appointed battalion commanding officer to disobey superior orders. There was Marty as well as Gal to answer to. Moreover, when Major De La Salle (sometimes referred to by volunteers as Lasalles) of the Marseillaise Battalion had been court-martialled and subsequently shot for his failings at Lopera, Nathan had been the chief witness. Later, Wintringham admitted there had been a 'communications blunder'.

An alternative explanation, which partly reconciles Wintringham's account with that of the men in the infantry companies, is that the messenger reached their forward positions *directly*, by-passing Wintringham's HQ either mistakenly or deliberately, following Gal's orders. There was a gap of more than 700m between the British positions and the Franco-Belge Battalion. If the messenger had come through the gap from the direction of the Morata-San Martín road, which is likely, he could have reached No.1 Company without being intercepted by battalion headquarters. In a report written in hospital a week later, Wintringham suggested that it was 'impossible' for him 'to hold back' No.4 Company because its four Colt light machine guns would be needed to support No.1 Company and No.3 Company, both of which had advanced as a result of 'interference' from the unidentified brigade officer.

In any event, all three infantry companies, including Kit Conway's, moved out of their positions on the lower ridge. They scrambled downhill for about 200m until they were almost on the floor of the valley, and still going forward, they climbed up to a further ridge along the line of a cluster of outlying hills below the heights. Although these smaller hills, beyond the plateau, were to be given individual names by the volunteers, taken as a whole they became known as 'Suicide Hill'.

The British position was now dangerously close to the Moors' forward *tabors,* offering little cover. Even so, the men charged forward beyond this line, down into the valley. At a stroke, the British Battalion had thrown away its biggest advantage in what was already an unequal struggle. At this point, where it was most exposed, the battalion encountered fire from enemy troops. Men later recalled that what they at first took to be birdsong was in fact the sound of bullets whistling over their heads. The support promised by Gal was nowhere in sight, and Wintringham had later to admit that the 400 men in his three infantry companies had been put in 'an untenable position'.

Almost by instinct, most of the men in all three companies retreated back to the higher ground and turned to fight along the ridge behind them – Suicide Hill. A small number went further forward seeking the cover of two small mounds of earth on the valley floor. Kit Conway's company took up positions on the right flank on what came to be known as Conical Hill. No.4 Company, commanded by Lieutenant Bert Overton, an ex-regimental sergeant major in the British Army, occupied the saddle between Conical Hill and the slopes leading up to the ruins of a conspicuous white farmhouse with a red roof, soon to be dubbed 'Casa Blanca'. No.3 Company turned to face the enemy on the other side of Casa Blanca. All three positions immediately came under devastating fire from artillery and machine guns. Clem and Sprigg dug in their Shosser and made ready to hold the line.

Immediately, the superiority of Nationalist armament, by way of artillery and heavy machine guns supplied by the Germans, became apparent. Shells began to land all around. On top of Conical Hill Conway's company, most exposed of all, was an easy target. Men trying to get below the skyline had nothing but thin grass for cover. There was no entrenching equipment other than the precious few bayonets that had not been chucked away. By midday the Franco-Belge Battalion to the north was in retreat. Moroccan troops appeared on the knoll to the right of Conical Hill. Nationalist planes strafed the British positions only to be chased away by Republican fighters. The men in Conway's company offered up a weak cheer, realising that their position remained untenable. Conway ordered his men back, but not before standing up and encouraging them to do likewise, to show they were 'not afraid of fascist bastards'. Moments later, he and his company commissar were mortally wounded. Volunteers who followed Conway's example were mown down.

What was left of No.1 Company pulled back to the saddle. By that time No.4 Company was being blown to pieces by shelling. As Overton lay weeping for lost comrades, survivors of his and the other two companies began to scramble back along the ridge, intending to take cover behind the white house, seemingly oblivious to the fact that it was serving as a range-finder for Nationalist artillery. The battalion's position was truly undefendable, but for desperate men Casa Blanca was the only alternative to being picked off by enemy fire as they lay on the skyline. Piled up bodies were being used as gun emplacements. Bill Briskey, commanding No.3 Company, managed to get a message to battalion headquarters: 'I have part of nos 4, 1 and 3 coys left … we are holding out well.' By the time Wintringham received the message Briskey was dead.

As the artillery barrage intensified on and around Casa Blanca, No.3 Company lost Briskey's replacement, Ken Stalker. Three battalions of Moors prepared to storm the ridge. Among the remnants of all three companies still resisting, Clem and Sprigg continued to fire the Shosser. As volunteer Frank Graham, a member of No. 3 Company, put it with generous understatement, 'We were in a very bad position indeed.' To compound the situation, most of what was happening was out of sight of battalion headquarters, so that Wintringham had little idea of the extent of casualties. He was also deceived by the fact that so few of the wounded were being evacuated, and that from what could be seen from his headquarters men were moving about, apparently 'casually', giving the false impression that the infantry companies were holding their own. Nothing could have been further from the truth. Within an hour, about half the battalion had been killed or wounded.

When the artillery barrage ended, the Nationalist infantry began advancing towards what was left of the British positions. By this time the line of retreat, uphill towards the Sunken Road, was being swept by enemy machine-gun fire, adding to the dangers faced by runners reporting to Wintringham. In spite of Gal's earlier insistence that the British should 'hold on at all costs', Wintringham at last issued the order to retire. But even then it had to be coaxed out of him by a runner sent back up from the front line. Still unaware of the extent of the slaughter, Wintringham allowed that the men should retire *if* outflanked or *if* they suffered heavy casualties (which they already had). Realising Wintringham had not grasped the seriousness of the situation, the runner had the presence of mind to seek clarification: 'Sorry, but this won't do. If you leave it to them – these *ifs* – they'll just stay there – and it's rare bad.' Only then was a definite order to retire given. The runner's insistence undoubtedly saved many lives.

On inspection of the ground today, it is easy to say, with hindsight, that battalion headquarters should have been better positioned, perhaps behind the ridge below the Sunken Road, nearer to the fighting, but still out of sight of the enemy. But on the day Wintringham was a dealt a very bad hand, which went well beyond 'the fog of war' faced by every soldier in battle. His dispositions, not to say his authority within the battalion, were fatally undermined by Gal's interference, leading to the stampede of infantrymen onto the valley floor. Likewise, the absence of detailed maps meant that the significance of a rippling series of ridges on the edge of the heights, which obstructed views towards Casa Blanca and Conical Hill, could not be anticipated.

If there was any hope left of defending Suicide Hill, or of providing covering fire for an orderly retreat, it would have to come from No.2 (Machine Gun) Company, under the command of Harold Fry, in position on the lower ridge. However, although they had the correct belts, Fry's company had discovered they had been supplied with ammunition for German Maxims which would not load into their older Soviet-version heavy machine guns.[2] The mistake was not discovered until the gunners were in position on the heights of Pingarrón, with the infantry companies already committed to attack. It was a tragic irony that the men were well trained in the use of these twelve heavy guns, and that in contrast to the Shossers they were regarded as reliable and easy to fire. In his written report, Wintringham claimed that he had delayed ordering the retreat from Suicide Hill because he was unable to provide covering machine-gun fire.[3] As if matters could not get worse, the driver bringing the correct ammunition up from Morata crashed his lorry, only to be found sitting by the roadside 'completely drunk'. As the situation deteriorated, Oldham volunteer Albert Charlesworth (like Clem, a nominal Yorkshireman born in Saddleworth), attached to No.4 Company, was wounded in the arm.[4]

The Moors, experienced and expert at moving quickly over open ground, came in for the kill. As they stormed over the knoll towards Casa Blanca, the survivors, also coming under attack from their left, attempted to retire 250m or so through the olive groves and back onto the plateau, dragging wounded comrades with them. As they did so, and with no help forthcoming from the useless Maxims, covering fire was provided by Clem and Sprigg, still at their Shosser and well dug-in. Clem scanned the olive groves with his binoculars, trying to spot the Moors as soon as they emerged from cover.

Reaching the relative safety of the Sunken Road, Frank Graham turned to see what had happened to the men behind. He recalled that after about half the retreating volunteers had 'got through', with Clem and Sprigg still manning the Shosser, it jammed. Fred Copeman, on the heavy machine guns above, and about the same distance away, gave a slightly different account. He reckoned that in the heat of battle Clem and Sprigg had forgotten to disable the Shosser before they had got away. Realising their omission, they ran back towards the gun to be met by a hail of fire and a volley of hand grenades. It was Clem's last dare. Both accounts agree that he and Sprigg were together, inseparable to the end, the last men in action on Suicide Hill.

Chapter Twenty-six

From Dolt to Hero

*'We can go on about the mistakes, and can regret them
when we look back. But then there's the selfless heroism
shown by those you and I knew, and ... above all the
absolute correctness of the Brigade and all it stood for.'*
Scottish volunteer John Lochore, writing to his
one-time comrade Maurice Levine in 1975.

Had Clem and Sprigg made it back to the plateau they would have lived
to fight another day. One of the last men to reach the shelter of the ridge
was gritty Mancunian Sam Wild, nursing four bullet wounds. Wild, a
future battalion commander, organised covering fire for the retreat and
helped get the walking wounded back up the hill. With the Moors in hot
pursuit, the battalion's luck changed. Fred Copeman, who had managed
to locate the crashed truck, arrived at the Maxim guns with a quantity of
the right ammunition. It was loaded into the belts by hand just in time.
As Clem and Sprigg lay dead or dying, the Moors swept across their
positions. Thinking the Republican defence had broken, they charged
over the outer ridge, towards the plateau. Now it was their turn to be
slaughtered. Copeman made sure the gunners held fire until the right
moment by laying out the Irish gunner who threatened to loose off
prematurely. The Moors suffered hundreds of casualties and eventually
withdrew.

The Battle of Suicide Hill was over, but the Battle of Jarama was to
go on for another two days. Many wounded were left behind, and during
the night their pitiful cries could be heard by survivors. One or two men,
tortured and mutilated by the Moors, were deliberately despatched by
their captors to crawl back to the British lines where they fell, helpless,
into the Sunken Road. Horrified comrades ended their suffering with
a bullet to the head. The series of disasters continued into the second

day. Early in the morning Fry's machine gun company was captured. Dressed in uniforms of Republican dead, and singing the *Internationale,* the Moors knocked out the strongest point of the British line, with the majority of the company being taken prisoner. Gal again issued a suicidal order for the British Battalion to advance, but this time Wintringham had the courage to ignore the order. He was wounded in the thigh as he was about to lead a diversionary bayonet charge.

A tank appeared in the Sunken Road. The British lines broke, with hundreds of men fleeing back down the heights. Some hid in the wine vaults at the Cookhouse while others got as far as Morata. And then the following day, when all seemed lost, there was a miraculous rally. Fred Copeman's threat to throw a hand grenade into the wine vaults brought out frightened men. Gal himself appealed to them, heart to heart, saying they were all that was left to stop the Nationalists cutting the Valencia road. In fact, Republican reinforcements were already arriving at the front, notably Lister's crack Fifth Regiment, on the left of the fragile British positions. Even so, the remnants of the British Battalion, led by Irishman Frank Ryan, marched back to the front, along the Sunken Road. Picking up stragglers on the way, and lustily singing the *Internationale*, they gave the impression, so the legend goes, of being a much greater force. The Nationalists halted. Madrid was saved, and the front stabilised. The *Daily Worker*'s wishful thinking had come true. Its optimistic anticipation of events three days earlier had been justified – but at a terrible price.

Makeshift memorials made of stones were built at Jarama, and the bodies of twenty-nine men of the British Battalion recovered from the battlefield were buried with due ceremony. But for the majority of the dead, whose bodies had to be left on Suicide Hill, there was no such formality. With the digging of trenches and the erection of barbed wire the front remained static until the end of the war, leaving the majority of British dead on enemy territory, to the west of and below the Pingarrón Heights. It was too dangerous to recover their bodies.

Of the 650 members of the British Battalion who fought at Jarama, only eighty survived unscathed. Of the 250 said to have been killed on 12 February, the majority were 'missing in action'. Some time later the Nationalists paraded the surviving members of Fry's machine gun company on the back of a lorry to give the false impression that prisoners were treated humanely. The real reason for their being spared, however, was to exchange them for Italian prisoners held by the Republic. Only at this point could it be said with reasonable certainty that those still unaccounted for were dead. Even so, confusion as to casualties at Jarama continued. The remnants of the British Battalion remained on the Jarama front for another four months, manning the line in dug-outs. For the rest of February they were cold and wet, then as spring advanced they were burned by the sun.

It fell to the Communist Party of Great Britain to be the bearers of bad news. Families of the dead were informed as soon as possible, but it was mid-April before Clem's death was confirmed to his family, and in other cases it was July before deaths were confirmed. As General Secretary of the CPGB, responsible for recruitment of volunteers for Spain, Pollitt had his work cut out. Political commissars had the task of supplying Pollitt with reports, particularly as evidence of death, which would assist dependants. Battalion officers appealed desperately to Pollitt to supply them with a bank of death certificates that would assist relatives to obtain grants of probate. There was doubt about what had happened to prisoners, and because men had arrived on the eve of battle there was uncertainty over the full complement of the battalion. Even Wintringham was at first reported killed. It was known that some volunteers had panicked, and that some were taken alive by the Moors, but these facts were, reasonably enough, withheld from relatives.

To this day, somewhere beneath the thin soil of the Jarama valley, amid the wild thyme and olive trees, lie the remains of Clem Beckett. There could be no place of pilgrimage for his grieving family, no grave upon which to lay flowers. They had but one consolation: that Clem's remains lay close to those of his friend Christopher St John Sprigg. Brave comrades in life and death, innocents abroad, and 'Unlikely Warriors' both.[1]

The Communist Party of Great Britain was rocked by the disaster at Jarama. Such heavy casualties, especially among the ranks of the Young Communists League, made the Party vulnerable to criticism, especially among relatives of volunteers. Some newspapers, notably the *Daily Mail,* insisted that recruits had been misled. In response, the Party undertook a campaign to salvage its reputation, portraying those killed in action as martyrs to the cause of democracy. In this they were helped by the humanitarian crisis soon to be created by the Nationalists in northern Spain. The bombing of Guernica and the plight of Basque children prompted a generous response in England to the cause of Spanish aid.

For Pollitt, a man of conscience, the rising casualty list was a bitter pill to swallow. But he did his best for families who needed both financial and emotional support.

The news reached Lida when she was in Denmark for the wedding of her sister. Notwithstanding that Clem's death occurred on the battlefield in a foreign land, and that there was no body, an inquest was held in England. The record of the coroner's perfunctory enquiries perfectly reflects official indifference. Name of deceased: Clement Henry Beckett. Place of death Harama (sic) Bridge. Near enough. That would do.[2]

On Sunday, 2 May 1937 the Party put on a commemorative event. The venue, significantly, was not in Clem's native Oldham but in Manchester, at the Coliseum Theatre, Ardwick Green. Proceeds were in aid of the Manchester Dependants Aid Committee, a charity established by the CPGB, but, in line with the Party's Popular Front tactics, partly administered and fronted by Labour Party councillors and officials. With politicians on the platform were actress Dame Sybil Thorndike, who presented a 'golden helmet' once won by Clem to Lida, and Miss Marjory Lees, daughter of a veteran women's suffragist from Oldham.

History does not record if the event was attended by Clem's friends from speedway days, but eulogies in a booklet produced shortly afterwards by the CPGB included an effusive tribute from none other than Eric Oswald Spence: Clem, he said, was 'the most dramatic figure of the tracks,' adding, 'He rode as no one else had ever done.' In the potted biography written by William Rust, Clem Beckett, 'Hero and Sportsman,' was praised for his loyalty to the Communist Party, his 'indomitable courage and love of principle,' and his desire to reform 'the rottenness of capitalism'. Barely three months before, commissars in Albacete had taken a different view, but this was no time to recall official reports of Clem being 'confused and muddled'. And certainly no one was going to mention his alleged role as leader of 'all the rotten dissident elements' opposed to the Party leadership there. Among the speakers at that May Day memorial event was Madrigueras Commissar Dave Springhall.

Lida Beckett was invited to add her own tribute to the booklet. It began with a reference to the atrocity at Guernica, a Basque village bombed by Hitler's Condor Legion only four days before the memorial service for Clem, which, through Picasso's famous painting, would soon become a symbolic denunciation of fascism. Clem had died 'defending his ideals'. Contrary to misinformation in the *Daily Mail*, volunteers in Spain were not mercenaries and adventurers, but defenders of democracy. Nor was the tribute devoid of tenderness. Lida described her shock on receiving the news: 'I could not understand it [...] it seemed too monstrous, even ridiculous, that a life such as Clem had before him could be broken long before its time.' And yet, for all she had to say of Clem as a dedicated Communist, she said little about him as a husband. It was a one-dimensional image, beloved by the British Workers' Sports Federation, and carefully sub-edited by the Communist Party's foremost wordsmith. Those who knew the real Clem – his family and friends in Oldham, his maverick speedway colleagues – might have been hard put to recognise him.

The absence of references to Clem's friends and family in Oldham indicated a rift between them and the CPGB. Indeed, many other grief-stricken families of volunteers blamed the Party for their loss. In the popular press the role of the International Brigades was being characterised as 'meddling', with great swathes of even left-wing opinion still opposed to war – any war – in principle.[3] The *Doncaster Free Press* of 22 July 1937 scathingly lectured the widow of local volunteer Herbert Tagg, 'said to have been a keen Communist,' pronouncing, 'It is not for us to say that poor Tagg was mistaken in his ideals, but we are at liberty to express the opinion that Englishmen should keep out of other people's quarrels,' especially, Mrs Tagg was heartlessly reminded, when it meant the 'loss of the breadwinner' for a wife and three children.

Whether or not Lida was a beneficiary of the collections raised for the Manchester Dependants' Aid Committee is unclear. On leaving for Spain, Clem had been particularly concerned about his mother's welfare, but he had not made a will. So when, on 13 July, Letters of Administration were granted to Lida by the Probate Division of the High Court, she alone inherited Clem's estate. Valued at £390 (approximately £25,000 in today's money) it was a tidy sum. Family friends subsequently said that Henrietta got nothing. Moreover, it was not long before Lida moved on. She married a Dr Hem Anand, brother of well-known novelist, Mulk Raj Anand, and emigrated to India with him.

Left-wing opinion was gradually shifting towards supporting intervention on the side of the Republic, and in the summer of 1937 it was by no means certain that it would lose the war. Memorial meetings such as that held for Clem and his fallen comrades at Jarama were greatly instrumental in popularising the Republican cause. Huge sums of money were raised for medical aid to Spain, and for sending food there, especially at first to the Basque country. The Labour Party, having deposed Lansbury and under the leadership of future Prime Minister Clem Attlee, reversed its policy on Spain and pressed the British government to intervene. Later, the British Battalion formed a 'Major Attlee Company' in an attempt to attract wider support in Britain.

Among the Republic's tireless supporters was the Unionist MP Katherine Stewart-Murray, Duchess of Atholl, and student Edward Heath, a future Conservative prime minister. As a seventeen-year old boy, Alfred Sherman, one day to become personal adviser to Margaret Thatcher, joined the British Battalion to became a machine-gunner in the Major Attlee Company. Even Winston Churchill became alarmed about the consequences of a Nationalist victory, and by October 1938 public opinion polls showed widespread support for the Republican government among Conservative voters. Above all, working people right across Britain, and especially in the north of England, continued raising money to relieve the suffering of the Spanish people.

Commemorations such as that held for Clem encouraged more men to volunteer. The secretary of the Oldham branch of the CPGB wrote to the British Workers' Sports Federation expressing the hope that Clem's death would inspire 'thousands' of men to fight for freedom in Spain. The British Battalion of the XV International Brigade fought bravely in battles at Brunete, Belchite, and Teruel, and finally, in 1938, in the last Republican offensive in Catalonia. Joe Lees, to whose sister Clem had once paid court, was killed at Brunete. Lees' family partly attributed his volunteering for Spain to the personal example set by Clem. Kenneth Bradbury, secretary of Oldham Young Communist League, died at Teruel. Clifford Wolstencroft was killed in action at Belchite. William Jackson, also a YCL member, died at Gandesa. On 22 September, as the British Battalion prepared to go into action for the last time, its former commander and hero of Jarama, Fred Copeman, addressed a memorial meeting at Oldham's Central Hall, Renshaw Street, intended to raise money for dependants. Of the ten Oldhamers who fought in Spain, only four – Albert Charlesworth, Charles Armitage, Charles Hanson, and Joseph Buckley – survived.

Memorial meetings such as those at Ardwick Green and Oldham were held all over the country, often addressed by volunteers on leave or recovering from wounds, and contrary to the view of some respected historians, they moved thousands more men and women of all classes to contribute to the Spanish cause.[4] Indeed, the campaign to support the beleaguered Republic became the most widespread mass movement in Britain since the days of Chartism. Huge sums of money, estimated at £2 million or more (with a present-day value of around £140 million) were raised to relieve the suffering of Spanish civilians and Republican fighters. Two hundred medical personnel and scores of ambulances were sent out. Towns and cities all over Britain raised money for hospitals and mobile dressing stations as well as canteens for refugees. Scores of British women served in Spain. Returning from leave, after being injured in an air raid, Madge Addy, a Manchester nurse, took back a Bedford truck loaded with medical supplies on board a ship running Franco's blockade of Valencia. Twenty-nine food-ships filled by donations from British workers reached Spain. More than a thousand committees were established nationwide, and millions of people attended fund-raising events, giving money, food and clothes. Lorries sent from Britain were used to evacuate children from Madrid, and to bring 4,000 Basque children to safety. Even after the International Brigades had been withdrawn, and when the defeat of the Republic had become inevitable, money was still being raised to help the Spanish people.[5]

Sacrifices made by British men and women who resisted fascism in Spain have seldom been acknowledged and often belittled. But in their selfless toil and bravery, and in the face of indifference shown by the majority of their countrymen, they were participants in an heroic struggle against evil.

Chapter Twenty-seven

The Department of Lost Causes

'They were fighting for us all, against the combined force
of European fascism. They deserved our
thanks and respect and got neither.'
American journalist Martha Gelhorn,
on the International Brigades.

'What a waste!' was the reaction of Captain W.E. Johns, author of the *Biggles* adventure stories, when he heard of the death of his friend Christopher St John Sprigg. His reaction echoed the feelings of many who knew Clem Beckett – his mother, Henrietta, his sisters, Mary and Hilda, his life-long friends in Oldham, and his fellow speedway riders.

Of the 2,500 or so British volunteers who fought in Spain, more than 500 died there. At least twice that number were wounded. As every last yard of Spanish soil fell under Franco's heel, the great dictator lost no time in ensuring the destruction and desecration of his enemy's graves and memorials. Bodies in cemeteries were disinterred. Scattered remains were reburied en masse in unmarked pits. In 1994 former commander of the British Battalion Bill Alexander gave the figure of 529 for the number of bodies of British and Irish volunteers lying in unknown graves in Spanish soil.

In Britain, the government and the popular press paid little heed to these outrages. While British volunteers in Spain were still dying in the Ebro offensive, Prime Minister Neville Chamberlain waved 'a little piece of paper' in the air bearing Hitler's signature and claimed to have achieved 'peace in our time'. But others, taking the lesson of Spain to heart, now knew that fascism could only be stopped by force. Re-armament was accelerated. In Oldham and in every other industrial town, air raid shelters were built; gas masks were issued. War was coming.

CLEM BECKETT: MOTORCYCLE LEGEND AND WAR HERO

The International Brigades were withdrawn from Spain in October 1938. Commanding the British Battalion at the end was Manchester man Sam Wild, and among the 350 or so men repatriated to England via a train journey through France was non-combatant Ernest Woolley. Mysterious as ever, Woolley had been attached to Battalion headquarters at Ripoll near Barcelona sending despatches to the *Daily Worker*. Addressing departing Brigaders, Spanish Communist Party leader Dolores Ibarruri, known as 'La Pasionaria', paid a tribute which has echoed to their memory ever since. 'Comrades of the International Brigades: Political reasons, reasons of state, the welfare of that very cause for which you offered your blood with boundless generosity, are sending you back, some to your own countries and others to forced exile. You can go proudly. You are history. You are legend.'

Did Henrietta Beckett ever read those words, and if she did, was she consoled by them? Would she, or even the departing brigaders, have understood what was meant by 'reasons of state'? In truth they amounted to a last forlorn appeal to western democracies to stand up to the evil of fascism. Yet everywhere, except among those who had taken part in the Spanish struggle, the appeal fell on deaf ears. At Christmas-time 1938, to publicise fund-raising for a Manchester food ship, repatriated brigaders Albert Charlesworth, Charles Hanson and Joe Buckley attended at the offices of the *Oldham Chronicle*. The paper's response was a patronising 'diary' piece, commenting on the men's return from 'sunny Spain' with 'healthy tans', and expressing doubts about their politics and 'the efficacy of meeting violence with violence'. There was no mention of the men's fallen comrades from Oldham: Kenneth Bradbury, Harry Heap, Clifford Wolstencroft, Joe Lees, William Jackson – and Clem Beckett. Photographed side by side, obviously sensing their interviewer's insincerity, Charlesworth, Hanson and Buckley look grim as death. How utterly betrayed they must have felt when they read the paper.

Six months later Franco achieved final victory. Though it meant little to ordinary people, the Communist Party of Great Britain had been right about Hitler all along. But when, on the eve of the Second World War, Stalin made a non-aggression pact with Hitler, British Communists gasped with incredulity. Pollitt resigned or was fired as general secretary. Other prominent leaders such as Wintringham had already broken with the Party. The official line was that workers had no interest in a 'capitalist war' with Germany. For many who had fought in Spain the

Party's *volte face* was incomprehensible. Many Communists resigned their Party membership, including ex-brigaders who volunteered for military service without waiting to be conscripted. Yet, then as now, Communists were entitled to point out that after the battle of Jarama it was another five years before the march of fascism on the Continent was successfully confronted again – at Stalingrad, by the Red Army.

A terrible repression, described as 'the Spanish Holocaust', followed Franco's victory. As Europe fought to free itself from Nazi domination, Franco was given a free hand.[1] For decades he presided over an appalling regime of mass executions, torture and abuse of human rights. More than 100,000 Spaniards were systematically murdered, dispatched to mass graves, either by Nationalist soldiers or functionaries of the Franco State. Republican graves and memorials were destroyed with a vengeance. Prisoners slaved over the construction of a vast war memorial, at the centre of which they prepared a marble tomb for Franco. With the onset of the Cold War, Franco secured his position in the new order by allowing American air bases on Spanish soil. The backward Spanish economy was revived by the arrival of sun-seeking holidaymakers from northern Europe, and after Franco's death in 1975 a precarious democracy emerged.

At reunions of surviving brigaders in the 1970s thankful reacquaintance was mixed with disagreement. When Clem's comrade in No.3 Company, John Lochore, brought up the infamous Burns supper in Madrigueras, Peter Kerrigan told him that it never happened. Later disputes between surviving brigaders centred on whether or not 'warts and all' accounts should be encouraged. Bill Alexander, who wrote the 'official' history of the British Battalion in Spain, was against raking up controversy or misdeeds. In the 1940s the Battalion War Diary mysteriously disappeared.

Percy Platt, who had maintained his contacts in northern Europe, even after Britain declared war on Germany, was unlucky – or foolish – enough to be in Denmark in April 1940 when the Germans invaded, and was interned for the duration of the war. Albert Charlesworth, wounded at Jarama, joined the RAF as a pilot, where his fellow airmen nicknamed him 'The Red Baron'.

A short distance away from Oldham's parish church, a statue of Annie Kenney dominates the pedestrian precinct. It proclaims pride in Oldham's most militant suffragist, with Ms Kenney's back turned to the porticoed facade of the old town hall and the faded blue plaque commemorating Winston Churchill's first election to Parliament. On 12 August 1985 Councillor Richard Postle, Conservative leader of Oldham council, opposed plans to commemorate the town's 'left wing' volunteer warriors in Spain. Describing them as relics of 'the department of lost causes', he echoed the sentiment of the British government fifty years earlier, as it sought to camouflage non-intervention. But he was overruled, and a plaque commemorating the Oldham men who died fighting for the Spanish Republic now hangs in the parish church. Yet few of the thousands of Oldham holidaymakers who have followed in the footsteps of Mr and Mrs Fort to Spain have any notion of the horrors that accompanied Franco's reign of terror, or of the fact that the bones of six brave Oldham men lie there still in unmarked graves.

In spite of the fact that monuments erected to Republicans and brigaders in Spain are regularly defaced by neo-fascists, a campaign to recover the 'lost historical memory' of Franco's victims is gaining ground. Spain is facing investigation for crimes against humanity. For as many of those who would let the anonymous dead lie undisturbed, there are those who would restore their memory by finding, exhuming, and reburying their remains. The *Generalitat* of Catalonia has built a memorial on the Ebro battlefield, and put aside land for burials when bodies are recovered. Gradually, the rest of Spain is following suit. The body of Generalissimo Franco himself has been disinterred, to be reburied discretely in a family grave. By matching descendants' DNA with that found in newly discovered graves, bodies have been identified and reinterred with due ceremony. Not all the 'disappeared' will be found. But, with access to long-forgotten and once secret archives, combined with modern methods of archaeology, many will be – perhaps even those of Daredevil Clem Beckett and Christopher St John Sprigg, who dared fight fascism on Suicide Hill.[2]

As for speedway, Clem's pessimism about its future was further confounded after the Second World War. A population starved by austerity of spectacle and thrills flocked to reopened stadiums as the sport enjoyed a post-war boom, echoing the glory days of the late 1920s. With the dawning of the television age, there was a contraction in the sport, but then – just as had happened in the late 1930s in the days of EOS – there was a rationalisation, leaving an elite group of big-name teams, including Belle Vue Aces, with a following which for a time made speedway the second-biggest spectator sport in the country. The ups and downs of dirt track have continued. With the demise of Belle Vue Zoo and Gardens in the 1980s, the speedway stadium, scene of many a Clem Beckett triumph, was sold to become the site of a car auction, and its famous Aces team disbanded. But then it was reformed thanks to the intervention of former star rider Peter Collins. Today, the Aces are back at a rebuilt track close to the greyhound stadium at Kirkmanshulme Lane – their original home. For older Mancunians with misty-eyed memories of Belle Vue's heyday, the survival of the speedway team is the last outpost of a vanished empire. Only the sign for 'Hoskins Close' on the nearby Wimpey estate recalls the glory days of the sport. Wall of Death shows continued to be popular up to the 1970s, but today only a few practitioners remain.

Nothing remains of Clem Beckett's birthplace at Stone Rake, high on the hill above Springhead, other than foundations pushing through rough pasture, and a ruined farm building. In contrast, Top o'th' Meadows remains an idyllic backwater, a half-dozen stone cottages and farmsteads tucked into the hillside. Clem's mother, Henrietta, having mourned the deaths of all four sons, ended her days living with her daughter, Mary, and son-in-law, Albert Whitehead, just across the meadow at Pastures Farm, where she died in 1949, aged seventy-six. Surrounded by fields and woods, Top o'th' Meadows is still comfortably separate from the town below, its buildings converted into desirable residences for professionals and business folk.

Clem's father, Alfred Beckett, died in Birmingham in 1957, aged eighty-two, never, it seems, having renewed contact with his family. Indeed, most of the men who influenced Clem Beckett in his formative years survived into old age, living long enough to experience the Second World War and the enormous social changes that followed. Tom Mann died in 1941, aged eighty-four; Harry Pollitt, reconciled to the CPGB, died in 1960; Ernie Woolley died aged eighty-eight, after emigrating to Australia.

Clem, the internationalist, who died fighting for the brotherhood of man, would not have disapproved of the diverse mix of peoples who have come to live in his home town, the majority from the Indian sub-continent. He might, however, be surprised at the rate of demographic change, concerned at the degree of separation between ethnic groups, and the apparent decline in community cohesion. In 2011 a report commissioned by Oldham Council lamented the limited social mixing between white and Asian people, with 'geographical segregation' being 'exceptionally high'.

Even so, apart from domed mosques, the towering Civic Centre, and the replacement of trains by trams, the present-day landscape of Oldham would be immediately recognisable to Clem Beckett, especially its sprawling mass of terrace houses beyond the town centre. For the most part, stone-built chapels and churches, manifestations of the town's wealth when cotton was king, still stand, though usually abandoned as places of worship. Many have been converted into warehouses or cash-and-carry businesses, others lie empty and derelict, awaiting their fate. In a similar manner, the remains of an empire of Co-op stores linger on. Date stones over ornately tiled frontages evoke their golden age when Clem was a boy. In style and hubris they are excelled only by the grand array of Victorian buildings in the centre of the town.

The splendours of Alexandra Park, a little tarnished by age, survive, but alas Oldham's Park Parliament sits no more, replaced by the mean and malevolent mutterings of social media. The town's newer buildings, such as its redeveloped shopping centre, typify soulless modernity, none more so than the concrete slabs of the 'new' County Court, opened in the 1990s and already abandoned, a victim of austerity and rationalisation. Once-thriving Tommyfield Market, a pale shadow of its former glory, perches on high ground adjacent to empty shops along the length of a still magnificent Victorian arcade, one-time location of Percy Platt's motorcycle showroom. Seemingly helpless to resist the rising tide of internet retailing, Oldham town centre faces an uncertain future. In contrast, the comfortable commuter villages of Saddleworth such as Uppermill, Delph, Dobcross and Diggle, set amid spectacular Pennine scenery, have become popular visitor destinations. Clem would be surprised to see signs close to his home in Glodwick advertising 'Saddleworth Tourist Attractions'.

South of the town centre, in and around Werneth, is the last little clutch of tall mill chimneys in England. In Clem's day their smoke rose from boiler houses which powered the most modern spinning mills in the world. At that time, the notion that they might one day shut up shop, worn down by foreign competition and lack of investment, would have seemed preposterous. Oldham's last cotton mill closed in 1998, but a surprising number of mills remain standing, their vast spaces hived off to small businesses of every kind. Some, notably in the commuter lands of Saddleworth, have been converted into 'high-end' luxury apartments. All around the town centre are signs of modern, thriving enterprises – software developers, sign-makers, pvc manufacturers, and all manner of light engineering firms – many of them market leaders using cutting-edge technology.

In July 2020, amidst the terrors of the Covid pandemic, the *Oldham Times* featured an enterprising local company producing digital menus for the hospitality industry, combining table service with test and trace technology; a few weeks later, Oldham recorded the second highest number of new Covid cases in England. In the same period the Department of Work and Pensions published data showing that the percentage of Oldham children living in poverty was the highest in the United Kingdom. Here, unfortunately, are echoes of the hopelessness which Clem Beckett experienced in the inter-war period and the Great Depression. Whether Clem would join the Communist Party if he were around today is anyone's guess. As to whether he would still be a daredevil? More than likely.

A hundred years after Clem Beckett and the Anderson boys revved their home-made motorbikes through the gorse and heather of Glodwick Lows, it remains a refuge for young off-road motorcyclists. Its elevation from wasteland to a special site of geo-diversity has not stopped local lads indulging their fascination with speed and machines on the rough tracks above Swinton Street and adjacent Jinnah Close. They, too, are exhilarated by the occasional pursuit of police officers. They have never heard of Daredevil Beckett, but they share his love of risk-taking and his impatience with old fogeys.

Appendix

People

Anderson, Eli (1906-1966)

Eli, youngest of ten children, Clem's life-long friend. During the First World War, while still at school, Eli and Clem formed a partnership to sell daily newspapers to workers at local mills and factories; the enterprise required them to rise before dawn. Along with Clem, he attended a Communist Party rally in Oldham, and the two of them joined the Party together. Clem was always able to rely on Eli in moments of crisis. In 1928 he accompanied Clem on his first visit to a speedway meeting at Audenshaw, and afterwards helped prepare a machine for Clem's first competitive race. After marriage, Eli settled down to family life in Oldham, just as Clem's globe-trotting career was taking off. When Clem was trying to keep the beleaguered Owlerton stadium afloat by performing on 'the Wall of Death', Eli joined the show as 'Spider' Anderson. When Clem arrived back in England, penniless, following his trip to the Soviet Union, Eli met him on the dockside in London, to give him a lift back to Oldham. Eventually Eli joined Clem in this motorcycle repair business in Manchester, but his involvement ended in 1934 when Clem brought his future wife Lida to live 'over the shop'.

Anderson, Irving (1906-1992)

Irving, no relation to Eli, was another of Clem's motorbike-mad boyhood friends in Roundthorn. At the age of fourteen Irving and Clem clubbed together to buy their first ramshackle motorbike for the princely sum of £5, and not long afterwards the two of them were in business repairing motor-cycles. Irving's recklessness astride motorbikes earned him the nickname 'Mad Andy'. As with Eli, his friendship with Clem was lifelong. And like Eli, Irving married and settled down to life in Oldham. His wife, Elsie (a niece of Clem's mother), responded to an appeal by Edmund and Ruth Frow, founders of the Working Class Movement

Library, as they gathered information about Clem's life. Irving also worked for Clem at his motorcycle business in Miles Platting, but like Eli, he quitted with the arrival of Clem's wife, Lida. In 1944 Irving and Elise named their fourth child Clement Henry. They lived the dream of many a working-class couple who had spent their lives toiling in smoky Lancashire mill towns by retiring to a newly built detached house in Blackpool.

Elder, James Lloyd (1904 -1957), known as 'Sprouts'

American Elder personified the dashing image of speedway as it took a hold on the imagination of the British public in the late 1920s. Over 6-ft tall (hence the nickname) he was immensely popular in England, and Clem's victory over Elder in the summer of 1928 pitched him into the 'star-man' bracket. The two became friends. Estimated to have earned £50,000 during his first three years riding in Britain, Elder's career followed the rolling-stone trajectory and typical buccaneering adventurers of those who followed the money from one meeting to another. He was typical of speedway stars who made and lost fortunes as the vicissitudes of the economy affected the sport. Retiring from racing to join the California Highway Patrol, he suffered serious injury in a road traffic accident. After the death of his wife, he committed suicide, at the age of fifty-three.

Franklyn, Arthur (1907-1983)

Arthur was Clem Beckett's alter-ego: his successful career in speedway and later achievements being what Clem himself might have enjoyed had he not become involved in politics. Born in County Durham, to well-off parents, and brought up in Ashton on Mersey, Franklyn achieved overnight success when he began racing. His style of 'riding the bends' on the inside of the track contrasted with Clem's broadsiding technique. He was among the first star riders at Manchester's White City, before going over to rival Belle Vue stadium. In the English close season of 1929-30 he was among Belle Vue riders who toured Argentina. Like Clem, he learned to fly, going on to compete in the King's Cup air race in 1931, where the majority of opponents were officers in the RAF. Following this, and a short spell as a TT rider, he obtained a commission in the Royal Air Force, returning to speedway as a promoter at Ipswich in the 1950s.

Henriksen, Eli Marie (1911-1979), known as Lida

Born in Denmark, daughter of a coal merchant, Lida was twenty-three in 1935 when she married Clem. The course of her life is difficult to follow because of changes of name, occasioned by four marriages, and an adopted forename 'Lida', also rendered 'Leda'. Her second marriage was to Clem. She grew up in the Horsens area of Denmark, emigrating to Canada in her teens, where she married Hugo Johnson, but appears to have been divorced from him when she returned to Denmark in the 1930s. By the time of marriage to Clem, in 1935, she had assumed the additional forename of Lida, and was a member the Communist Party. Practical and businesslike, she was able to run Clem's motorcycle business after his departure for Spain, and even after his death. She was in Denmark when news of Clem's death reached her, and one of the speakers at the memorial event in Ardwick, as well as the author of a tribute published after news of the Nationalist atrocity at Guernica. In 1938 she married Dr Hem Raj Anand, brother of novelist Mulk Raj Anand, and went to India with him. However, little more than a year later, on the eve of the Second World War, the couple were shown on the National Register as living in Hazel Grove, a Manchester suburb, with Lida's occupation given as 'Director, Motor Cycle Firm', and doing war work as an ambulance driver. Dr Anand's practice was in Miles Platting, the same area as Clem's motorcycle business. Lida divorced and remarried again. Her fourth husband was Niels Steen, a Norwegian pilot. After the war, the couple lived in Bedford, where Lida died, aged sixty-seven.

Hart, Edgar (1883-1960)

Entrepreneur Edgar Hart was an influential figure in Clem's life through his role as speedway promoter. During the First World War he served overseas with the British Red Cross. Hart almost certainly saved Clem's life by arranging private medical treatment following his accident in Newcastle. His company, Provincial Dirt Tracks Ltd, appointed Clem and other riders as directors. The company also owned a stadium in Cardiff. With the onset of the Depression, Hart was forced to sell out to rival International Speedways, and as a result of the takeover the value of Clem's shares crashed. Hart then resumed his career as an exhibition organiser, travelling to the United States. He became a director of the Mere Country Club in Cheshire. Following the death of his first wife, he remarried, and lived in a flat in the grounds of the club for the last twenty years of his life. In spite of Hart's middle-class credentials, Clem remained loyal to him, even praising him in the columns of the Communist Party's paper *The Worker Sportsman*.

Jeans, Arnold (c.1903-1936)

Son of White Russian émigrés who fled the Russian Revolution, Jeans was a mysterious figure among volunteers who went to Spain. In spite of suspicions aroused by his background, Jeans' knowledge of languages and military experience qualified him to travel to Spain with Clem. Jeans (possibly a *nom de guerre*) had been a language tutor to the Bowes-Lyons family, although his occupation is given as 'scientist' at the time of his death. Fluent in German, he joined a small contingent of British volunteers attached to the Thaelmann Battalion, composed mainly of German Communists. Killed in action, at Boadilla del Monte, Jeans's courage was recorded by fellow volunteer, Winston Churchill's nephew, Esmond Romilly, in his book, *Boadilla*: 'If there was one who deserved the appellation hero, it must have been Arnold Jeans.'

Kerrigan, Peter (1899-1977)

Kerrigan personified the professional British Communist. Born in Hutchesontown, in the Gorbals district of Glasgow, he became Scottish organiser of the Party in 1930 after attending the Lenin School in Moscow. Tough and demanding, Kerrigan believed in the essential Communist quality of discipline and was notoriously feared by subordinates. Said to have a chest 'like the Dneprostroi Dam' he communicated 'in roars' and often reduced comrades to tears. Bob Cooney, a volunteer in Spain, told of being so afraid of Kerrigan when he was a Party organiser that he would hide when a visit from Kerrigan was expected. As political commissar in Madrigueras, Kerrigan took a dislike to Clem, reporting him as the ringleader of dissident volunteers, and having him arrested. On the eve of the battle of Jarama, British Battalion commander Wilfred Macartney, a non-Communist, was mysteriously shot and wounded by Kerrigan, who claimed the incident was an accident. Unlike volunteers who broke with Communism in later years, Kerrigan remained loyal to Moscow. He served the Party in various capacities, including national industrial organiser, and as unsuccessful Communist Parliamentary candidate in Glasgow following the Second World War.

Levine, Maurice (1907-2000)

Born in a tenement block close to Strangeways Prison in Manchester, Maurice Levine was the eighth of eleven children born to Jewish immigrants from Lithuania. He worked as a clothing cutter, but left England for Australia when he was nineteen. Back in Manchester, and as a member of the Tailors and Garment Workers Union, he was one of many Jewish recruits to the Communist Party in the 1930s who saw the Party as a bulwark against fascism and as a means of combatting poverty. He was at Benny Rothman's side on the1932 Mass Trespass on Kinder Scout. One of the first Manchester volunteers for Spain, he arrived there shortly after Clem, but went into action before him. At Jarama he and other Lopera veterans provided a guard for brigade headquarters. Wounded at Brunete, he served with the International Brigades in an administrative capacity until they were withdrawn. Resuming life in Manchester, he eventually became a director in his brother's clothing firm. He was a founding member of an old comrades association for brigaders, the body which became the International Brigades Memorial Trust. In later years he defended historians who gave a 'warts-and-all' picture of life in the International Brigades, and was a critic of those who sought to sanitise the record. In the 1980s he collected money to support striking miners, and in retirement he campaigned against the threatened privatisation of the Forest of Dean.

Mann, Tom (1856-1941)

A Marxist from his twenties, Mann was a prominent figure in the development of socialism in Britain, and in the formation of the Communist Party of Great Britain. Acquiring a reputation as trade union leader and a public speaker, he persuaded the Trade Union Congress to campaign for an eight-hour working day, and played a key role in the London dock strike of 1889. By the time he came to speak on behalf of the CPGB in Oldham, in 1924, his flamboyant and checkered career had included a period in Australia where he helped found the Australian Labour Party, and a notorious conviction under the Incitement to Mutiny Act for urging British soldiers to refuse to shoot strikers. Revelling in publicity generated by prosecutions against him, Mann, an Anglican, cited Communism as an expression of Christianity. He called for British 'soviets' to be formed, emphasising the need for revolutionary action, and fronted the National Minority Movement believing that trade unions should have the major role in organising industry. The first unit of British volunteers to fight in Spain, the Tom Mann Centuria, was named in his honour.

Platt, Percy (1887-c.1945)

From humble beginnings Platt worked his way up, becoming a well-known Oldham businessman with wide interests in the world of motorcycling. Like Clem, he grew up in Glodwick, and attended Roundthorn school. His mother, who worked as a cardroom hand, was widowed before he was five years old. After serving his apprenticeship and working as a motor engineer, he opened a shop selling motorbikes, expanding into car dealerships. Platt was Clem's tour manager in Scandinavia and Germany for both speedway and Wall of Death events. By the early 1930s he was acting as agent for Skid Skinner. In 1934 he promoted events as far afield as Baghdad and Palestine, returning to England with strongly anti-semitic views. He maintained business contacts in Denmark after Clem's death, and during the Second World War was unfortunate enough to be there when the country was occupied by the Germans. Interned, he remained in Denmark for the rest of his life, dying in hospital in Aalborg shortly after the end of the war.

Pollitt, Harry (1890-1960)

The most significant figure in the history of the Communist Party of Great Britain, Pollitt played an influential role in the life of Clem Beckett. Born in Droylsden, brought up in poverty, Pollitt attended a Socialist Sunday School and became a leading member of the Openshaw Socialist Society. A founding member of the CPGB, he worked alongside Tom Mann, making several visits to the Soviet Union. Imprisoned in 1925 for incitement to mutiny, Pollitt helped recruit volunteers for the International Brigades, interviewing Clem Beckett. He played a key role in raising funds for Spanish Aid and Dependants Aid for families of volunteers killed or wounded. Pollitt was general secretary of the Party from 1929 to 1939, and from 1941 to 1956, the two-year interruption being prompted by his opposition to the Nazi-Soviet pact. Otherwise he remained loyal to the Comintern policy line, persuading himself that human rights abuses under Stalin were largely the responsibility of subordinates. In 1995 a plaque commemorating Pollitt was erected on the wall of Droylsden library. Another smaller plaque underneath states that the memorial was 'partly funded' by Droylsden Labour Party, echoing the uneasy relationship between different elements of the 'Popular Front' during the Spanish Civil War.

Morley, Ellen Alma (1911-2008), later Skinner

It was through Skid Skinner that Clem became acquainted with Yorkshire-born Alma Morley, one of the most colourful figures in the Wall of Death mania which swept England and northern Europe in the 1930s. Determined, glamorous, and business-savvy, her extraordinary career was launched at Billy Butlin's Skegness holiday camp, at the age of eighteen. Alma made regular tours of Scandinavia, mainly in Denmark, teaming up with various partners. She shunned protective leathers in favour of satin blouses and breeches, adorned with sequins, and capped by a beret. Unlike Clem and Skid, she hardly ever fell off and, bruises apart, her only significant injury was a cut chin when a splinter ricocheted from the wooden 'tilt'. When Percy Platt took over as her agent, Clem accompanied them on visits to Denmark as Platt's assistant. She met Skinner in 1931, although they did not marry until 1940. Alma kept a diary illustrating her bravery as well as the everyday hazards of 'the wall'. Her collection of newspaper cuttings, including those amassed by Skid Skinner, was continued for more than sixty years after Skinner's accidental death in 1944.

Skinner, Hector (1905-1944), known as 'Skid'

'Skid' was typical of the larger-than-life characters attracted to speedway in its early days, and more resourceful than most in reacting to the end of the dirt track boom. Of all Clem's fellow adventurers, Skinner was the closest, his career running parallel with Clem's up to and beyond Clem's final suspension. Born in Epworth, north Lincolnshire, son of a cycle-maker, he soon showed the same 'motorbike mad' enthusiasm as Clem. His small (5-ft 4-in) stature, combined with incurable bravery, attracted the attention of Edgar Hart, and like Clem, Skinner became a favourite with the Sheffield crowd, also joining him in the Marseille adventure. In contrast to Clem, Skid dressed immaculately in the latest fashion, and was invited to model raincoats by Burtons the tailors. He acquired a garage business in Tinsley, Sheffield, and attempted to set up a speedway venue at Hellaby, near Rotherham, coincidentally the home of his future wife, Alma. In 1930 he joined Clem to put on a Wall of

Death show at fairgrounds and fêtes, and like Clem, suffered a series of injuries as a result of frequent falls. His tour of Denmark with Clem was foreshortened by Clem's fall in front of the Danish king. Afterwards, Skinner teamed up with Alma (billed as Alma Johnson) in a Wall of Death double act, being obliged to drop the nickname 'Skid' in Scandinavia because of its vulgar slang meaning in Danish. His purchase of a lion cub to accompany him in a sidecar on the Wall of Death prompted an investigation by the RSPCA. Forever striving for novelty, Skinner came up with the idea of integrating a Wall of Death show with a trapeze act. The project was quashed because none of the trapeze artists who auditioned could overcome dizziness on the wall. Skinner died after accidentally shooting himself in both legs while hunting rabbits in his native Lincolnshire.

Spence, Eric Oswald (1895-1947)

Universally known as 'EOS', Spence became one of the most important figures in early British speedway. Born into a Leicestershire farming family, he saw First World War service in the Royal Navy. As honorary secretary of the Camberley Motor Club he organised the 1924 'Camberley Scramble', reputed to have been the first 'motocross' event. A keen amateur motorcyclist, Spence excelled in sidecar events, competing in long-distance trails events in the early 20s, before moving to Manchester. Following the initial speedway boom in 1928, he became Clerk of the Course at Belle Vue. With the backing of International Speedways, EOS guided Belle Vue to success in spite of the closure of other stadiums brought about by falling attendances. He exerted a dominating influence on the setting up of a new Northern Speedway League, and on the introduction of a new system of remuneration which benefited 'star' men but penalised younger riders. The takeover of Sheffield Owlerton by International Speedways wiped out Clem's investment and ended his career as a company director. Spence did, however, help to improve track safety standards, and remained steadfastly opposed to the introduction of betting in speedway stadiums. When, in the depth of the Depression, stadiums came under pressure to allow betting Spence led the successful opposition. Clem called him 'the Mussolini of speedway', and other commentators labelled him the 'monarch' of the sport. A journalist described him as 'a chain-smoker, who rarely smiled, and was never heard to raise his voice'. Towards the end of his career at Belle Vue, Spence even picked a fight with the ACU, threatening to break away and set up a new regulatory authority. In spite of all this, EOS paid Clem a glowing tribute when news of his death reached England. Spence's final position at Belle Vue was as general manager of the zoo.

Sprigg, Christopher St John (1907-1937), also called Caudwell

The close friendship between Christopher St John Sprigg and Clem Beckett, as volunteers in the British Battalion of the International Brigade at Madrigueras, reached a poignant denouement with their deaths, side by side, at the Battle of Jarama. From a middle-class background, Sprigg achieved a prodigious output as journalist and writer, much of his work influenced by his conversion to Communism. Born in Putney, London, both his father and grandfather were journalists. Leaving school at fifteen, Sprigg joined his father in Bradford, then working as literary editor of the *Yorkshire Observer*, beginning his career as a reporter on the same paper. He became editor of *British Malaya*, reflecting the life of rubber planters and British influence in the Far East. With brother, Theodore, he launched various publishing ventures focused on the development of aircraft and airlines, but their schemes were confounded by the Depression, and in 1933 the brothers were declared bankrupt – an experience which encouraged Sprigg to question capitalism, anticipating his conversion to Marxism. Like Clem, he achieved expertise in 'nuts and bolts' engineering, as well as theoretical science. His *Crisis in Physics*, written in 1936, stunned the academic world. A true polymath, and using the *nom de plume* Christopher Caudwell, he wrote a series of detective novels, as well as poetry, together with literary and philosophical treatises, the best known being *Illusion and Reality: a Study of the Sources of Poetry, Studies in a Dying Culture, and Romance and Realism, a Study in English Bourgeois Culture*. Much of his writing, however, was published posthumously. As the driver of an ambulance donated by Londoners, he, like Clem, determined to take on a fighting role once in Spain. His grasp of mechanical matters led to his appointment as machine gun instructor at Madrigueras, alongside Clem, and sharing the same billet. A poem written for the Battalion Burns Night in January 1936 is one of his least-known works, but perfectly expresses the idealism of most British volunteers in Spain.

Wild, Sam (1908-1983)

Born in Ardwick, Manchester, of Irish parentage, Sam Wild personified the tough breed of ex-servicemen from whom the British Battalion of the International Brigade drew many of its officers. He joined the British Navy aged sixteen, serving for eleven years. As section leader in Kit Conway's No. 4 Company, and nursing four bullet wounds, he helped get survivors off Suicide Hill, assisted by covering machine-gun fire from Clem and Sprigg. He fought in later battles at Brunete (where he was wounded again), Teruel, and Belchite. His outstanding leadership and organising ability played a vital part in preventing the Aragon retreat from becoming a rout. Wild received the Spanish Republic's highest decoration for bravery, and was promoted to major. He was the last, and generally regarded as the best, commander of the British Battalion. After withdrawal of the International Brigades in December 1938 he led the battalion back to England where it was enthusiastically welcomed at London Victoria station. He married Bessie Berry shortly afterwards, and joined her in fund-raising efforts to alleviate suffering in Spain. Like many returning brigaders, Wild struggled to readjust to civilian life. His daughter, Dolores, lamented: 'He never really found anything that he was as passionate about as Spain.' After volunteering to fight in the Second World War, and in spite of his immense military experience, his reputation as an active Communist ensured rejection.

Wintringham, Tom (1898-1949)

Son of a prosperous Grimsby solicitor and an Oxford graduate, Wintringham was prominent among middle-class recruits to the Communist Party of Great Britain, who envisaged themselves playing important roles in bringing about a revolution in Britain, along the lines of that which had been achieved in 1917 in Russia. In 1925 he was imprisoned after being convicted of seditious libel and incitement to mutiny. As journalist and writer with the benefit of active service in the First World War, Wintringham became military correspondent of the *Daily Worker*, leading to his being despatched to Spain soon after the outbreak of the Civil War. He tutored volunteers of the British Battalion in machine-gun use, alongside Clem and Christopher St John Sprigg. Unexpectedly promoted to command the battalion, he admitted that heavy casualties at Jarama were the result not only of enemy superiority in weaponry but also 'blunders' on the Republican side. The rout of three companies of infantry on 'Suicide Hill', in which Clem and Sprigg were killed, is generally attributed to the fact that they advanced beyond the relative safety of strong defensive positions. Wintringham blamed this on confused orders from brigade, but another factor was the positioning of his HQ in a dip from where he was unable to observe the extent of casualties. Wounded on the second day, he was evacuated to hospital, and after a further spell as instructor, was repatriated. Wintringham was a notorious womaniser, and his affair with an American journalist (whom he subsequently married) got him into trouble when she was accused of being a Trotskyist spy. His break with the Party was hastened by the Nazi-Soviet pact. During the Second World War he pressed for the formation of a Local Defence Force, forerunner of the Home Guard, and was allowed to set up a training school, teaching guerrilla warfare and street-fighting. Even so, Wintringham's Communist past ensured that he was refused a commission in the army. Ever the idealist, his attempt to form a new 'Common Wealth' political party was dashed by the Labour electoral landslide of 1945.

Woolley, Ernest (1900-1989), known as Ernie

Older than Clem Beckett, Ernie Woolley was Manchester and District Organiser of the Young Communist League at the time of Clem's recruitment to the Communist Party of Great Britain. He was an inspirational figure, not least because of his belief that preparations of a quasi-military nature were necessary to pave the way for imminent revolution. Amid rising industrial discontent following the First World War, Woolley was the moving force of the Manchester District Communist Party Cycle Corps, intended to provide an infrastructure for Party communications and the distribution of Party literature, should it be declared illegal. Along with Harry Pollitt, he had been a member of Openshaw Socialist Society, which contributed to the formation of the CPGB in 1920. Born in Abbey Hey in east Manchester, service in the Royal Flying Corps added to his reputation as a man of action. Later, as the Party's first Industrial Organiser, and a member of its Central Committee, he was jailed for activities during the General Strike of 1926. He served further terms of imprisonment, and even Pollitt accused him of having a 'police complex'. A leading light in the National Minority Movement, whose aim was to infiltrate trade unions, Woolley also spent time in the Soviet Union. Under constant surveillance by British security services, along with his German-born wife, Emma Elizabeth Jansen, Woolley's precise role in the Civil War remains mysterious. Papers issued to him suggest he was assisting the Republican air force, though not as a pilot. At the end of the war he was attached to the headquarters of the British Battalion, ostensibly as correspondent of the *Daily Worker*. After the Second World War Woolley emigrated to Australia. His death, aged eighty-eight, came just a few months before the fall of the Berlin Wall which presaged the collapse of the Soviet Union.

Selected Bibliography

ALEXANDER, W., *British Volunteers for Liberty* (Lawrence and Wishart, 1982)

APPLEBAUM, A, *Gulag, A History of the Soviet Camps* (Allen Lane, 2003)

BARRY, B., *From Manchester to Spain* (Working Class Movement Library, 2009)

BAXELL, R., *Unlikely Warriors* (Aurum Press, 2012)

BECKETT, F., *Enemy Within, The Rise and Fall of the British Communist Party* (Merlin Press, 1998)

BEEVER, A., *The Spanish Civil War* (Cassell,1982)

BROWN, G., *Maxton* (Collins, 1986)

BUCKLEY, H. *The Life and Death of the Spanish Republic, A Witness to the Spanish Civil War* (Hamish Hamilton, 1940; Taurus, 2014)

BULLARD, R.,eds., BULLARD J., and BULLARD M., *Inside Stalin's Russia, Diaries 1930-34* (Day Books, 2000)

BURLEIGH, M., *The Third Reich* (Macmillan)

COLLINS, Tony, *Sport in a Capitalist Society* (Routledge, 2013)

DALLING, P., *The Golden Age of Speedway* (The History Press, 2011)

DAVIES, G., *You Are Legend* (Welsh Academic Press, 2018)

DUNN, R.M., *Wall of Death, Smoke and Mirrors, A study of motives of International Brigade volunteers, focussed on Clem Beckett and Christopher St John Sprigg* (University of York, 1992)

FERSOV, F.I., KLEHR, H., HAYNES, J.E., *Secret Cables of the Comintern 1933-1943* (Yale University Press, 2014)

FROW, E & R., *Clem Beckett and the Oldham Men Who Fought in Spain* (Working Class Movement Library, c.1980)

FYRTH, J., *The Signal Was Spain* (The Camelot Press Ltd, 1986)

GREENING, E., *From Aberdare to Albacete, A Welsh Brigader's Memoirs* (Warren and Pell, 2006)

SELECTED BIBLIOGRAPHY

HILL, M., *Red Roses for Isabel, Highlights from the Life of Isabel Brown* (Preston Community Press, 1982)

HOPKINS, J. K., *Into the Heart of the Fire, The British in the Spanish Civil War* (Stanford University Press, 1998)

IMLACH, G., *My Father and Other Working Class Football Heroes* (Yellow Jersey Press, 2005)

INGLIS, S., *Played in Manchester* (Manchester City Council, English Heritage, 2004)

JAMES, T. & STEPHENSON, B., *Speedway in Manchester 1927-1945* (Tempus Publishing Ltd, 2003)

LAW, B.R., *Oldham, Brave Oldham* (Oldham Council, 1999)

LEVINE, M., *Cheetham to Cordova, A Manchester Man of the Thirties* (Neil Richardson,1984)

MANCHESTER I.B. MEMORIAL COMMITTEE (ed) *Greater Manchester Men Who Fought in Spain* (Manchester Free Press, 1976)

MAYNARD, C., *The Murmansk Venture* (Naval and Military Press, 2010 [reprint])

ORWELL, G., *Homage to Catalonia* (Penguin Books, 1962)

PAVEY, A., *Speedway in the North-West* (Tempus, 2004)

PHILLIPS, T., *The Secret Twenties, British Intelligence, The Russians and the Jazz Age* (Granta, 2017)

PLOWDEN, W., *The Motorcar and Politics* (Bodley Head, 1971)

PRESTON, P., *!Comrades! Portraits from the Spanish Civil War* (Harper Collins 1999)

PRESTON, P., *The Spanish Holocaust* (Harper Press, 2012)

PRESTON, P., *We Saw Spain Die, Foreign Correspondents in the Spanish Civil War* (Constable and Robinson, 2008)

PURCELL, H. with SMYTH P., *The Last English Revolutionary, Tom Wintringham,1898-1949* (Sussex Academic Press, 2012)

PYE, D., *Fellowship is Life, The Story of the Clarion Cycling Club* (Clarion Publishing, 1995)

REDFERN, N., *Social Imperialism in Britain* (Brill, 1999)

REYNOLDS, D., *The Long Shadow, The Great War and the Twentieth Century* (Simon and Schuster, 2013)

ROGERS, M., *The Illustrated History of Speedway* (Studio Publications [Ipswich] 1978)

RUST, W., *Clem Beckett, Hero and Sportsman*, 1937

SEEBAG MONTEFIORE, S., *Stalin, the Court of the Red Tsar* (Phoenix, 2003)

STUART, N.A., T*he Memory of the Spanish Civil War and the Families of British International Brigaders* (De Montfort University, 2001)

TAYLOR, A.J.P., *The Origins of the Second World War* (Hamish Hamilton,1961)

THOMAS, H., *The Spanish Civil War* (Eyre and Spottiswoode, 1961)

WEBB, S., *1919: Britain's Year of Revolution* (Pen and Sword, 2016)

WILSON, A.N., *After the Victorians, 1901-1953* (Hutchinson, 2005)

Endnotes

Chapter One: King Cotton's Doorstep

1. Elsie appears to have lived in Oldham, but not with Henrietta and Alfred, until an early death, aged forty-seven; Herbert's adult life remains mysterious although, like Elsie, he attended school in Glodwick. There is a suggestion that he died in the war, which, if true, begs the question as to why such a tragedy went unremarked upon by friends, family and commentators after Clem's own death.
2. By coincidence the Second Battalion of the Royal Lancasters was based at Whittington Barracks, Lichfield, some 11 miles from Walsall. The Battalion sailed for South Africa in December 1899 at the outbreak of the Boer War, and did not return to England until the end of the war in 1902.

Chapter Two: Top o' th' Meadows

1. Redfern, N., *Social Imperialism in Britain, The Lancashire Working Class and Two World Wars.*
2. After the war, these three campaign medals were (and still are) popularly referred to as 'Pip, Squeak and Wilfred', after a hugely popular cartoon strip which appeared in the *Daily Mirror* from 1919-1956, and featured a dog, penguin and rabbit, respectively.
3. Webb, S., *1919: Britain's Year of Revolution.*

Chapter Three: Mad Andy

1. 'Card-rooms' housed key processes in the manufacture of cotton goods, typically involving rollers fitted with metal 'cards' which combed and prepared raw cotton or cotton waste for subsequent treatment. Such precision-built machines required constant

maintenance, generating work for a range of occupations, such as 'strippers and grinders', 'doffers', 'card-fettlers' and 'card-dressers'. The card-room was a notoriously dusty environment, giving rise to high rates of respiratory illnesses.

2. C. Maynard, *The Murmansk Venture*.
3. Law, B.R., *Oldham, Brave Oldham*.
4. Ominously for the town's post-war future, Bradbury's had failed to secure a contract with the War Office for the provision of Army motorbikes: during a rigorous six-day trial in 1914 the chassis of the firm's flagship machine, powered by a twin-cylinder V-type 750cc engine, broke.

Chapter Four: Bill o' Jack's

1. According to a witness, Clem took the full force of the kick 'in the tram lines'. Naturally, his quoted reaction entered recorded history shorn of the industrial language in which it was originally couched.
2. The LYR carriage works at Newton Heath was already building 'motor lurries' (contemporary spelling) for local collections and deliveries.
3. Borough Watch Committees were nominally in charge of policing but often acted as the guardians of public morality, and survived until they were replaced by police authorities in 1968. Self-elected from the great and good of the community, they had surprisingly wide powers, including that of banning cinemas from showing particular films.

Chapter Five: Temperance Hall

1. Although CPGB accounts of Clem's life place his attendance at a Tom Mann meeting in Oldham in the autumn of 1924, newspaper reports of Mann's appearance at Temperance Hall at that time cannot be found. Mann certainly spoke at other venues in the Manchester area in November of that year, but according to information provided by Eli Anderson the meeting attended by Clem took place in 1923.

Chapter Six: Besting Mr Toad

1. Once dirt track racing had become popular, the High Beech venue became known as King's Oak.
2. In spite of claims to the contrary, racing at Droylsden was in what became the conventional anti-clockwise direction, although events at Camberley were conducted clockwise.

3. James and Stephenson, *Speedway in Manchester 1927-1945.*
4. In the early days, would-be broadsiders put their machines into a slide by cutting out the engine, laying the bike over at the start of the bend, and then restarting the motor creating a surge of power to the rear wheel. The technique was known as 'buttoning' because the drive of early bikes not having a clutch was controlled by a button. A 'pure' broadside involves *both* wheels sliding, with the rider appearing to steer the front wheel outwards in parallel to the rear wheel. In fact, the rider does not turn his handlebars; rather the machine is laid over with the throttle closed as a means of slowing for a bend, causing both wheels to slide. Once in the slide, the rider is able to steer by turning the bars, steadying himself by dabbing his inside foot on the ground. Pure broadsiding was harder to achieve on the smaller tracks, and Clem, among the handful of British pioneer riders who mastered it, was reputed to take the bends flat out, 'ignoring the button entirely'. Naturally, aficionados resented the condescending description of broadsiding as 'a skid narrowly averted'.
5. James and Stephenson, *Speedway in Manchester 1927-1945.*
6. A 'flapping' track was a term used to describe an unregistered greyhound track (few of which now survive) indicative of the early association between speedway and dog tracks, whose unused centre oval proved ideal for speedway circuits.

Chapter Seven: Flying High

1. Breaking chains, usually attributable to 'frame whip', were to dog Clem's early dirt track career, but eventually a solution was found. See Chapter Ten.
2. 'Roughyeds' was, and is, the nickname for Oldham's Rugby League team. In spite of their relative proximity, only 9 miles apart, Oldhamers maintained a civic identity distinguishable from their Manchester neighbours, their speech infused with stressed vowels and Lancashire dialect.

Chapter Eight: Taming the Beast

1. The first speedway fatality in the UK was Charlie Biddle, who died of injuries on 30 May 1928 after a collision at the London Stamford Bridge track a week earlier.

2. Douglas was being a tad disingenuous. Only a few months earlier, at the height of the controversy over dirt track racing, and fearful that its manifest danger would damage sales to the public, his firm had actually obstructed the purchase of DTs to the mighty International Speedways, obliging it to camouflage its order for fifty machines through agents.
3. Apart from worn or split tyres, engines parts, notably valves and piston rings, required regular replacement. Brutal 'buttoning' (cutting the engine in and out) imposed tremendous stresses and was the cause of most mechanical failures.

Chapter Nine: Icicles in Marseille

1. Fraser G., and Henry J., eds, *Speedway Researcher*, 2012.
2. Following the end of the 1928 season in Britain, a seventeen-strong group of dirt track riders sailed from Liverpool to Egypt, intending to race on a new track being built in Cairo under the supervision of West Ham idol, Ivor Creek, while A.J. Hunting went to Argentina with the idea of setting up several ISL tracks in South America.

Chapter Ten: Tin Cans and Dead Cats

1. Van Damm's involvement in speedway was short-lived. He later became an impresario, and became well-known, if not notorious, as manager of the Windmill Theatre, presenting revues featuring female nudity.
2. The Golden Helmet was generally awarded to the winner of a challenge match (which might extend over several heats or several meetings). Some were ornate and valuable objects; others no more than ordinary crash helmets covered in gold paint.
3. 'Talmage' was R. Morton, speedway correspondent and commentator of the *Motor Cycle*.
4. James and Stephenson, *Speedway in Manchester 1927-1945*.

Chapter Eleven: Shirt-tails and Lamp-posts

1. The frequency with which remounted riders went on to collide with the leaders eventually prompted the ACU to consider a rule change forbidding fallers to rejoin the race.
2. Fay Taylour, the best known woman rider, was well used to falls and injuries. She confided to a journalist that she always packed a pair of silk pyjamas in her track kit in case of being hospitalised.

3. One exception in the early days before ACU regulation was Skid Skinner, who frequently raced *sans* protective leathers.
4. Plowden, W., *The Motorcar and Politics 1896-1970* (Bodley Head, 1970). Estimates of the carnage on the roads of the United States at this time put casualties as high as million every year. Most accidents involved motorists, but casualties among motorcyclists were also rising steeply. Echoing the concerns expressed by Oldham Watch Committee, the Vicar of Thames Ditton, worried about accidents on the main road through his parish, supported their calls for a ban on pillion riding.
5. Later, Renold produced a superior chain adaptable to all machines, with deep inner plates fitting tightly over the sprockets.

Chapter Twelve: Slump

1. Another organisation purporting to represent riders – the Dirt Track Racing Riders Association – had been formed at the outset of the speedway boom, but its members appear to have been limited to riders under contract to southern stadiums such as King's Oak, Greenford and Stamford Bridge.
2. *The Great Depression in Germany*, Alpha History (website).
3. If true, Clem's experience in Hamburg portended an episode in the Spanish Civil War which is credited with ground-breaking medical advances in blood transfusion, famously carried out in the later phase of the war in the 'cave hospital' at La Bisbal de Falset by Dr Reginald Saxton.

Chapter Thirteen: The Mussolini of Speedway

1. Unsurprisingly, this practice of using animals gave rise to objections from the RSPCA, although it did not stop Skinner from introducing his own variation on the theme by obtaining a lion cub to sit beside him on the wall.

Chapter Fourteen: Capitalist Sport Bad, Workers Sport Good

1. According to right-wing critic Giles Udy, in *Labour and the Gulag* (2017), more than a million people, forced into cattle trucks, were dispatched to labour camps in Soviet Karelia and Siberia; hundreds of thousands were shot, or died as a result of their privations. Of Moscow's 500 churches in 1917, more than half had been closed

by 1930. In the same period thousands of mosques were shut down. *In Gulag, A History* (2003), Anne Applebaum maintains that Stalin was an admirer of Peter the Great's use of forced labour in building roads, factories, ships, and the city of St Petersburg.

2. Speedway authorities moved quickly to keep the sport 'clean' in response to the threat posed to the integrity of speedway by 'bookies', aided by 'runners' with unsavoury criminal associates. It was generally believed at this time that fixing of results in horse racing was widespread, and that totaliser betting (the 'tote') supervised by stadiums, involving the distribution of total amounts staked between winners, would be the thin edge of the wedge. Speedway's successful resistance to betting is all the more creditable given the sustained efforts of bookmakers to move in on dirt tracks during the early years (and all the more remarkable in the light of betting in contemporary sport, amplified and promoted by commercial television and online media). In fact, EOS took his lead from A.J. Hunting, managing director of ISL, with riders under its control entering into a gentleman's agreement not to ride where bookies were present.

3. Manchester rider Frank Varey got a bad name for overzealousness, typically being disqualified in a race at Belle Vue for fetching off a slower rider while trying to force himself through on the inside. In mitigation, Varey gave his reason for taking up speedway as the need to earn extra money to pay for radium treatment of his mother's cancer. In any event there was a fine line between outright 'boring' though other riders and gamesmanship arising from the will to win – especially in the dash to gain advantage on the first bend. Whether or not Varey deserved his reputation is lost in the impenetrable cloud of dust and cinders that settled long ago on the pioneer contests of speedway gladiators.

4. The problem of false starts – sometimes as many as six or seven – was eventually solved with the invention of the starting gate by New Cross promoter Harry Mockford, and built by Bristol rider Harry Shepherd. But it did not come into use until 1934 – too late for Clem's career.

5. Two years earlier Australian star Frank Arthur appears to have escaped censure when he admitted that he was often happy to stay in second place, without risking his neck by overtaking the leader, content with picking up second place prize money, and in the hope that the leader would come off.

Chapter Fifteen: Wall of Death

1. Failure to understand this perspective has given rise to woeful blindness towards Communists who fought fascism in Spain and later. When in September 2019 the European Parliament passed a resolution ascribing moral equivalence to Communism and fascism, the International Brigade Memorial Trust countered with a resolution condemning Europe's failure to acknowledge the part played by Communists in the war against Hitler, citing the bravery of partisan fighters and the role of the Red Army. In its foray into historical revisionism the European Parliament also ignored the defeat of the Spanish Republic as a factor hastening the advent of the Second World War – omissions which the IBMT correctly described as 'alarming'.

2. ROP pursued a policy of 'dumping' on the British market, with ZIP usually selling at two or three pence per gallon cheaper than other brands.

3. The JAP company, which went on to produce early aircraft engines, took its name from founder John Alfred Prestwich, a genius precision engineer who was also responsible for creating cinematic projectors. With the appearance of the Speedway JAP in the early thirties it became the engine of choice for dirt track riders until the mid-1960s.

4. As stadiums struggled to survive against a background of declining attendances, promoters tried various gimmicks to attract spectators. 'Trick cyclist' teams, such as that sponsored by motorbike manufacturers *Ariel* began appearing at ISL tracks, with riders typically lying over the front wheel, or standing with one foot on the saddle. It was a development that anticipated the Wall of Death craze.

5. Her expedition to Germany did not last long. By mid-September promoters of the Hamburg track were in voluntary liquidation.

Chapter Sixteen: By Royal Appointment

1. Rudge designers were on the offensive; they had improved their Ulster engine, no longer encumbered by heavy struts, and by providing better gear changing. They could usually outpace the Douglas on 'shallow' tracks, but the Douglas could hold its own on deep cinders. Later, many riders adapted their machines by fitting new JAP engines. One experienced dirt track manager summed up

the practical issues: 'The Rudge wants driving,' he said, whereas, with its low centre of gravity, a Douglas 'will do its own broadsiding'.

2. The guinea (a favourite measure of currency in the world of horse racing) was equal to one pound and one shilling. That said, the ACU later insisted that its scale of charges was expressed with all due modernity in 'pounds, shillings and pence' and that its fee for officiating per meeting was a mere £2.

3. The issue of banking the bends to allow riders to approach them at faster speeds gave rise to some controversy. Managing director of International Speedways A.J. Hunting was strongly against it on the grounds that it would detract from the art of broadsiding.

4. The Right Honourable Leo Amery M.P., Secretary of State for Dominions and Colonies, appropriately invited to present golden helmets and gauntlets to Australian winners, was an early supporter of Mussolini, but went on to redeem himself. His immortal parliamentary interjection in 1940 ('Speak for England, Arthur!') is generally credited with sparking the move to replace Prime Minister Neville Chamberlain with Winston Churchill. Alas, his son John, a died-in-the wool fascist, was hanged for treason at the end of the Second World War after supporting Hitler and Mussolini, and broadcasting Nazi propaganda.

5. *Speedway Researcher* website.

Chapter Seventeen: Dagenham Blacklist

1. An artificial rule which linked the pound sterling to the quantity of gold held by the Bank of England, and therefore restricted the supply of money. Economists such as John Maynard Keynes had been arguing for some time that the policy was a fallacy.

2. At the same time the brother of Joe Lees, a CPGB member who followed Clem to Spain, was beginning work in the Vauxhall plant at Luton.

3. William Rust, writing up a summary of Clem's life for propaganda purposes, claimed that he worked at Dagenham *after* his return from the Soviet Union, some twelve months later, and that he was fired after only two weeks. This is inconsistent with the evidence of several newspaper reports confirming that once back in England, Clem went straight to the Manchester area to set up in business, and, more importantly, with the timeline described by Ruth and Edmund Frow in their short biography.

Chapter Eighteen: Speed and Spondulicks

1. Four years later Rothman volunteered to fight in Spain, but was rejected. He remained an active trade unionist, and in later life, when the Kinder Scout Mass Trespass had become historically respectable, he achieved celebrity status. Like Clem, he had been obliged to turn down the offer of a scholarship because of poverty.

2. The growth of speedway had generated a literature of performance analysis in the trade press. Diagrams criss-crossed by dotted lines illustrated the right and wrong lines to take round the track, with 'X' marking the correct spot to cut out to broadside, and 'Y' as the place to turn on the power. Paradoxically, the *Motor Cycle* approached London rider Jim Kempster to lend authority to their piece. He, like Clem, was famed for broadsiding away from the 'white line'.

3. Alma Skinner Collection.

4. Not to be confused with Harry Riley 'Ginger' Lees, also of Bury, who after riding in the first speedway event at Audenshaw, went on to achieve star status in regular competition with Clem. His track career continued with various teams until 1937, including an appearance in the third test match against Australia at Wembley.

Chapter Nineteen: The People's Broadsider

1. Named after the Chairman of the People's Commissars of the USSR.

2. Eli Anderson, Sound Archives, Tameside Local Studies Library.

Chapter Twenty: Mosley's Manor

1. 'Money for Speed' (1933 film) directed by Bernard Vorhaus, starring Cyril McLaglen, Ida Lupino, John Loder and Moore Marriott, provided cameo roles for real-life speedway stars such as Ginger Lees, Frank Varey and Johnnie Hoskins. Against a backdrop of speedway crashes, as well as romance, the storyline featured a banned dirt track star taking up stunt-riding.

2. The part played by Denmark in the careers of Skid, Alma and Clem arose partly from the geographic proximity to the East of England, with regular sailings to Scandinavia from Hull, as well as similarities of language. It was said that the nineteenth-century dialect of coastal Yorkshire was so akin to Danish that North Sea fishermen from the two countries had no difficulty communicating with each other.

Chapter Twenty-one: Look After Mother

1. Years later Bebb candidly admitted that he knew the true purpose of his mission all along.
2. A significant number of volunteers, prominent among officers, turned out to have experience as soldiers, sailors, or airmen in the British armed services, including Peter Kerrigan. Trade unionist Jack Jones joined the Territorial Army in 1934, specifically 'to learn the use of weapons'.
3. Firsov F.H., Klehr H., Haynes, J.E., *Secret Cables of the Comintern.*
4. International Brigade Collection, Russian Centre for the Preservation and Study of Recent Historical Documents (RGASPI), Moscow.

Chapter Twenty-two: Rotten Dissident

1. The Foreign Enlistment Act of 1870 was enacted to deter British citizens from involvement in the Franco-Prussian War. It was always something of a dead letter in practice, but the British authorities, committed to appeasement of Germany and Italy, and non-intervention in Spain, were prepared to invoke the threat of enforcement proceedings by way of sequestration of assets.
2. The figure of forty-five has been disputed, the alternative figure of sixty-seven being put forward by Bill Alexander, later to command the British Battalion. The discrepancy may have arisen from the fact that a number of Lopera survivors were hospitalised with hypothermia, delaying their return to Madrigueras.
3. Nathan's reference to 'guardsmen' helped explain why he gained a reputation as a former officer in the guards. In fact, he came up through the ranks to be commissioned in the Royal Warwickshire Regiment.

Chapter Twenty-three: Friends and Flunkers

1. Many years later, recalling Manchester comrades at Madrigueras, Maurice Levine had to be prompted to include Clem in their number, and in memoirs of other Mancunians and Salfordians, such as Joe Norman, there is little reference to association with Clem. Likewise, volunteer Albert Charlesworth, a Labour Party member and self-confessed 'loner', born and bred in Saddleworth, felt no particular bond with Oldhamers, let alone Mancunians.

2. Roger Dunn, *Wall of Death, Smoke and Mirrors* (1992), interpreting correspondence between Theo St John Sprigg and Harry Pollitt.

3. Some eighteen months later, in training for the Ebro offensive, volunteers met to decide a new name for the reformed battalion. Reasonably enough, the Irish took exception to 'Cromwell', and there was equal opposition to the alternative nomination of 'Winstanley' (a reference to the leader of the seventeenth-century Diggers movement). When, in exasperation, someone suggested 'Fred Karno's' the meeting broke up in comradely disorder.

Chapter Twenty-four: The Worst Machine Gun Ever

1. The Nationalists also had the benefit of oil provided by American company Texaco, which, in spite of President Roosevelt's nominal support of 'non-intervention', supplied Franco and his German and Italian allies with unlimited amounts of fuel for aircraft, tanks and trucks, on credit, after cutting off supplies to the Republic.

Chapter Twenty-five: Suicide Hill

1. Jarama was the first and only occasion when the British Battalion was able to benefit, albeit marginally, from superior Republican air power. Within weeks, with the steady stream of aircraft sent to join the German Condor Legion, the balance had tipped decisively in favour of the Nationalists.

2. Problems stemming from old and out-of-date weaponry were matched by problems with second-hand ambulances donated through the Spanish Medical Aid Committee, which were prone to break down, and for which spare parts were difficult to obtain.

3. Apparently influenced by a report made after the battle by Overton, Wintringham echoed suspicions that the mix-up of ammunition for the Maxims had resulted from sabotage. Overton also claimed that the Colt light machine guns issued to No.4 Company were wrongly filled with Maxim ammunition. But Overton's credibility was questionable: he had panicked in the fighting on Suicide Hill, and was to do so again when the Moors renewed their attack the following day. Subsequently court-martialled and sent to a labour battalion, Overton died in the Battle of Brunete 'carrying ammunition to a forward position'. The driver of the crashed ammunition lorry,

Sergeant Hornsby, was also recommended for court-martial by Wintringham. Wounded later in the battle, and again at Brunete, he survived the war.

4. It was a remark from Charlesworth, a man of relatively few words, that summed up the inexperience of the British volunteers at Jarama: 'It wasn't until eleven o'clock in the morning that I realised that the birds that (I thought) were singing were bullets whistling past.'

Chapter Twenty-six: From Dolt to Hero

1. The title of Richard Baxell's authoritative book *'Unlikely Warriors'*, together with his detailed research, perfectly encapsulates the wide variety of backgrounds of members of the British Battalion.
2. How times change. Given that Clem died in the service of a lawfully elected government, today's human rights lawyers would have argued for a verdict of unlawful killing.
3. Any bitterness towards the CPGB felt by Clem's family was matched by the anger shown towards Harry Pollitt by Christopher St John Sprigg's brother, Theodore. He suggested that the Party had taken advantage of his brother not being in his right mind after receiving a blow on the head at a Mosley rally. The episode paralleled expressions of incredulity concerning Clem's 'suicidal' attack on the ACU while he was still recovering from a fractured skull and concussion following a speedway accident in Germany.
4. While the claim made by A.J.P. Taylor (*English History 1914-45*) that most English people displayed little concern for Spain may be allowed, his assertion that 'The Spanish war remained very much a question of the few, an episode in intellectual history' may not. At the height of the battle of Jarama the *Daily Worker* devoted its entire front page to stories referring to the war, and its readers – who were by no means all intellectuals – were kept informed of developments throughout. Hundreds of thousands of working people donated to charities supporting the Republic and its beleaguered people.
5. Fryth, J., *The Signal Was Spain*.

Chapter Twenty-seven: The Department of Lost Causes

1. Preston, P., *The Spanish Holocaust.*
2. Excavations of the battlefield at Jarama were commenced in 2018. There are also plans for housing developments in the area, which may provide opportunities for historical 'digs'. In other areas, however, such as the Brunete battlefield west of Madrid, local authorities, unsympathetic to the cause of rescuing historical truth, have obstructed efforts to carry out research, typically by expediting building developments when notified of wartime remains.

Index

230